Crossing My Rainbow Bridge

CAROL ANN ARNIM

BALBOA.
PRESS
A DIVISION OF HAY HOUSE

Some names of canine and humans have been changed.

Balboa Press books may be ordered through booksellers or by contacting:

Balboa Press
A Division of Hay House
1663 Liberty Drive
Bloomington, IN 47403
www.balboapress.com
1 (877) 407-4847

Because of the dynamic nature of the Internet, any web addresses or links contained in this book may have changed since publication and may no longer be valid. The views expressed in this work are solely those of the author and do not necessarily reflect the views of the publisher, and the publisher hereby disclaims any responsibility for them.

The author of this book does not dispense medical advice or prescribe the use of any technique as a form of treatment for physical, emotional, or medical problems without the advice of a physician, either directly or indirectly. The intent of the author is only to offer information of a general nature to help you in your quest for emotional and spiritual well-being. In the event you use any of the information in this book for yourself, which is your constitutional right, the author and the publisher assume no responsibility for your actions.

Any people depicted in stock imagery provided by Thinkstock are models, and such images are being used for illustrative purposes only.
Certain stock imagery © Thinkstock.

Printed in the United States of America.

ISBN: 978-1-4525-8550-5 (sc)
ISBN: 978-1-4525-8552-9 (hc)
ISBN: 978-1-4525-8551-2 (e)

Library of Congress Control Number: 2013919289

Balboa Press rev. date: 12/02/2013

Contents

DEDICATED
EQUALLY TO
THE GOD
WITHIN ALL
TO ALL MY DOGS PAST PRESENT AND FUTURE
THROUGH ALL TIME AND SPACE
AND TO MY FOREVER LOVE
ROBERT CHARLES

Message from My Four Legged Angels

My human companion Carol Ann and myself as a labrador retriever named Laverne; later renamed Spirit were both led to our highest good as agreed upon prior to birth. Each event of my thirteen year life was a stepping stone in our joint evolution.

It has been all about the journey of opening her heart. Life can close one down. When a being gets hurt the wounds create walls but they must be removed. I witnessed the process in Carol Ann. She dismantled her wall brick by brick. It is difficult to become open and to maintain the openness. One can be so fragile. She called herself Humpty Dumpty after the death of her beloved Robert yet she became whole and this cannot and will not be undone.

I guided her yet she did the real work. She found her centre. The writing of her journey was therapeutic for herself and others she shared it with. Carol Ann has shared her brokenness most eloquently and tenderly. She left her fears behind embracing trust to climb victorious to the top of her own personal Mount Everest.

My labrador tail is nonstop propeller whirls knowing it is now in book form. Of course her Robert love is now and always still her number one fan. All of her dog gang on the other side, Saber, Terrace, Mystic puppy, Amber, Spookie, Maggie and Treasure salute her work. Her bravest Mystic Love and courageous retired service dog Serna are howling their joyful support. All of us are honored for her portrayal of our lives and to see our contributions within the pages of her book.

SPIRIT

Author's Note

This book came to be due to the death of my husband Robert Charles. A few months after his spirit flight I was blessed to become a puppy raiser for Guide Dogs for the Blind. Four more puppies followed the first. Over the years of sharing stories of my life with family, friend and stranger I heard countless times you ought to write a book. How to write of my life journey was a daunting task so I began with short stories.

Time and life marched on creating more synchronistic blessings compelling me to share. The story count grew.

In the summer of 2013 a dear friend emailed me information about publishing which had just appeared out of nowhere from a stranger. This email had a link to another and I hit the send button. Magically a couple days later I received a phone call from Balboa Press. I could not ignore this huge nudge from the universe. I was being supported and guided. It was time to make my book dream a reality.

I thank all the beings who crossed my path in a small way or big way, each one playing a vital role in encouraging and inspiring me to sit down and write.

Thank You Roger

I opened the door to the shack of the rig's dining room and there before me was the man I would marry nineteen years later. This would be the man whose son I would bear, give up for adoption and find twenty years later. This would be the man who would perish from lung cancer five weeks short of our fourth wedding anniversary. This would be the man despite our twenty-nine year age difference that would be my best friend and support leading me into living life to my highest potential. This would be my first love that in death would comfort, restore and guide me into rebirthing a new Carol Ann open to all the magical wondrous possibilities and belief that my best is yet to be.

And how did I end up on an oil rig you may be wondering?

Thanks to my older brother Roger, who had begun a life homesteading outside of Athabasca, Alberta, I decided to head west from my home of Stratford, Ontario, at the age of twenty. His wife, Beth and I needed jobs. We heard about the oil patch requiring cooks for their bush camps. This sounded like a marvelous idea and the two of us were quickly hired on. Adventure was already part of our lives living in Roger's hand hewn log cabin without any amenities, so going further into the bush to live suited both of us. The rig was miles north of Manning, Alberta down a long bush road. It was a bit of a shock to see my new home away from home. The day was December 26, 1973. Little did I know how this co-creative effort was about to rock my world.

It was a few days after arriving to the rig that I wanted to do my wash, yet to my dismay upon inspecting the laundry shack I discover

I cannot manage the ringer washer. I headed to the kitchen shack in pursuit of a man. Upon opening the door, I stood timidly as I caught my first glimpse of this future love. He was conversing intently with another. The two men turned and the older one greeted me with a disarming welcome smile.

"Would one of you be kind enough to assist me in a lesson with the ringer washer?"

The older man jumped to the ready setting me at ease. "Hello, my name is Bob." He opened the kitchen shack's door for me to step out before him and off we went into the snowy night. I was mesmerized by his attire in a blue down jacket, blue jeans and white shoes. How very odd. We were in the bush surrounded with deep snows and he had on no hat and spiffy clean white shoes.

To my amazement I watched this friendly gentleman thread my dirty clothes into the ringer. Then came the invitation that would launch our destiny. "Carol Ann, could I offer you some New Year's Eve celebration in my shack?"

I hesitated as I recalled my employer's strict instruction to not become involved with the men on the rig. Bob is the petroleum engineer in charge of the drilling. But it was New Year's Eve after all. "Thank you, yes that sounds good."

Shortly after being in his shack the other man from the kitchen popped his head in the door. "Do you guys want to go for a ride?"

"Dwight come in here and meet Carol Ann." He stepped all the way inside as Bob continued. "Dwight is our driller. Do you think Beth would like to join us?"

A few minutes later the four of us sat bundled in the warm truck for a ride down the dark bush road. Where does one drive to in such a place so late at night I pondered. Dwight expertly manoeuvered the snowy bush road to the landing strip carved out of the trees.

"Shall we go for a walk, Carol Ann?"

Moments later I found myself plopped in a large snow bank with this man who awhile earlier had helped me with my wash. Funny thing about that laundry interest of his, it would be years later that he took great delight in patiently hanging up all of my "ditties" in our Arizona backyard.

I prefer to use whole names and began to call him Robert which seemed to please him. He was known to everyone as Bob. I declined his offer of Scotch whiskey. It was a chilly place to visit in a snow bank close to midnight and his arm became wrapped around me.

This Robert effortlessly crept his way into my young heart and I found myself going over to his shack every night when I was done in the camp kitchen. He was very creative in finding excuses to invite me over. At that time he had a moustache and would ask me to trim it for him. On an outing to civilization he had come back with red wine and this became our drink together. Initially, I had refused to partake in this because I had become indoctrinated into the Mormon Church prior to leaving Ontario.

The odd fact is that this was also due to Roger. He was a friendly soul and had invited into his Stratford home two young Mormon missionaries. I had become enamoured with one and we had envisioned a future together.

I became a Jack Mormon enjoying our evening wine with this handsome moustached charmer and our kinship evolved in the long dark hours of the northern winter. We had the very best time getting to know each other.

Despite being in the middle of the bush we found a lot of entertaining things to do. He would take me with him in his blue Jimmy blazer over the camp roads to check on his other rigs. He let me drive which landed us in the ditch with great laughs and a call on his radio for help from the rig. Robert was a pilot of bush planes also. Often he would go by plane to other sites to check on the wells although most of the time there was a hired pilot for these outings and a few times I went along for the ride. Sometimes a helicopter was our mode of transportation. I never knew what was up his sleeve next.

We would often just go for long walks down the camp road away from the rig and I would drop myself into the blanket of white to make snow angels. With little boy delight and great chuckles he would join me in these snowy creations.

I was often in the large cooler getting kitchen supplies. He would make it his mission to find me, flinging open the door to my surprise and with long legged strides cross the floor to envelop me in a bear embrace. Then a moment later with a grin, he was gone back to his work. Without any effort our hearts had become entwined. It was rather a shock to me due to the age difference and the fact that he was married with four sons. His oldest boy was older than me.

Yet neither of us gave any consideration to the consequences of this bush camp romance. That fated first night came that I did indeed stay in his arms. No doubt the night crew on the rig were placing bets for this. Our shenanigans did not go unnoticed. Somehow the news was passed on to my employer.

My behavior with Robert was not taken lightly and my days as a second cook came to an abrupt halt. I had nicknamed myself Spud and now Spud was asked to put down her potato peeler. Mashed potatoes for a hungry rig crew calls for a massive amount of potatoes to be peeled. Wowsers! I was most dismayed and yet Robert was unfazed. I could continue to stay with him at his shack he happily suggests.

I had gone into this bush camp without any birth control and soon I had indications of pregnancy. My brother David in Ontario was about to be married. I was expected to be home for this family event and so I made a tearful goodbye from Robert. While in Stratford a pregnancy test revealed I was indeed with child. I remember standing outside the doctor's office in a payphone calling Robert and tearfully telling him this scary news.

What was I going to do? I had to head back west and said farewell to my family. I was greeted with big hugs by my love. He took me back to the scene where we had lovingly co-created this new life forming inside me. Long discussions ensued into the night. I remember him broken hearted as he collapsed on the floor of his humble rig shack in tears when I told him my decision.

"Robert, I believe I will give up this baby for adoption. I do not believe in abortion for a situation like this. And I do not want to raise a child without a father."

The possibility of him leaving his family was not an option. His marriage with Marion was never a true partnership in genuine love and yet they shared the birth of four sons. The boys were raised by Marion due to Robert's oil and gas consulting taking him overseas for extended time. Their home was in Calgary, yet he was rarely there.

He agreed to stand by me and support my decision. There was never any moment in my mind of him abandoning me. This potential child held us committed and bound together although the endless questions of how this and how that were unanswered. We were both in shock and needed to absorb this life altering news.

Robert knew a lot of people and kept in touch with many of his buddies. "I know a man in Spokane, Washington whom I would like you to meet, Possum." He had started calling me Possum and my nickname for him was Toad, as in J. Thaddeus Toad from the "Wind in the Willows".

"Who is he and why do you feel this?"

"Walt is a dear friend who is a psychiatrist and I believe he would help us to make sense of this situation."

I was not going to disagree with him and so we went off on this trip together. We met this Dr. Walt and indeed it proved to be a very wonderful time. Both of us shared our hearts with this kind soul and yet in reality this was more about Robert working through his turmoil. It did seem to put his mind at ease to talk to a buddy. Robert had to get back to the rig and I had someone of my own to visit.

Near to Spokane was the home of the Mormon missionary I met in Stratford. Looking back at this I cannot believe I even did such a thing and yet in my circumstance my desire to have this baby was motivating me down a strange path. I had written a letter to the missionary and advised him of my situation. The visit with his parents was truly not wise yet desperation had led me astray. I was searching.

I loved Robert and yet marriage was not possible with him at that time. Yet for me to have to give up a baby was not something I really wanted either. This ridiculous visit to their home proved to be very hurtful. Religion certainly can cast ungodly standards and judgments wherein it is no one's place to do so. In their eyes I was deemed a sinner and an adulteress.

The fact that our future baby was conceived in love had no bearing on their harsh judgment. This event forever steered me clear of religious dogma and enforced my belief in my own spiritual strength and convictions.

I went on to Duncan, Vancouver Island to stay with my Uncle Russ.

They were going away and I was able to be there alone. I went into Duncan in search of answers to my dilemma. I wanted to remain living out west to be near Robert. I could not advise anyone in my family of my situation nor risk visits from them during my pregnancy.

My angelics were watching over me. I was lovingly steered into an office of a Catholic nun who worked with family services counseling people during trauma. Her name was Sister Freida Raab and she held the answer to my prayers. She listened patiently to my pleas for guidance. "I may have an answer for you if you are willing to live in Prince George."

"Yes, I need to stay out west."

"I know a family who has a daughter named Vivian about your age that has her own apartment. I can explain your situation and see if she would be willing to have you as a roommate."

"That would be marvelous, thank you."

The call was made and thanks to the family's kindness to strangers they agreed to this plan. My obstetrician was a kind British man named Dr. Phillip Woods. My case was a welcome change for him he explained because he performed more abortions than births.

After several weeks he confided he may have a potential family for my baby. I was relieved but found myself hesitant at the same time. I did want to keep this child and yet I could not see myself as a single Mom without his father by our side. Yet that was definitely not possible.

My heart ached over this agonizing decision creating many a sleepless night. There seemed to be no end to the questions in my mind which had no answers and the fear I may never see this child again pained me beyond measure. Who are these people my doctor is considering? Do they really want another baby and will the child get as much love as I could provide if I kept the child? Vivian was glad I was having the baby and yet seemed to think I would be capable of raising him myself.

Thankfully, my light in the darkness was Robert's constant support and our visits together. My roommate was not approving of this Robert love of mine which added to my strain. Yet I was most grateful to her compassion and the kindness of her family which welcomed me into their home.

I wanted to find a job and decided to try tree planting. I enjoyed this outdoor fresh air adventure and yet it was very tiring for me. Camp life can be challenging and there is a lot of time for gossip. I did receive looks from folks as my little love growing within me had begun to show. One day I could no longer feel the baby kicking. I worried that overexerting myself constantly bending over all day had put the baby at risk. This was not true and yet my concern for the baby stayed on my mind.

Some of the women bet a male tree planter to streak through the camp and to great guffaws from a cheering crowd he took up the bet. After about three tours of tree planting I decided to hang up my shovel. I left the streaker behind. I returned to Prince George and spent most of my time swimming in the apartment pool, bicycling and walking. Phone calls and mail from Robert were a blessing.

Once my mind was finally made up about the adoption I knew I could stick with my decision. The last time I saw Robert prior to delivery I was very close to my due date and he was worried that I should not be flying in that condition. Yet I insisted we see each other. We met in Banff staying a couple nights at a cozy log cabin in the trees. His open romantic attentions to me in public created a lot of stares since I was heavy with child.

Robert was distraught by my decision to not allow him to be with me when I gave birth. I knew it would be tough enough on my own yet believed in my heart this was for the best. If he saw the baby I knew it would make it harder for both of us and add to his guilt about not being able to raise the child.

We shared a teary farewell with my promise I would call at the point I was on my way to the hospital. A few days later, in the middle of the night my waters broke and I made my phone call to Robert. "I am on my way and shall call you after the birth."

Vivian drove me to the hospital and had been my coach during child birthing classes so she was by my side. In all honesty I wanted only to be alone and yet I was so grateful for her help I agreed. A few hours later about 8:00 am a healthy kicking nine and a half pound baby boy greeted my startled eyes. It was October 15, 1974. Tears of relief poured from me as I gazed into his blue eyes for the first time. In that moment I was his one and only Mom. A few minutes later I was alone in my own hospital room and the baby in the nursery.

I needed to telephone Robert and found my way to a phone down the hall. "We have a magnificent handsome healthy baby boy." Robert was beside himself. "Are you alright, you sound terrible."

"Well I am on the floor right now with an agonizing sore back, Possum. I did not want to tell you when you phoned at 3:00 a.m. on your way to hospital but I was flying yesterday with a couple rig guys and I crashed the plane. We hit a tough crosswind and I lost control of the plane and it flipped over. We landed upside down and all three of us were scrambling as fast as we could to undo our seatbelts to get out of the plane in case of fire. All of us are ok but it was quite a scare."

"I guess my heart was with you instead of paying attention to my flying. I have been feeling so bad that you are alone in this and my mind became very distracted with worry."

I silently pondered this reality as I listened to him chatter away telling me he loved me and what a brave soul I was. In my mind I kept repeating, thank you over and over to his angels for watching over him. It was indeed a miracle that he was alright. Within a mere few hours of our son's birth unknown to me, his father was having a struggle for his own life. Robert was dangling upside down in a crashed bush plane on the same airstrip of our New Year's Eve celebration.

We agreed to talk again a bit later and I went to the nursery to gaze upon our miracle boy. I was overcome by tears when his crib showed no last name. Instead it read, "Boarder." Thankfully, a nurse was able to get a black and white photo of our lovely co-creation. She placed him in my arms and I went back to my room to savor each moment of our togetherness.

The day arrived for me to depart the hospital and leave behind this bundle of love. Dr. Phillip, and the lawyer handling the private adoption were waiting outside to greet me as Vivian and I approached. I walked slowly up to them with my son for the last time. Photos were taken. I planted a kiss on his forehead and whispered a silent prayer to keep him safe and well. He was taken from my arms and given to the lawyer.

I turned and walked away promising myself that the day would come he would stand before me as a young man to meet the woman who gave him life. Words are pointless to describe the pains and aches overtaking my whole being as I silently got into Vivian's car. She drove us to a park on a hill next to the hospital and we sat in the fall colors. I began my grieving for this baby which would carry with me wherever I went for the next twenty years plus. For the first few years every baby I saw gave me heartache.

Yet the depths of courage and strength we all carry within us astounds me and I was to learn that I was indeed well blessed in this regard. It was during this early time after our son's birth that Robert began referring to me as a "brick." He spent many an hour writing out long letters on legal length note pads. Along with one such letter I received in the mail a copy of a letter Vivian had sent to him. I was so touched he had sent her kind words on to me.

One day a rather bumpy envelope arrived from Robert. I opened it to find peanuts taped inside. Goodness knows how long it took for him to compose and tape peanuts on to a page. It read, "Once upon a time there were two little peanuts"; with two peanuts taped apart. "Who somehow found each other"; two peanuts are taped side by side. "Don't they look like happy peanuts. And then there were three peanuts, my my." Next there are three peanuts taped together. "And even today there are still three little peanuts even though sometimes they look like this." There were three peanuts taped apart from each other. It ends with, "Now isn't this a sad and beautiful and lonely and lovely and tearful and happy story and one without an end because they will live happily together forever wherever."

On the back of the envelope he had written, "By Jove, I do believe it is wax" and affixed a blob of candle wax. I envisioned my love in his rig shack with the jug wine candle burning like we used to do while he sips his scotch admiring his creativity.

I worked part time for my doctor Phillip. I shall always remember a picnic we shared after the birth. We enjoyed the scent and colors of the fall leaves. I captured photos of the sky above. I missed Robert and it was time to leave Prince George. I bade my teary farewells to everyone and headed for Peace River, Alberta.

Robert sometimes spent time at the Travelers Motel in town and thanks to his contacts was able to help find me a studio apartment with a lovely lady named Shirley. We became the best of friends and she spent many an hour listening to my tales and welcomed Robert into her beautiful home overlooking the Peace. Thanks again to his contacts I was accepted at the local Sutherland Nursing Home as a nurse's aide. I had forged a new life thanks to my love.

I became good friends with a couple of the other aides named Donna and Erna. Sometimes I would go spend time with one of them as they began the night shift. I had a bottle of wine which added to our silliness. We shared many a giggle about this and that. My aching heart was comforted in sharing my tale of Robert and the baby with these women. Erna, herself was familiar with adoption since she and Pete had adopted two children. Thus we were able to have some great heart to hearts. This job proved to be just what I needed.

My memory shall forever hold the hearts of those elderly who left their imprint. Elsa, was a Dutch woman who endured the Hitler death camps and her arm bore the insignia of this horror. Often during the night I would go in to comfort her as she cried in her sleep talking in Dutch. She was a lady of utmost dignity and immense strength.

Another favorite was Isabelle Evans. She was a short, feisty soul who could be quite combative when she did not want to comply. She loved to sing her favorite refrain, "My name is Isabelle Evans and I am from Glasgow, Scotland." She had a twinkle in her eye and an unforgettable smile.

For the next three years I moved tenderly through my grief and saw Robert as much as possible. During my alone time I spent all my time outdoors. I had purchased my first Pentax camera and some lenses. This was a godsend. I often spent all day hiking the train tracks and wandering the hills with camera in hand and a bag of snacks to keep me going.

Roberto was born in Santa Ana, California and as the oil business began to change due to the Canadian government he made the decision to close up his own company and head south. It was a tough farewell. With his big arms enveloping me he promised, "We shall be together again somehow, somewhere and sometime. Believe me Poss, Poss, I am not letting you out of my life." He headed to his beautiful second home in Carefree, Arizona, yet this was short lived. Soon he found himself in Denver, Colorado in search of work. Thankfully, his hard efforts paid off and he became a drilling manager for Exeter Drilling Company.

We stayed in touch by phone and mail, however it was a full year before we were able to see each other. I had become restless and wanted something more to my life. My job at the nursing home I loved and yet it was taking a toll on my tender heart.

The day came that the world outside of idyllic Peace River beckoned to me. Thanks to my parents I share a love of travel and seeking foreign lands. I was drawn to Mexico. It was a big step back into embracing life. With my camera friend I boarded a plane for Mexico City. For about ten days I saw as much as I could and took a train into the Yucatan and was mesmerized by the Mayan ruins of Chichen Itza. After a couple days in lovely Guadalajara I flew home to Alberta.

This adventuresome trip had opened my mind. I was not able to happily resume my duties as a nurse's aide and realized I was burnt out. It was time to leave the safety of my Peace River cocoon. Carol Ann was ready to step out into the big wide world. At the age of twenty-four, I decided to go back to school. Robert was pleased and suggested a small women's college in Denver. This sounded good to me since I was not willing to be part of a large campus life and it offered the chance for us to be together again.

More Big Changes

Prior to the start of my campus life Robert flew me to Denver from Edmonton. I was enthralled with my future home of Colorado Women's College. It was during that timeframe that my sister Valerie was making plans to be married to her love, Dick. They had been living and working in Tehran, Iran and decided to marry in Edinburgh, Scotland.

I shared this news with Robert as we sat on his deck overlooking the city of Denver and the Colorado Rockies in the distance. For a time Valerie had lived in Calgary and had actually met my Robert. As we chatted I came up with a great idea. "You know what I am going to do, Toado, I am going to take my bicycle to London, England and meet up with Valerie and Dick. I shall be their photographer for their little wedding at their Scottish chapel. I will cycle the British Isles and maybe I could get a train pass to see a bit of Europe."

As always he was supportive and we saluted this grand scheme with a toast. I returned home to the hills of the Peace River valley and began to train for my cycling journey. I hiked up and down, down and up the many hills and rode my bike for hours. The hill with the twelve foot Davis monument was hiked many a time. The view was well worth the effort.

I was so excited to be making my first overseas travels on my own. My bicycle and I headed across to merry London where I put us both on a train to Edinburgh. Needless to say, I received a festive welcome from the future Mr. and Mrs. Hodge upon my arrival to Edinburgh with bike in hand.

After their wedding ceremony, it was time for me to begin my marathon bicycle adventure. I captured a memorable photo of Dick riding my wheel. Big hugs and off I rode leaving them waving happily. My little pup tent and gear were strapped to the back of the bike. I eagerly cycled towards whatever was waiting over the beautiful rolling Scottish hillside.

For the next month I cycled several hours each day and found an appropriate place to pitch my little pup tent for the night. The first few days were tough. Yet I soon got my leg muscles up to the task happily peddling away enjoying the ever changing delightful greenery and manoeuvering my way through the many sheep wandering the roads.

I crossed the channel into Northern Ireland and experienced the unpleasant body searches and checkpoints of life in Belfast at that time. Bombed blackened buildings and armed stern looking soldiers was the way of the world there. I was glad to depart this warzone by train heading south. There were some other bicyclists on the train and we all shared the fact that Belfast was not a place to hang about in happily.

I knew the Irish folk were speaking English and yet it certainly could be a challenge to discern some of their wording. The Irish were a welcoming lot. After the initial shock of seeing me at their door requesting the use of their nearby field I was often invited in for a cup of tea and goodies.

I crossed the waters again landing in Wales and more cycling back into London where I stored my bicycle. For the last two weeks of my trip I toured France, Spain and Portugal by Euro Rail Pass. I camped out on the lovely sandy beaches of Portugal and spent hours in the warmth of the sun tanning and becoming a very light blonde. The beaches had many vendors selling delicious fresh concoctions of their catch from the sea.

My light blonde hair caught the eye of a tanned, young handsome Portuguese beach dweller and we spent time sharing the beach cuisine and Portuguese wines. Soon it was time to fly away and we said our farewells.

I returned home to Canada with iron legs and a sack full of film to be developed. It was then time to pack up my belongings to get ready to head south of the border for college. My life at the nursing home was over and I made many a tearful goodbye and hugs that did not want to end. Peace River had proven to be the ideal setting to restore my zest for life and inspire me to greater heights. It had served its purpose in my recovery over our son's adoption. Now it was time to move forward and onward in a new direction. I flew into my life in the good old U.S. of A. Canada would not be my home again until twenty-six amazing, eventful years later.

The timing was right for this. I leapt into my studies and campus job with the exuberance of a joyful labrador puppy. I was in my glory and reveled in my new world of college life. Robert and I were back in each other's arms. To my surprise and delight he had quit smoking. When we met on the rig he smoked cigars and cigarettes. He shared with me that one night when he reached for a smoke he looked at it saying, what the heck am I doing. It was thrown into the toilet and that was his last smoke of any kind. He had quit cold turkey and had been a serious smoker for many years. "It was a filthy, dirty habit Poss and I am best to be over it."

He was still married and I was an unknown part of his life so this did create challenges but we were up to the task. Being together was all that mattered and I was grateful for all of these precious times. I loved my studies and job in the admissions department and breezed my way through the four year program in three years.

Robert invested his well-earned monies in a small condo in the mountain ski town of Steamboat Springs. This became our getaway place for frequent weekend jaunts. His wife Marion had no interest in his company so this was fine with her. She would take off on her own excursions which meant we had more time for us. I was his wife in many respects; it just was not a marriage.

In the last year of my bachelor's degree, my need to travel took hold again. My craving for new adventure led me to be accepted into a semester abroad program in the other worldly Shangri la of Kathmandu, Nepal. My Nepalese was put into practice living with a Hindu family in an outer village with two young children. The father wore white always since he was in mourning for a year for his father's death. The mother was a year younger than myself and could not understand why I had neither children nor a husband.

Third world lifestyle was a real culture shock. Most Nepalese are very poor. The village children welcomed me home each day on my rented bicycle and I did my best to fit in. The children loved to play with my film canisters and some balloons which I blew up for them. I was the centre of attraction for the nearby neighbours and relatives.

Being alone and solo is not an issue for me. For my independent study I excitedly found myself at a Tibetan Buddhist monastery for ten days involved in a meditation retreat for westerners. It had a lovely view of the valley below since it sat above the village. The colorful streams of Tibetan Buddhist prayer flags greeted us every morning and waved our intents into the mountains. I was not adept at holding the meditation position so the days were quite long. We had a day of total silence which proved to be very interesting. This certainly gave me a different perspective on people interaction.

I hold the greatest admiration and respect for these lovely peace minded people of Nepal and Tibet. Their greeting Namaste is to this day my favorite word which translated means, "I honor the place in you in which the entire universe dwells. I honor the place in you which is of love, of truth, of light and of peace. When you are in that place in you, and I am in that place in me, we are one." When one greets you with "Namaste", the hands are placed together at heart level and you bow to the other. To this day I have a fondness and affinity with Tibetan Buddhism.

Of course I missed my Roberto love, yet everyday was a new adventure and I wanted to savor every moment of this breathtaking foreign land. I had come a long way from my life in the hills of northern Alberta. Part of the program involved time to travel on your own and I found myself trekking in the footsteps of countless others before me reveling in the otherworldly beauty of the Himalayan foothills. Somewhere over the horizon was the majestic Mount Everest. At one point I was totally alone walking down a long winding path into a mountain village below. It was liberating!

My fear of heights was a challenge when having to cross the various rope swing bridges. I gasped in terror upon seeing the first one before me. It was either cross it or turn back and cross it I did. Throughout the trek there were stupas and many a prayer wheel which I happily turned as I hiked past.

After my trek I headed into the south of Nepal with a totally different terrain where elephants roamed. With the aid of a Nepalese to boost me up, I found myself enjoying the slow swaying ride of an elephant.

Head lice, bed bugs and upset tummy became a part of my life yet it was worth every minute of the physical unpleasantness. My most repeated Nepalese phrase was, "My tummy hurts, where is the bathroom?" I sent postcards and many a letter off to my Robert and family. He sent me countless telegrams expressing his excited plans for my return and a trip for the two of us to Baja, Mexico.

One of the parcels he sent me gave me great chuckles. I opened it up to discover birth control pills for me to restart before my return; my silly thoughtful boy. I had the biggest laughs when he shared with me later how he convinced my doctor to allow him to fill such a prescription.

Another silly parcel was a wool hat which he had spent countless time attaching little love notes all over it.

The time in this majestic kingdom came to an end and I flew into Delhi, India and spent a few days exploring. I was blessed in being able to set foot into one of the wonders of the world, the Taj Mahal.

I flew back into New York City and will never forget my state of culture shock when I stood in a phone booth speaking to Robert. I returned home to Canada for a brief visit with my parents. The contrast of lifestyle between the west and an underdeveloped country took me awhile to readjust to and I was overwhelmed by the luxury of life. I no longer had to stoop over an open pit with maggots to do my business and I had safe tap water and a cozy, warm, comfortable bed without any creatures.

Then it was another plane ride back to Denver, Colorado. My unpleasant case of intestinal parasites was cleared up with medication. Bobby and I had a most pleasant reunion and memorable vacation at a lovely resort on the sea of Baja. He pampered me with only the best.

He had another delightful surprise for me upon my return. I had been living in an apartment in an area of Denver which held some safety issues. Just prior to leaving for overseas I had been mugged while walking to the college and my purse was stolen. Robert was beside himself with agitation and unknown to me while I was studying in Nepal he had made it his mission to find me a suitable new place to live. The rent was higher yet my on campus job would fill my needs. And it was indeed a lovely step above my former place. It was quite the treat to get used to after life in Nepal.

My college advisor was a dear Chinese man named Dr. David Yu. He was most excited and approving of my Nepal adventures and we shared great visits upon my return. The Dalai Lama made a trip to Denver for a public audience and to my great thrill; Dr. Yu and I were at the event. This certainly was a cherished evening.

My love affair with Nepal opened the door to further education. I was accepted into the Master's program at the University of Denver. Graduate school proved to be harder and not as much fun for me. My socializing was spent with the foreign students. Friendship with a couple men and a woman from Indonesia provided many happy moments. Life was busy with schoolwork, part time work and of course the closeness of Robert.

Being a Canadian I was allowed to study with a student visa which would expire upon my graduation. My initial plan upon getting all that expensive education was to have an international job or work for the World Bank. My head was in the clouds for sure with that as a plan. I came to realize that I was fooling myself. I had now invested eight intimate years in my relationship with this married Magoo.

Despite wanting to pursue a career to use my education I knew my heart belonged with my love. I was not capable of leaving Robert or Denver. I had given up our son and I could not give him up also. My graduation was approaching. The year was 1982 and at that time Denver was still a bustling oil and gas city. With Robert's encouragement I applied to the U.S. immigration for a working visa in hopes that I could continue to stay in Denver. However, my education and skills did not deem me a suitable match according to United States immigration. My request was denied.

Years ago through unknown means to me Robert had arranged for me to get an American social security number. This proved to be a blessing and he insisted that I ought to ignore the decision of the American government. "The heck with them, Possum, you do not have to leave. You have a social security card and can get a job no problem." This man's faith in me was unwavering.

"I will become an illegal alien, Robert. You will have to call me a snowback." My tears turn to chuckles with my silly remark.

"This will work itself out, you shall see. Have heart; Carol Ann, we shall hatch a new plan of action."

Both of us are chuckling now and have overcome the disappointment. I am buoyed with his trust that all will be in perfection. And indeed it was. We were being watched over and meant to stay together and this is exactly what we did.

It is not obvious the difference between a Canadian and an American unless you can detect this in a person's language. I did frequently use the Canuck expression, "eh," with my sentences and became more conscious of this habit doing my best to eliminate it from my vocabulary. I found work with a temporary agency and jumped from one assignment to another, often working for oil and gas companies. Then the happy day came I was hired on as a full time employee in the land department of an oil company. Funny thing was that my new employer was a Canadian oil company based out of Calgary. Robert and I took the greatest delight in this ironic twist of fate.

Life was very good. I had an interesting job analysing oil and gas leases in the land department. My petroleum engineer buddy and I now had something wondrous in common. He gave me his own education into the various agreements which involve drilling a well. We would meet for lunch together and drinks after work surrounded with oil field trash as he affectionately called them. I became known to a few of his friends and was greeted with knowing smiles. We spent a lot of weekends at his mountain condo.

Every year on October 15 we were always together to mark the anniversary of our son's birth. This was never a very happy day. The fact I had a son somewhere was kept secret to my family and friends. Over the years I did share my story with women I became close to and this was a source of comfort. It did pain me to not be able to shout it out to the world that I had a son and yet silence was a safer option.

My sorrows did take a heavy toll on my relationship with Robert. I added to his guilt over the situation and my tears on the birthdays of our son could not be squelched. Of course, he had his own sorrows for our son. Yet he was a father to four boys and I had only one son whom I did not know was alive or dead.

The oil business started to have layoffs of anyone over the age of sixty. They hired younger folks for less money. Unfortunately, after his sixtieth birthday this happened to Robert and he was put into forced retirement. This was a man who loved his oil business or mostly gas as added humorously, being a great farter.

He did not know what to do with himself, yet soon found a suitable solution to help him have a new routine. He rented a small office which he shared with another laid-off oil buddy. The three of us often shared lunches and I would listen to them reminisce and tell tall tales of the good old days in the oil biz. The times had indeed drastically changed from the day that an oil well agreement was made in a bar with a mere handshake.

It was a sad fact of life that most of the older experienced employees were let go and younger guys came in for less money and less experience. The oil and gas companies began to hurt and people were let go regardless of age. Then the downturn hit my own company and I was laid off. It was a very sad day. I had become very fond of my budding career as an oil and gas lease analyst.

I knew that I would not be able to find another good job in Denver and I pondered what the answer to this predicament was. Robert had purchased another lovely home in Carefree, Arizona. It was situated within the exclusive five star golf community of The Boulders. He used it as a rental property and occasionally a vacation destination. I was blessed to get to know the Arizona desert with him in hand during a couple trips to his home. By then, I had lived in Denver for ten years and thought it was time for a change. I decided a move to Carefree would prove to be a good idea because he owned property there.

This time I was the one to make the move to a distant city. Perhaps one day he may be the one to follow me I mused.

My decision was made and he helped with the big move. It was another adventure for the two of us after all. I rented a small U-Haul trailer and hitched it to my mustang and happily said goodbye to Colorado. It was the fall of 1987.

Robert had begun his love affair with old corvettes. He drove his 65 roadster to Arizona. It was great fun driving beside each other on the freeway, honking and laughing as we head into Albuquerque, New Mexico to stay the night and then on to Phoenix the next day. Once again, thanks to his contacts of spending a lot of time himself in Carefree, a realtor friend named Joyce arranged for me to rent a small condo.

The valley of the sun was in a downturn also and finding a job proved difficult. I did whatever I could to pay my bills. I had a short lived career of cleaning pools. Working in the triple digit heat did not agree with this Canuck and I was a lousy pool cleaner anyway. I went on to become a self-employed caregiver for a homebound elderly woman. Then I was blessed to become a temporary at an oil and gas refining company only a few minutes outside of Carefree.

As anticipated, Robert and I set up housekeeping together at his home in the Boulders. He had a membership to the Boulders and he often enjoyed sitting up at the bar chatting with the bartender. I would join him. On one such occasion he greets me with an extra-large smile wrapping his arm around me saying, "Kristy, I would like you to meet Carol Ann."

I was greeted with a lovely, smiling blonde woman who was very glad to meet me. The three of us develop a rapport and soon Kristy is enveloped in our lives. There was always a lot of merriment between us. It was great fun for me to share my Robert love with someone about my own age.

Upon a trip back to Denver he shared with me that he wanted to find us a chocolate labrador retriever. I knew he was in a difficult place in his life being unemployed and without me nearby. A dog sounded like a great idea. I had moved into a bigger apartment across from the post office.

We enjoyed daily visits by phone and contemplated his next planned trip to the desert. Albuquerque was a halfway point and often I would fly there to meet him and then drive on to Carefree with him. We saw a fair bit of each other and yet endured many a difficult goodbye. It was great being together and yet it always had to end for him to go back to his Denver home.

On one of these occasions, I remember standing at the side of Cave Creek Road waving as I watched him drive away in his roadster with the top down. A few moments later, he turned the car around and came back for another embrace. Again I stood waving. Yet still he did not want to leave. I watched as he pulled up to me again for a third time. There were tears in his eyes. We again said our farewells. This time he kept driving and I slowly walked with a heavy heart back to my little abode.

After that loving experience whenever he drove away from me I made it a point to watch and see if he would turn around. During the times I would drive with him to Albuquerque and fly back to Phoenix, even at the airport this tender turnaround manoeuver was standard even though it took him longer. I waited and sure enough a few minutes later he showed up for another embrace.

Then he began to start moving things from his Colorado home since we were spending so much time together in Carefree. On a phone visit he shared his plans to fly into Phoenix. He had purchased a car which he left parked at his desert home and this I drove to the airport to pick him up.

I went inside to greet him as he was retrieving boxes off the baggage claim. "Could you bring the car around out front and I shall meet you." I was perplexed by his behavior and yet complied with his request.

As I pulled up to the curb I could not believe my eyes. My Bobby love greeted me with a big boyish grin and a magnificent chocolate labrador by his side. I jumped out of the car and was welcomed by a big woof. "Carol Ann, I would like you to meet Saber."

"Oh Robert, you found your puppy and have kept him a secret from me."

"Yes, I have had him about a month. I wanted to surprise you."

"Where in the world did you find such a beautiful creation?"

"A lab breeder named Dodie, in Loveland, Colorado. The moment I laid eyes on him I knew he was the one and I told her I want that dog. She said you can't have him because I plan to use him as a stud for breeding. But I insisted and finally she agreed."

"Well I am so glad your charms were not wasted. Thank you to this Dodie, whomever you are for complying with my lovie's wishes."

The three of us happily drove out to the desert and Saber became acquainted with the swimming pool. I saw immediately that Saber was Robert's dog. This labrador was no ordinary dog that was for sure; there was something very remarkable about him which oozed from every pore. I felt a Namaste resonance with him and knew the three of us were soul bound together. I was very grateful for this decision of Robert's. It was a providential manifestation without any doubt!

Robert was now living most of the time in Carefree and yet for whatever reason he felt the need to return to Denver. He became upset about leaving. This began to take its toll on our relationship. Over the years although the word divorce did come up in conversation I knew he was not in favor of this and thus it was rarely discussed. As he lay on the couch one day moaning about having to leave my company I could not take his ridiculous attitude anymore. "You know my dear man; there is a solution to our situation. And the word begins with a "D."

I was referring to divorce and unbelievably I had to spell it out for him. Slowly a smile forms and the light went on upstairs as the saying goes. "Well now Poss, Poss, I do have a buddy that could get such a venture under way." He got up off the couch and made the call that would change our lives for the better. His wife Marion had been living her own life for years and undoubtedly would welcome this proposal of divorce which in turn could lead to our own proposal of married life. What a thought to finally envision as our potential truth.

A meeting was set up to file for his divorce and he was on the way to Denver. Our customary farewell had a different feel to it this time as we realized that perhaps we had an opportunity to finally put an end to all of these comings and goings. The notion that we could actually be married one day seemed quite foreign to me and yet held great promise. I was sighing inwardly with the most profound grateful relief.

I returned to my own apartment and he headed down the road with Saber dog by his side. He would be in need of his four legged angel as he headed into this venture so I was very grateful he had been guided to the right place at the right time to discover his soul mate pup.

On the eve of my Dad's birthday, March 7, 1991 my phone rang in the middle of the night. Robert was at his condo in Steamboat Springs when he had received a phone call from Marion. I fell to the floor as I heard his words, "Mark has killed himself."

Unknown to both of us as Robert was about to forge a new path for our lives together, his son Mark was about to end his life. "Yes, he is dead."

Robert had four sons. His boy named Mark lived in Salt Lake City, Utah with a wife and two boys. He ran a successful toxicology lab. He was living the American dream or so we thought. Robert had recently visited with him and shared with me how well he was doing. Mark was a very compassionate quiet soul and yet unknown to anyone was in a lot of inner turmoil. Of his four sons, this was the one Robert had chosen to confide our story with and now I would never get to meet him.

Mark had gone into his garage about 1:00 a.m. and climbed into his old restored truck with a shotgun. The silence of the night was erupted with his last breath. Death is a tough enough challenge, yet suicide by such means is an indescribable horror with no answers. Needless to say the divorce plans were put on hold.

This Is My Wife, Carol Ann

Saber was left with Dodie so he could fly to Salt Lake. Dodie asked if she could use him for stud services and in payment he could pick out a puppy. Prior to this we had discussed getting a puppy and yet Robert was never in agreement. However, this crisis changed things. The prospect of a puppy was what we all needed.

After the death of his son I moved in with him and we were together full time. His trips to and from Colorado stopped. My job at the refining company had turned into a permanent fulltime job in the land department.

I was very grateful that we could be together. Robert's grief had overwhelmed him to the core. He confided that it was good he had me in his life otherwise he would not still be alive himself. I could say nothing but hold him close at the reference to suicide. The time came that our puppy was ready to be picked up and Robert drove to Colorado. The divorce which had been put on hold with Mark's death was now back in the works.

The day I met Saber's puppy is etched in my brain as another magical day. She was a black lab and we decided to name her Spookie. I was at work on the day he arrived back in Carefree and to my surprise there he was in the parking lot when I went out to my car. With the biggest grin he passes her into my welcome arms. It was love at first sight. I happily drove home with this cuddly bundle looking up into my eyes for the first time. Father and daughter labradors quickly became the closest of buddies as Robert and I joyfully watched their relationship evolve.

Our friend Kristy joins us one day for photos on the golf course with the two dogs. It was great fun as always sharing time with her. Bob, as she referred to him kept all of us in smiles and laughter.

It was shortly thereafter that my job was terminated due to layoffs. Yet this turned into a blessing to be able to finally be fulltime with my Robert and the two dogs. A puppy can do wonders to an ailing heart. The divorce was finally over and behind us. We began to make plans for our marriage.

Years ago while still in Alberta I had told my parents about him but this news had been met with disapproval. It was tough on my Mom and Dad to envision their daughter involved with a much older married man. Sometime after my move to Arizona they had flown to California to meet us. My Dad travelled a lot with his high position within the Canadian Masonic Lodge. Our initial meeting was a little awkward but Robert was adept at putting people at ease. I was very grateful to my parents' willingness to finally embrace this man as part of my life. The next year we met in Dallas, Texas. Robert knew that our wedding plans would ease their hearts and suggested that we be married at my parents' home.

The news of our potential wedding is well received by his old Carefree friend, Joyce. She had been the one to help get me settled initially. During a private conversation with her one day she shared, "I am so happy for the both of you. Bob spoke to me more than once how he hoped he would be able to take care of you in the manner you so well deserved and now he shall fulfill his wish. Congratulations to you Carol Ann. Your patience is outstanding."

The long awaited day arrived which was October 10, 1992. Our son had been born on October 15 and this date prior to his birth was chosen intentionally. We drove with Saber and Spookie in his old eldorado cadillac convertible to Canada.

Shortly after crossing into Ontario we found a lovely fishing camp with comfortable cabins. Unfortunately, I forgot to take the box of milk bones from the well of the back seat of the car. We were now in bear territory. In the night I heard a ruckus and to my horror looked out to see a black bear cleaning up the dog food which had spilled by the stair. It had rained recently and when I placed the bag on the

26

ground momentarily the bottom fell out. There was still some left on the ground.

I went back to bed and in the morning we were greeted with a most upsetting sight. The bear had clawed his way through the convertible top. He had clawed through the front seat to the back and devoured the dog treats. Needless to say we could not continue our trip. A top had to be ordered and the interior reupholstered as well. Robert was most displeased and yet this misadventure had happened in a beautiful spot.

We enjoyed an extended stay and even took a seaplane ride to a little island to fish and came back with our supper. Finally the car was done and with big grins and farewell to the bear we continued eastward. Our next stay was a visit with my brother Dave. My brother Roger who had led me to Robert had divorced Beth and returned to life in Kitchener, Ontario with a new wife named Wendy. Rog welcomed Saber and Spookie and my Roberto. He was most pleased of our marriage plans. He agreed full heartedly that my following him out west years ago had ultimately saved me from marriage to the Mormon missionary which would have ended in sorrow.

We arrived in Stratford to say hello to my Mom and Dad and pick up my brother Mark. Our labs cannot be at my parents and we found a superb kennel in the country with heated floors and woods for the two labs to run in twice a day. Mark and Robert formed an instant rapport and the three of us share many a good laugh. Robert loved to fart and delighted Mark by telling him. "Pull this finger Mark." My brother happily complied and then the three of us are rolling in laughter as my soon to be husband displays he can fart on command. What a talent!

October 10 arrives and the two of us stood in my parents' living room for our wedding vows. My Robert sheds a tear as we become husband and wife. We are both overjoyed. As everyone mingles about afterwards I am with my sister Valerie, when Dave comes to me with a big grin saying, "Your husband is looking for you."

I am momentarily speechless to hear these words for the very first time and have a startled look on my face which my dear brother Dave chuckles over. "Hey, I thought you would like to hear those words." I am all smiles as Dave congratulates me and I go find my husband. He is sharing the bear story which becomes one of his favorites.

After a lovely time visiting with everyone it is time for us to depart for our honeymoon. Robert had arranged for us to take the train from Toronto to Halifax. We stay at the Royal York hotel in Toronto for the night and start our train safari in the morning. After a few memorable days in the Maritimes we head back to Ontario to then begin our driving safari back to where we just came from.

Mark joins us when we go to pick up the dogs. He is a true lover of dogs and enjoys every second with an exuberant Saber and Spookie reunion. Our farewells to family are made and it is now time to head down the road with our joyful labs.

American immigration requires a three month waiting period of us living within Canada prior to my becoming legal. We spend a lot of time exploring all around Nova Scotia and take the ice breaking ferry across to Prince Edward Island. A couple nights are spent in Charlottetown and sometime exploring this lovely green isle home of Anne of Green Gables. The beaches are lovely stretches of open sand. Our favorite one is a place called Panmure Island. There is a lighthouse and I captured a great photo of our two beloved angel dogs with my husband sporting an ear to ear grin. Chester, Nova Scotia welcomes us with the labs and we frequent a charming pub with both of them. All of us love our time in the Maritimes.

Life was a magical time spent as Mr. and Mrs. Arnim. Robert never tired of introducing me as his wife. Good things can indeed come with patience and we were both reveling in our new life. With my green card from immigration in hand we return to the U.S. and take the long way home. Valerie's husband Dick is also American and they live in Jacksonville, Florida. It is a joyful happy time sharing our married bliss with my sister and husband. We finally arrive back in our desert home.

A phrase I often began to hear Robert say to me was, "So why didn't we do this before Possum?" It had been a long journey to get this love of my life to realize that our marriage was meant to be and to just do it. I was too beside myself with joy to chide him on this at this point, so I merely chuckled at his comment. "You are a silly boy. It does not matter anymore my love, that is past and this is our now."

I loved to take Saber and Spookie on long treks around the neighbourhood. The golf course was up the road and we often walked its pathways. I let the dogs off leash and delighted in watching them run and roll on the fine greenery. Serious golfers took great offense to Saber's game of charging onto the green and stealing golf balls. I quickly gathered both dogs back on their leashes and hurried away with apologies. One day the doorbell rings and I am greeted with the stern face of the town sheriff. "Mrs. Arnim, we have had numerous complaints of your dogs running loose on the golf course. You must refrain from any such actions in the future."

Robert inquires who was at the door when I see him at his desk. "I just got told off by the sheriff for letting the puppies loose on the golf course."

"Well now my fine Possum, that is amusing for sure that you are creating a ruckus. That's the spunk in you I know and love, you are not one to follow the rules. No doubt Elmer was miffed for sure."

"It was a brief conversation yet he was doing his job. Jerry was outside on his driveway so likely wonders what the sheriff is at our door for."

"How funny, you have created some good gossip."

He delighted in sharing his new life with his Red Baron buddies. This is a small group of men he went to school with. Robert had an admiration for Baron Von Richthofen, the flying ace from World War I, thus the name the Red Barons. He had even designed his own letterhead with the name and a sketched red triplane. The five men would take skiing trips without any wives allowed. It was a time of reminiscing along with the irreverent pastime of gazing at cookies and studying panty lines. Certainly a very fine time was always enjoyed by all. It was friendships of a lifetime so very special indeed the bond they shared and maintained.

It was harder for him to share this news with his sons yet I persuaded him to do so. I did not want to be kept a secret anymore. It was months after we were married that he sat at his desk over two days composing a letter which he read to me upon finishing. I was startled by his sentence, "At this time there is no evidence of cancer in my lungs." I refuse to envision these words and do not even want to discuss why he said such, so do not question him. It was a very beautiful letter and not short on words. I was grateful. The phone rang as a result of this and I got to have my first hello with his three sons. His oldest, Skip was shocked to learn his stepmom is younger than himself.

The truth was now out with everyone and our lives as a married couple begin in earnest. Robert decides to replace the flooring in the entry and kitchen area with Mexican saltillo tile. He discovers a place that does custom tile design. We take a drive in to the city and choose some unique designs for our floor and also the fireplace area. He surprises me in asking for some wet clay to take home. "We can place the paw prints of both dogs with their names in our floor. What do you think of that idea wife of mine?"

"That is great, I love it. The dogs will leave their permanent paw prints in our floor."

"I am also going to ask them to design a toad and possum tile. You as my possum shall be dangling upside down from a tree limb above me while I as J. Thaddeus Toad shall be reclining below smoking a cigar."

"Oh my goodness, that will certainly be a one of kind tile."

"But of course, just like us."

"How neat that a symbol of our love will leave a permanent expression in our home even after we leave it. Thank you Bobby boy."

The tiles with the imprints of the dog paws turn out well. A couple are strategically placed on the front walkway. Von Spook's is placed in front of the oven since she was always in the kitchen whenever cooking was happening and Saber's was placed nearby.

Robert had sold his corvette roadster and acquired a bright yellow 1972 corvette with Ttops which I occasionally drove. While he stayed home one day doing his paperwork I drove it into the post office and parked it in our carport upon my return. Later as he passes the front door he asks me, "Poss, why is the corvette on the road?"

To the shock of both of us the car had rolled out of the driveway hitting the corner stop sign and thankfully came to a stop at the edge of Boulder Drive. "It seems you forgot to put the brake on."

"Indeed yes. I must have been distracted by something and rushed to get back inside."

He carefully inspects his lovely riding machine stroking the back end. I breathed a sigh of relief when he says, "There does not appear to be any damage. However, this broken stop sign will have to be uprighted. But there is no harm done." I am thankful my error has not resulted in anything further.

It was not long after that a bill arrived in the mail for the cost of putting the stop sign back up. Roberto was more miffed by this than the incident itself. Yet it proved to be another addition to his bag of tales and he lovingly smiles at me whenever he recites it.

We loved to travel and Robert wanted to show me his home state of California. We took several little jaunts by plane. His home area of Santa Ana, along with Balboa Newport, Del Mar and Santa Monica and wherever else caught his fancy were a destination more than once. Fortunately, we had found a great dog sitter who came to our home to care for our pampered labradors.

Both of us loved our Carefree home and yet were getting tired of the desert heat and wanted to live in four seasons again. It was a dream of Robert's that we build a Lindal cedar home on some treed private land somewhere. He dearly loved Canada so it was a tough decision. It was in the fall that we drove up to Washington and rented a home in Anacortes by the sea. We spent a lot of time exploring and went by ferry across to Vancouver Island.

Over the years we discussed the possibility of finding our son when he became old enough at the required age of nineteen. I did not know how we would accomplish such a challenge and yet believed there was a way to resolve the puzzle.

Robert was very concerned about finding the boy and afraid I would be hurt in the process. "I assure you Robert that I cannot be any more hurt than what I have endured over these long years and I believe your worries are unjustified. I very much appreciate and understand your concern, yet this needs to be put aside. There is no choice in the matter, whatever the outcome we must do this."

"Yes you are right again, my Possum for sure we need to do this and so we shall. This is for him as well."

I do not remember the details of how we were led to our answer and yet somehow it fell into our laps. There was a government agency in Vancouver, B.C. who handled adoption searches. I dug out the private adoption paperwork and the letters from the lawyer and the birth certificate I had made for him, naming him Robert Charles Mennie.

The fee was enclosed along with the application and sealed with trust in my heart this was the right choice at the right time.

Certainly both of us were very anxious and pondered whether he would even want to meet us. After all not everyone involved in these situations desires to meet the other party. I just always believed that our story would evolve to the best for everyone.

Our trip to live in Anacortes proved to be a divinely guided decision and we made the trip across the border to meet the man handling our case for the past months. A most exciting yet frightening time it was. Our application and process had been in the works for a while. There was no definitive timeframe when an answer would come but we were told it could be a few months.

Another blessing to this trip was being able to reconnect with the two women who were my salvation during my pregnancy. Sister Freida Raab was contacted and Robert was able to thank this woman. Thanks to Freida I was able to reconnect with Vivian who was now living in Kelowna. It was a very festive time. It was a welcome surprise to both women to meet the father of the baby who was now my husband. Everything was progressing as if in a fairy tale and yet the best was soon to be.

Our time in Washington proved to be most propitious indeed. One day the phone rang and it was the search agency. They had discovered the whereabouts of our son! The next step was for them to contact him to find out if he wanted to be found and have any contact with us.

We were a mix of fear and jubilation upon hanging up the phone. Spookie came to our rescue and provided relief with laughter as we discovered that she had found the apple tree. Both her and Saber were taking delight in bringing their new treats into the house to gobble up and then go back outside for more. Thank Godness for dogs! What a joy they were to us and especially now.

We returned home to Arizona with our hearts full of anticipation. The trip had reconnected us with a painful past which soon could be turned around. The gods of serendipity had graced our path. The door was now wide open to the possibility of meeting our son.

We settled back into life in the Carefree desert and waited. The day arrived we were provided the information of our baby boy's name and address. As I sensed he had agreed to release his address and wanted contact. My heart was speaking the truth. His name was Jade Kenneth Watson and he lived in Chetwynd, B.C. It was a familiar town to Robert and yet I had never heard of it. He got a map to point out its location and delighted in sharing that he sat a lot of rigs in years prior to our meeting in the vicinity of this area. I was surprised that Jade was living so close to where he had been born in Prince George. Warm fuzzies filled my body and spoke to my truth that I knew somehow this was going to be perfect.

Next we both sat down and wrote our letter to him and included photos. I held great expectations mixed with high anxiety upon taking this life changing letter to the Carefree post office. I held it momentarily in my hand before releasing it as I envisioned our desired outcome. Then I let it fall from sight into the bin mixed in with everyone else's wishes and dreams waiting for the universe to respond.

Life went on as we waited for a reply. I contemplated the real possibility that our years of unknowing would end. Both Robert and I were a mixture of wonder, fearfulness and joy.

About a month later I came out of the post office to Robert waiting in the car. In my hand is what we had been anticipating. I twirled the letter around triumphantly as I walked to the car. I jumped inside with the exuberance of a labrador puppy and waved the letter under his nose. "Look, look it is from him."

"Marvelous, you must open it up right now and right here."

I tore open the envelope and read a short note from our son. The two of us wept with grateful heartfelt joy to see his photos. Saber and Spookie were allowed to sniff and put their stamp of approval upon his photos.

"Did he include his phone number?"

"Yes, it is here, we can phone him."

I was overjoyed beyond belief that I held in my hand a letter and photos of our son. Our excitement was beyond measure. After wiping our tears we drove home and I snuggled close to my husband, the father of this handsome young man. I kept the photos in hand studying his face as we drove. I silently talked to him, "There you are my son, soon to be in our lives for real. Thank you God and all of our angels

33

assisting in this miraculous manifestation." Robert wrapped his arm around me as he drove and we both breathed life into this memorable extraordinary moment.

"You did it my love, you truly are a brick."

"Yes, congratulations to both of us Magoo, I could not have survived all of this without you. It has been an arduous journey for me all these years and I have given you a lot of grief regarding this, yet it is behind us now."

I am dancing around our living room with Saber and Spookie. "Well, so shall we make a phone call, Possum?"

"You mean call Jade? Oh my Robert, I love his unusual name."

"This is your moment, Carol Ann. You need to be the one to dial the number and talk to him first." I gazed at my husband and silently thanked my angels for blessing me that he was the one who fathered our child.

I dialed the number and held my breath waiting to see if he would answer. Robert was sitting opposite me at the dining table his face anxious and determined. Yet God was smiling on us as I heard a male voice say hello.

"Is this Jade?"

"Yup, you got him."

"Jade, this is Carol Ann Arnim, your birth mother. We just received your letter and wanted to phone right away."

I cannot recall his reply yet his voice said it all and my body responded with the biggest sigh of relief as I exhaled the stress held within my heart for over nineteen years.

Both of us were a bundle of nervous excitement each trying to get a question out at the same time. He had a sense of humor, how wondrous and magical. Robert also got on the phone and the three of us delighted in hearing each other's voices for the very first time. It was truly exhilarating and miraculous that life had blessed us with this gift.

"Would you like to meet us?" Robert asks.

"You betcha, could I come to Arizona? I have never been there."

"Absolutely, we shall make arrangements to fly you into Phoenix."

Upon hanging up the phone I wanted to share this happy news with my family. My brother David was the only one who knew about our son. Years later after Jade's birth on a visit home at his place I had shared it with him. His son Matthew had been born. It was too difficult to keep secret while in the presence of his baby boy. Robert shared his concerns for me about informing my family. "Are you sure you want to do that?"

"It is time, yes. Our son has been a secret for years and I cannot do it anymore. This is a great opportunity now with our discovery of him."

I called my parents and shared the news. "I have kept something from you but now want to tell you that you have a grandson. While on the rig with Robert I became pregnant and gave the baby up adoption. The happiest news is that we have found him and he is coming to see us."

The other end of the phone was dead silence momentarily and then my Dad steps up saying, "These things happen." I breathed a sigh of relief and thanked them.

It was a short time later that our long awaited day arrived. Saber and Spookie excitedly jumped into the car eager to meet this young man they had been hearing about so much. Robert surprised me by parking the car at the arrivals. "Ok, Possum this is something you need to do by yourself."

"You aren't going inside with me to meet him?"

"No, I want you to do this yourself and I shall wait right here. Go inside there my brave brick and meet our son."

We held each other in a tight embrace as I wiped away tears telling him thank you over and over. I walked into the airport with a lightness in my step and my heart beating loudly. I had seen his picture so felt confident I would recognize him. I am gazing at all the faces coming at me and then we catch sight of each other. I let out a gasp of shock and walk towards him and put my arm around him.

"Where is Robert?"

"He is parked at the curb with the dogs."

"You brought the dogs too?"

"Of course, you are a very important person and they have to meet you right away."

We are both chuckling and laughing as we collected his bag and head outside. The oven like heat hits him and he reacts, "Oh my God."

"Welcome to the Arizona desert Jade, it is summertime heat unfortunately."

"We are so glad you could come Jade, welcome to Arizona." I stood quietly witnessing my two men share a hearty handshake. Saber and Spook welcomed him with gusto. Upon arrival to our home, his face lights up as he views the backyard pool. His curiosity and enthusiasm for everything delight me. This is a whole new world for him so different from his home in northern B.C. He is awestruck by the saguaros and the desert landscape.

We have about a week together and every day is a delight as we all revel in getting to know each other. "You can ask me anything you want, Jade. I shall keep nothing secret from you. I am willing to answer anything you desire to know."

Robert sat silently, watching intently as Jade and I asked and answered each other's questions. I can feel years of heaviness lifting off my hubby's tired heart. Oh thank you God!

One of my fears over the many years was whether he would know he was adopted because not all children are informed about this truth.

"Yes, I was told very young."

"How did your adoptive parents, Norman and Mary feel about this trip?"

"They wanted me to come but yes they were nervous about it. It was my decision and they agreed I needed to do what I wanted in this regard."

"I am very grateful for their support to allow you to make your own decisions. I understand the risk they took, but they do not need to be fearful in any way because we have found you. You are their son, we are your birth parents and ecstatic to have you in our lives, but would not jeopardize your relationship with your Mary Mom or your Dad."

"I have worried and dreamt about this for so long now. I cannot believe you are really here. I have to pinch myself to believe this is truly you sitting here before me." I was very touched by how understanding he was to everything I shared with him and he agreed that I had done the right thing upon his birth.

I could not have asked for anything better in how our first visit transpired. It was remarkable! Another thing I pondered for years was would he have the traits of his genetic makeup from Robert and me, or would his environment have played a stronger role in his personality. We both agreed that he was indeed our son and possessed many similarities to us. What a blessed relief this was to me.

Saber and Spookie had a new playmate in the pool as I watched with disbelief as he jumped off the pool wall into the water. "My God, Robert, he is part labrador. Look how he is flying off the wall."

He joins me at the door with his arm around me, "You are a Mom for real now, my dearest Carol Ann."

With Saber and Spookie we took a trip to our favorite retreat at the Tubac Resort, south of Tucson. During our supper Jade shared a disturbing story from his youth at about thirteen years. A friend and he were involved in a near fatal car accident. He was flown by helicopter to a Vancouver hospital and he was in a fight for his young life. He was comatose for a very long time and when he awoke had to learn to walk again. After his difficult recovery he shared that he dealt with suicidal urges for a long time.

That evening neither Robert nor I got much sleep. Due to his son Mark's suicide, this news about Jade living with such thoughts at a young age was too much for Robert to bear. "I lost Mark to a shotgun and now I have to learn that our baby you gave up and we magically found again could have been lost to such thoughts also. I cannot bear to hear such a story, Possum."

"Neither can I, my love and yet it is good that he confided in us. I am glad to know anything and everything about him, even any unpleasantness. We must consider how painful that was for him and the memories of it would be very difficult."

"Yes of course you are right; it was just such a shock to hear."

Our time together went very fast, every moment cherished and treasured. We shared hugs of farewell and promise to stay in touch. I watched him turn and walk down the runway into his departing plane. Robert put his arm around me as we strolled slowly back to our parked car. "Good work Possum, you were a real brick as always. Forgive my doubts about this discovery of our son. My worries were unnecessary."

"Yes and yet I am grateful for your concerns for it points to how much you love me."

"We must have him come again before too long, it has been a splendid time."

The next month of July we took an impulsive trip to Baja, Mexico. We were going from Arizona heat to Mexican heat but Robert found a deal he could not pass up. We had been to Cabo San Lucas before yet this time we stayed at a huge resort rather than our usual smaller type. It was a Westin. The most colorful bright colors greeted us. While he enjoyed the pool and shade with a corona I had a great time with my camera. A few shots were later enlarged for our home and Robert took great delight in sharing his wife's photos with anyone entering our home.

Again in month of August he planned another getaway to San Francisco and into the wine country. Looking back at it now it was almost like he knew something was coming in the wind. I also recall while at Baja that he was not in his usual merry mode of past Mexican trips. I remember sensing something not quite right with him and yet he said he was fine.

By fall there was definitely something amiss. Robert was always good about going to doctors. A visit to his doctor resulted in a prescription for valley fever medication and he was told he ought to be good within the month. Well, the pills did nothing and Robert continued to feel poorly. A bronchoscopy was scheduled at the end of November. Another month went by and still no improvement.

We were visiting with our son Jade and he inquired if he could come to see us again. Despite Robert's poor health he did not want to miss another visit with him and so we arranged for another plane trip. During his stay we had a scheduled needle biopsy for Robert. The intense strain we were under during this time did not make for a happy visit with Jade. Unknown to all of us that farewell would be the last time for Jade to see Robert and my last time to hug Jade until almost five years later.

Tests had revealed that fluid was building up in Robert's lung and he had a fluid drain on January 15. I was standing near the room of his procedure and saw Dr. Hammond in the hallway. He slowly approached me with a serious demeanor saying, "I think that the valley fever may turn out to be a red herring, Carol Ann." At an appointment with us in December he had discussed the possibility of lung cancer. Unfortunately, lung cancer and valley fever can be mistaken for the other as the symptoms are similar. It was two days later we both sat with Dr. Hammond. In my mind I recall Robert's statement in the letter written to his sons about no evidence of lung cancer in his lungs. My love had foreseen his lung cancer.

"This is very hard for me, Bob. I do not normally get sentimental about my patients and stay unattached, yet you are different. I need to tell you that you have lung cancer. You will need to get set up to see an oncologist to discuss chemotherapy and your options."

The appointment was made with a cancer specialist. His blunt words, "You have six months to live," left us staggering arm in arm back to our car. His approach did not sit well with either me or Robert. We believed that a person's time of death is between ourselves and God. The power of one's mind replaying this statement over and over, of only six months to live, can set oneself up for it to manifest.

The next morning was spent with a lawyer named David to make changes to his will and set up power of attorney. I was made his executor. I listened in shock as he shared with David about my remarrying one day. The very next day we met his oncologist at the renowned Mayo Clinic.

Surgery or radiation was not an option. He recommended chemotherapy saying it would buy us some time. His current stage of cancer was 3B.

That evening we went for supper at our favorite Italian restaurant and had a quiet heart to heart. I shared, "Robert, if this cancer takes you I promise that you shall be at home in our own bed with Saber and Spookie when you die." He replied with a quiet thank you and held my hand for a very long time.

A few days later we sat through his first all day procedure of chemotherapy. I silently watched the steady drip of the toxic medicines enter my husband's bloodstream. He had to be given GCSF shots in his belly and I was given a lesson in this procedure and every day I would poke him with a needle. During this time Robert had arranged for a visit from my parents and then soon after my brother David. This was a difficult time for visiting and yet he had done so in compassion for me.

A few days after the chemo we had an unpleasant trip to the emergency. His temperature was on the rise. A call to his doctor told us to get him immediately to the hospital. I stood next to him as the doctor examined him. My husband's eyes as they looked into mine were filled with terror. He was admitted to get his blood levels back to normal. I shall never forget the doctor's words as he checked in on him prior to leaving about 1:00 a.m. "I guess I gave him too much chemo for the first dose. He is a big man but he should not have gotten such a high dose." He walked away without another word leaving me shuddering in fear. I knew death sometimes resulted in such cases.

Due to his fever, Robert was highly agitated. I had to force myself to walk away and allow the meds to do their work. I needed to get home to the dogs. A nurse was putting a sign on the door, "Neutropenic condition." I asked her what that meant and she curtly replied, "Go home and look it up."

I stumbled slowly to the elevator with my head reeling from her unkind words and the doctor's words replaying as well. Gee wizzers man! Somehow I got myself home safely through the dark desert road. The sight of our two labs' tails wagging at the door was just what I needed. I collapsed into their furry embrace.

I spent the next morning with him in hospital mask and then left to go to Barnes and Noble Bookstore. It was Valentine's Day. I studied the books before me and left with a couple clutched to my heart hoping I could find some answers better than the poison that was running through my husband's veins. That night just after midnight, I sensed something amiss; I phoned his room. The nurse informed me that my husband had gone into the washroom and pulled out his IV. There was a bloody mess everywhere. She was not enthused and cut my call short. My Robert was not being a good patient.

From my readings I purchased supplements and Essiac tea. I had various vegetables in the fridge ready to make him concoctions. The day before my birthday of February 17 he was to be released. I happily greeted him with a yellow balloon. Saber and Spookie pranced about joyfully sniffing as we made our way to the bedroom door which I had kept closed.

"What have you done here Possum?"

He opened the door to be greeted with a big bundle of yellow balloons floating over our king size dog bed. "Robert these balloons represent how many more years we have together. We must believe you will be alright through this."

He held me in a tight embrace. "Is that all? We must have more time than just these few balloons, my Muffin."

"Of course, but there is not enough balloons to fulfill that and no matter what happens we have all the time of eternity to love each other I reckon. Even if you are to die, the love does not stop with death, right."

"I am sure that must be true dearest Poss. And you know that life is terminal anyways right?"

The month of March presented a second dose of chemo and visits from two of his sons. He was losing weight and having stomach problems and digestion issues. The doctor put him on antibiotics and he became more tired, weaker and very pale. I was always running to the pharmacy for some remedy for this or that ailment. Mouth sores became a bother also and he lost his taste buds. That was a very sad discovery. "Poss, you know this horrific treatment is worse than the disease it seems to me. When will I ever begin to feel better, this was supposed to buy us some time but this is the shits, pardon my lingo."

The end of March he saw the oncologist and had an X-ray. His third dose of chemo is cancelled. He is scheduled for a fluid drain and a talc pleurodesis where talc is put in the lining of the lung to aid in fluid not returning as fast. He spent two nights in the intensive care unit and thankfully was released two days later. It was a massive amount of fluid and he joked later about the amount equating to several measures of beer bottles.

Shortly after this cancer news we had started a walking regimen together. He did not want to walk in the Boulders so we went to a golf course development nearby called Legend Trails. There were no homes as yet and it was a good quiet place to walk instead of our neighbourhood. Saber and Spookie happily joined us. The surgical procedure took a heavy toll and he became more exhausted. Another of his sons came for a short visit. His days were mixed with bad days, very bad days and an occasional fair day.

"Possum the treatment is worse than the disease. When will I ever begin to feel better and this unpleasantness stop?"

This became a frequent question. He now looked to me for answers and yet I had no adequate reply other than to tell him that we must keep going. The bit of hair he had all fell out and I bought him a baseball cap with a black lab on it. In early May I was very disheartened to see my love in such suffering. I suggested that we take our labs down to our favorite spot, Tubac. He agreed. I set it up and drove us to our little retreat away from home. It was a brief respite from our hellacious routine.

He wanted to fly to Salt Lake City, Utah for some business with the company of his deceased son Mark and to see his grandsons, Andy and Nathan. With typical Robert fashion, he made a special trip of it, booking us a room at the lovely Sundance Resort of Robert Redford's. He was unable to eat the cuisine and thus we spent our evenings in the room. I made us grilled cheese and tomato sandwiches which suited him just fine. His breathing was not at normal capacity with a compromised lung and the fluid returning. The elevation proved to be a challenge for him and yet he insisted that we continue our stay. He enjoyed reading a book about flyboys I had found for him. As he read on the outdoor deck, I wandered camera in hand through the woods nearby.

We returned home to a joyful reunion with Saber and Spookie. He was having some better days and next he wanted us to fly over to California. So we took off on another two night adventure. We flew home out of Ontario, California.

Back home every day I was creating healthy concoctions with a juicer and blender, presenting him with various drinks. He began to have difficulty sleeping and bad night sweats for several days in June. Then unpleasant back pains started and he resorted to a physical therapist. He was put on meds for the sore back. I talked to the pharmacist and changes are made again. He enjoyed a couple good days and goes out for lunch with a friend. The doctor then gave him a series of B12 shots. His back pain intensified and I quietly pondered that the cancer had spread to his bones.

The long, hot Arizona summer was becoming very tedious and he contemplated a trip to Portland, Oregon next. Prior to his illness we had been discussing finding another state to call home and we both had loved the Oregon coast. I telephone his oldest son Skip, to discuss the possibility of him meeting us in Portland. He agrees and before you know it we were having supper with Skip. We were not enthralled with Portland and next he wants us to go to Washington.

"You must let me drive the rental car Robert or else I cannot agree to this idea you now have."

"Of course Possum dear, let's head north and see where we are led next."

Anacortes beckoned him and he remembered an old school buddy who happened to be a realtor. Contact was made and to my disbelief we are next actually looking at a couple homes for sale. He just would not stop! He wanted us to get out of Arizona and vainly was making any effort to lead to this. He had grown up on the Pacific shores and loved to sail. He boasted about the fact that during his youth he had crewed for Humphrey Bogart or Bogey as he was known. The bed and breakfast where we were staying offered a sunset sailboat cruise. This proved to be a real blessing as he finally relaxed and I breathed a sigh of relief.

Upon arrival back into Phoenix our friend who operated an airport shuttle service took one look at Robert and ran to get a wheelchair.

This trip had taken a heavy toll on him. He was beyond exhaustion. He was becoming thinner by the day and the back pain was intensifying.

I did my best to make him smile and would offer him a peanut for a taste test. Ever since we met he had loved peanuts. The toxic chemo had forever taken away his taste buds however. His smile turns to frowns as he replies, "Nope Poss, Poss, it still does not taste like a peanut."

He went out to Mayo for X-ray and blood work to discover he was anemic. The next day he had two units of red blood cells pumped into him. Mouth sores returned and insomnia. A couple of days later, August 13; he had a bone scan and cat scan. The next day he was in a good mood and we enjoyed a quiet restful day together.

On August 15 we went to see his oncologist. He was now stage four. The cancer was in his bones and spreading throughout his frail form. Morphine was prescribed. The doctor had nothing else to suggest and told us he needed to be put on hospice care. Both of us had already discussed this. I drove us home in quiet contemplation with his hand firmly gripped in mine.

His son, Gregory arrived for a brief visit and next came youngest son, John. On the day of their departure I drove us all to the airport and Robert was chattering away happily with his "Baben John" and "Gregyor." Our drive home was in total silence. A couple days later the hospice nurse came and we had a long visit. His feet were now swollen badly and very uncomfortable. A wheelchair was delivered to the house and oxygen in case it was to be needed.

He spent a lot of time in sleep. Conversation became less with him as he began to retreat more into himself. "I have no regrets Possum. I have lived a great life."

One night while I was lying on the bed next to Robert awaiting sleep, Spookie began to bark. It was not her normal bark and I got up to investigate. To my horror, there was a tarantula crawling slowly across our floor in the bedroom.

"Spookaton, you are a very good, good girl. Thank you for barking. Robert, my God, there is a tarantula in our bedroom." He did not respond or move in any fashion and I rushed to the kitchen to find a glass. I retrieve this scary looking creature and take him out into the desert outside our back gate. I collapsed back onto the bed pulling

Spookie toward me with gratitude. Saber and Robert had not moved throughout this ordeal.

Gregory arrived again and helped out with fixing our hot water heater and also took our car in for repairs. Upon my request he went to Pet Smart to buy a couple big dog crates.

I sat for a long time alone under our palm trees in the backyard and as I entered the living room he asked, "So what are you thinking, my dearest Carol Ann?" He rarely called me by my given name; it was time for a serious talk.

"Robert, I know about your fear of fire from your days flying B24's with an engine aflame. I know you would not want to be cremated. I have decided that I do not want to bury you in your family plot in California."

"That all sounds good to me, what do you have in mind?"

"I am not sure as yet, but it must be somewhere amongst greenery and trees."

"I entrust this to you alone, my dearest wife. You are fully capable of making all the appropriate decisions on my behalf. I thank you for your bravery as always my brick."

Robert is now too weak to get up and stays in bed. I had a quiet heart to heart with Gregory. "I am most grateful for all of your assistance but I need to be alone with your father and you must leave now." It is August 30.

The hospice nurse had been encouraging me to get an aide to stay at the house. She was concerned that I would not be able to carry on my hands on duties with my dying husband. I refused to have someone come in to stay but agreed that an aide would be alright for a couple hours so I could have a break.

The next day a young hospice aide named Aly appeared at our door. I left Robert in her capable hands and went for a drive to the grocery store and post office. Upon returning she was finishing up with Robert. I shared that the hospice nurse was insisting I needed more help and yet I wanted to be the one to provide his hands on care as much as possible.

"Carol Ann, I shall show you what to do. I am sure you will be able to continue for whatever time remains." She took a mouth swab and tenderly showed me how to moisten his drying lips. I was very grateful for her understanding helpful attitude. She shared about her goal of becoming a nurse.

The puppies and I walked her out to her car. "Aly, we are forever indebted to you and I know you shall make a stupendous nurse. I can share that I know Robert is in full agreement. He is beyond speech now. Yet I can hear his voice loud and clear in my head encouraging you to follow your heart. If he could, he would be filling your heart with such a burst of confidence you would be floating down the road. It has been a real pleasure to meet you."

We gave each other big hugs and I slowly walked back in to check on Robert.

*******Author's note**********
At this point in my tale, as I stepped back into our home to embrace my new life as a soon to be widow, due to this life changing moment the remainder of my book I address you, my readers in present tense short story format.

"I Am Sorry"

Prior to climbing into my bed of sleeplessness I sit in the dark looking out into the blackness. Quietly I whisper, "Please give me the strength to continue caring for my Robert. Please help me be brave. I need to be the one to see him through." I resume my vigil next to my husband's still form with only the sound of ominous rattled breath. Saber and Spookie are asleep. I have only the comfort of my angelics, my invisibles as I call them. Yet this does not seem to be working. I study the night sky as I vainly attempt to calm myself.

I recall the enthusiastic encouragement from young Aly and my spirits are buoyed. Yes, I can and will do this, I tell myself. I toss about and sleep finally overtakes my exhausted self for a brief time.

At some point in the darkness of our very long night, a little miracle occurs. I am aware that the dying are capable of remarkable feats prior to leaving this world and even hang on for days awaiting something only they know of. Somehow from my husband's semi-comatose body three little unforgettable words escape his lips, in the lowest whisper. "I am sorry."

I lean over him and there is no evidence of any consciousness. Only the death rattle greets my ears. With grateful awe I close my eyes and tell him I love him and it is alright.

Morning arrives as it always does. I kiss him gently good morning and moisten his lips and give him his morphine. "I need to go feed the puppies Toad, but I shall return in a few minutes." I pause at our bedroom doorway studying him. I sense his death is coming very soon.

He is no longer in denial. Death has taken its firm grip and will not let go. Communication is over and this has made my own denial fly out the window. I am now witnessing my dying husband. This cold hard reality hits me. Like it or not, Mrs. Arnim he is soon to fly away without needing an airplane.

My morning chores are finished and I return to his side when the telephone rings. I take the call in our living room and am greeted with the voice of his Red Baron buddy, Jose. Tears come as I share, "He is in very bad shape, Jose. He no longer responds in any fashion. I need to ask your help to find an appropriate cemetery and funeral home in Montana."

Jose lives in northern Montana and is very familiar with his home state. It was a place that Robert and I had planned to go rent a home to investigate the possibility of building our dream home. This dream was to stay only a dream. As I sense, he responds positively. "Yes, I can suggest a lovely little town called Livingston and the name of a pretty cemetery overlooking the Paradise Valley."

"I believe you have given us our answer with a name like that, Jose. It sounds perfect." I write down his information with profound gratitude and return to my Roberto. In the very moment of approaching the bedroom I feel a sense of dread. In that very second I know he has taken flight. They say a person can choose the time of their actual death and indeed I am now a witness to this truth.

His breath is silent, he is gone. He has been on the runway waiting for his exact departure time to be in the right moment while I was out of the room. He is now literally flying free on that mystical trip which requires no luggage and no actual plane. His spirit has piloted him into the light and left me behind.

I lose control of myself and the bedroom explodes into a tirade of wails. My departed husband's spirit is now a witness to my own living hell. I catch my breath and realize I must call hospice. The nurse asks for his time of death saying, "Yes, you can be the one to officially record this time." Thus on September 1, 1996 at approximately 8:00 a.m. my journey as a widow begins.

I make phone calls to family and begin the difficult task of funeral home calls. My promise to Bobby that our two lab pups would be by our side at his burial needs to be fulfilled. As I visit with the Montana funeral home I share this information about needing the dogs by my side as a fact that must be agreed upon and thankfully my request is granted.

The evening is very stormy and the skies are rumbling loudly. I stand quietly in our backyard crying and then I feel him. He is surrounding me in a sky hug. "Oh thank you my love, I sure need that." His presence is palpable, enveloping my whole being. There is no mistaking that my Robert is with me.

The next day is Labor Day and I stumble numbly through the day making the necessary phone calls. In the afternoon I answer the phone and to my delighted surprise it is Aly. "Carol Ann, I was just notified of Robert's death. I am not supposed to be talking to you, but I had to call."

"Oh Aly, I am so happy to hear from you. Thank you for following your compassionate heart instead of following rules. You most definitely are a heavenly emissary when I need it the most."

"I could come see you if you like?"

"Holy smokes, could you really? That would be marvelous."

And indeed she appears along with some yummy homemade cookies. We spend the evening with Saber and Spookie by our side. "I could not just ignore the news of his death. From the moment I walked inside your home I could feel the embrace of love everywhere. When I was working with him I felt so connected with him. He is my first patient to die and I shall never forget him."

We chatter away like two reunited souls from a past lifetime. Definitely Aly crossing our paths is another heavenly orchestration at play. She is a godsend.

A couple days later I find myself looking out the plane window as I envision his casket in the cargo hold. Our two labs are also in the belly of the plane so he is in good company. At the funeral home I lean over his casket to plant my last kiss and place a photo of us with beloved Saber and Spookie into his shirt pocket. I place some goobers into his jean pocket and sense his smiles with this touch. He is wearing his running shoes, blue jeans with a blue shirt and a labrador Tshirt peeking out underneath.

I have chosen to wear all white; black is devoid of energy and not at all uplifting. I have his unique gold ring with the nuggets on a long chain dangling next to my heart. Also I am wearing his air force wings which he gifted to me years ago on a silver chain.

At the gravesite Saber and Von Spook sit next to me. Spookie expresses her sorrows loudly and will not let up. I have a couple poems to read although I do not know how I shall find my voice. Yet somehow the words come out. I read the Irish blessing and another lovely poem about death. As the casket is lowered I step forward and throw more goobers into his grave.

Afterwards everyone meets at the lodge in Paradise Valley. My requested delivery of yellow balloons has arrived and I ask everyone to gather around to release their balloons. The blue Montana skies smile as the sunshine yellow balloons float upward. Everyone's heads are turned skyward as we intently follow the love floating his way. Saber and Spookie are mingling amongst us. It is a perfect sight which I know he is witnessing.

Eventually people go their separate ways. My brother David who kindly had come to this sad occasion departs. That evening I share a quiet supper with Mom and Dad. I pick at my salad without eating and share with them, "I do not know where these words are coming from right now, but I believe I am going to become more like Robert." My wise heart is indeed foretelling the truth that my introverted self shall blossom allowing the world to see my authentic self.

My Robert had been the one person who saw me as I truly am. Many years ago I asked him, "Why did you fall in love with me?"

He always gave the same reply whenever I asked, "It was because I saw the potential in you."

Again morning arrives as it always does. To my surprise I have indeed survived the toughest day of my life as I buried my husband gazing upon his face for the last time. It is time for my parents to depart. We embrace in a threesome tear-filled hug not wanting to let go.

I am now all alone. Thankfully, my earth angel pups are by my side however. It is time to take them for a stroll. As the three of us wander I am greeted by a wondrous surprise. In the Montana sky a small plane is approaching.

Robert loved to fly such planes. It is about to land. On the road nearby the little plane comes in. I am spellbound with teary smiles. I know I am being comforted by him from the other side. The dogs and I watch from the grassy hill as the plane bumps along to a gentle stop. The timing of this is unbelievable! Who are these people and what are they doing?

I am taken back in time to when we first met in the bush on the oil rig when he used to fly us around in a similar plane. Such high flying times our adventuresome falling in love days.

My heart is comforted in knowing that this is a heavenly orchestrated event for my benefit. Robert did take his final flight and yet this plane landing right in front of me tells me that he is now piloting me onward. On the first morning of my solo life after his burial this is very magical indeed.

He is here for me. I am not alone.

Labaru Driving Safari

After watching our Bobby plane take off the pups and I climb into our rental car and begin our driving expedition. I do not want to return to our empty home so I plan to spend the next few days exploring Montana. Jose has kindly invited us to stay a night and we spend a lovely evening filled with reminiscing and many toasts to our Robert. Saber and Spook get to have some great runs in the Montana fields of big sky country. It certainly is a beautiful state. I leave Jose and continue to explore for a few days.

It is now time to head home. We are welcomed back to our Boulders home with a warm desert heat embrace. The three of us wander from room to room. Saber is grieving deeply and does not stop barking. He displays his displeasure by lifting his leg a couple times on the hall planters. Grief is certainly stressful on animals as well. The phone rings a lot and I make more calls as I comb through his personal notebook notifying more of his death.

I am immersed in shock and numb to the core. I can feel him in everything I touch and yet he is gone from sight. It is unbelievable! He feels so close I cannot allow myself to acknowledge what has happened. He begins to make his presence known by playing with the lights. In the evenings the table lamp turns on and off. The phone rings and no one is on the other end. I grow to appreciate his playfulness from the other side. He seems to be taking boyish delight in his new abilities.

Every evening I take our two labs for a leisurely drive. The air is cooler. Saber and Spookie put their big noses out the window sniffing the desert scents. I like to drive around the Legend Trails area where we had walked with the two dogs. As I am driving along my mind reflects back to the first oncologist we visited who had bluntly stated, "You have six months at the max to live." In truth he had survived for about two months longer. As I am pondering perhaps the chemotherapy had given him more time in that very instant he replies loud and clear. "It was not the chemo dearest wife of mine. There was no benefit from that poison. It was you that kept me going. It was all because of you." I can now hardly see the road through the sobbing which racks my being with his words.

We return home to crawl into our king size dog bed. For a short while sleeping pills lull me into slumber. Sometimes in the night the owls sing their hoots to me and I am comforted in this sound remembering the times he hooted back to them. I have no appetite and get through the days drinking Ensure. This had been his daily cocktail many a time.

I am the executor for his estate and begin the task of handling the legal duties. Our lawyer named David patiently walks me through this maze. Christmas is coming closer. Mom and Dad do not want me to be alone and ask me to come home for the holiday. I reply, "I cannot be without Saber and Spookie, if you will allow them to come then I shall too." They agree.

Our jeep wagoner is acting up again and I make the decision to get a different vehicle. I am talking everyday with Robert and ask for his help regarding this big decision. One day at the Carefree post office I pull up beside a woman in a white Subaru. I remember our many trips to Steamboat Springs and his comments about Subarus being great cars in the snow. I begin a conversation with the woman. She astutely notes my downhearted demeanor and asks if I am alright. I feel her genuine interest and answer her honestly. We exchange phone numbers and agree to meet someday.

I had been spurred into full honesty with a stranger as I recalled a conversation with another widow recently. She had shared about the death of her true love and a second marriage. She did not love this man as much but had done so because she wanted to share. In that moment I had decided right then and there that I would learn to open my heart. Already I was becoming as I had told my parents on the eve of his burial.

I know that Robert has just provided my answer about our car. The next day with the two pups I drive into a Subaru dealer. Both the dogs are greeted happily and facilitate in trading the jeep for a brand new Subaru which turns out to be white. I call my family to share the exciting news. While talking with sister Valerie we are discussing possible personalized license plates. Labs are my constant companion now more than ever and she suggests, "How about Labaru?"

"Oh Valerie, thank you. That is a perfect name for our dog car."

Somehow I am staggering through my shock on auto pilot. Each day seems so tedious and long. Through my haze I decide I need to find a new focus. I pick up a pamphlet from the United Way which lists organizations soliciting volunteers. When I read the name of the American Cancer Society I ponder the possibility of being able to turn this hellacious grief into something useful. I make the phone call to discuss this opportunity and share my tale. There are many people in my shoes who make the same decision and become great volunteers due to personal understanding of the journey. I tell the woman about my planned trip home to Ontario and that I shall set up a meeting upon my return.

I begin to make plans for this Labaru driving safari. My parents are pleased about the new car and my plans. I recall that Mark's wife at the funeral of Robert had encouraged me to visit her anytime. I decide to take up her offer. She replies to my ideas, "That is a very long trip to take alone, Carol Ann."

"Yes, I know. However I must do it and I want to come see you. I will have Saber and Spookie."

Heading north through Utah is certainly not a direct path of driving to get to Ontario yet I am in no rush. I could continue further northward and make a visit to Robert's grave so this sounds like a grand plan and in style with my lovie. Around the beginning of December we head off. My two faithful navigators, Saber and Spookie are by my side and my co-pilot is Robert. My ability to fully focus on my driving is impaired by my ever constant companion of shock. I am still very numb. I am just three months plus after his death driving down the road talking aloud to him as if he is actually with us. I realize he is certainly around because my driving ability is not at its best. There is more than one time that I narrowly escape an accident. I heave a sigh of relief and thank my guardian angel and my Bobby in spirit.

I have always carried a fascination of the paranormal and the spiritual side of life. I know that spirits have the ability to enter into other forms. One day while driving without adequate sleep and very overwhelmed by sorrow I experience such a phenomenon.

I feel a pulsing whooshing energy flow through me and I know that his spirit has come into my body to aid in driving the car. Immediately, I feel completely different in my body as if my hands on the steering wheel are his hands. There is no mistaking what has just happened although it is rather a shock to say the least. I weep with joyful gratitude.

We arrive safely at Becky's and spend a couple nights of good visiting. One of the many condolence phone calls I had received after his death was from a man named Bob Garland of Douglas, Wyoming. He had offered his home anytime I was in the vicinity. Wyoming is my next state so I give him a call and thankfully he answers his phone with a friendly welcome. The evening is a lively one with lots of storytelling. He shares about a female ranch hand who survived two near death experiences. Needless to say, I am enthralled. This Bob certainly is a marvelous chap. His living room is abuzz with tales of spirits and Wyoming rig stories. I am blessed with a big manly hug wishing us safe travels and we are on our way again.

I am now heading to Montana for the dogs and I to lie next to Robert's grave. We spend a night in Livingstone and after a long sojourn at his gravesite it is time to finally head eastward. "Ok, my dearest labradors we have a bit of driving ahead of us, it is time to hit the road."

As I drive through a small town while studying a map at the same time I am disenchanted to see flashing lights behind us. Oh boy, guess I am being too much of a lead foot on the gas. I stuff the speeding ticket into my glove box and carry on. We have places to go and people waiting for us. But reckon I better watch for speed limits, I chuckle to myself. Well it is good to have a laugh with Carol Ann. Robert did not help me avoid this so even he is telling me to pay closer attention. Thank you lovie.

The rest of the trip is uneventful and we finally pull into the driveway of my Stratford home. The first Christmas, and any of the firsts as a widow are very tough so I am grateful for my parents' compassion. It is wonderful to be home and also have my faithful four footers by my side. The holidays come and go. I spend time at my brother Dave's.

I am in no rush to go home but the time comes that I must return and continue with the legal duties of Robert's estate. Our trip takes a direct route and we arrive tired but happy to climb into our bed at night. It has been quite an adventure but our first Labaru driving safari is safely behind us.

Describing experiences of the paranormal are very difficult to put into words which make sense to someone else. At some point after arriving home I receive a visual energetic presence of my love. I know without any doubt that it is him. There is a strong presence in the bedroom doorway as I lie on our bed. His form is more light than anything else. There is a huge glow around him. In the next moment as I accept that it is actually him, I see and feel a beyond words sensation of a light beam travelling from him over to me as it enters my heart. I am filled with a sense of otherworldly peace as tears flow. I fall asleep and awaken with its memory which I carry with me.

I set up an appointment with the American Cancer Society and a day is arranged for training on their toll free information line. Ironically it is a man named Bob whose wife died of cancer. Tuesday morning becomes my time to assist others who unwillingly walk the cancer path.

There are many times I take a call from someone asking about lung cancer. Every time I drive home in tears. Why am I doing this? It makes me feel worse. Yet each Tuesday I return. I have let the gardeners go and am out raking the front yard one day. Again I see the presence of my lovie. He is there watching and following me in his glow body. I am comforted in knowing he still watches over all of us. What a blessing! Perhaps he is showing me his approval of my new life. Yes, this must be so I tell myself as I slowly enter our home alone.

Bobby Magic Angel

Today is March 7, 1997, and it is my Dad's birthday. It is six months plus since my husband's death. Every day since has been pure torture and I have forced myself to do something different. I have bravely come to the Phoenix Symphony by myself. During intermission I am outside under the stars talking to Bobby. Out of the corner of my eye I see a dog. On the other end of the patio, there is a woman with a group of people surrounding her. The dog is wearing a green jacket which reads, Guide Dog Puppy in Training.

During our trip to Washington I had found a calendar from the service dog school, Canine Companions for Independence in a pet store. I had discussed raising a puppy with Robert but he vetoed the idea saying, "Possum my love, how could you possibly ever let such a puppy go after the intense time of training the pup?"

I had replied with a girlish pout, "Yes, indeed you are right but it sure sounds neat."

I am drawn towards the working puppy yet my heartache keeps me from making contact. Something tells me I ought to go inside and check out the balcony seats out of curiosity. So I walk upstairs and snoop around. A couple minutes later, intermission is over and I need to get back to my own seat so I start down the steps. Well, guess who is coming up the steps with her dog? I have been well guided.

The woman smiles at me and my face lights up. Without any conscious thought, the words tumble out of my mouth, "How do I do this, can I do this? I have two labs already, is that ok?"

"Yes", she grins secretly and hands me her card, "Call me."

I drive home from the symphony with an ear to ear smile and my heart has a sense of hope for the first time in many months. My belief in synchronicity tells me this is no "fluke." Meaningful coincidence or synchronicity only magnify when one learns to be open to such and one pays good attention. It can lead one into synchrodestiny. I believe this door has been opened for me and I jump through with a big whee.

On March 17, Nancy, the guide dog raiser comes to our home to interview me as a potential puppy raiser and also to meet our dogs. One of my first questions asked with the zeal of a silly puppy, "When can I start? I want a puppy right away."

"I need to check with the school and will call you in a couple days."

"Can I get a labrador retriever?"

"Yes indeed you can, we use only labs and goldens."

Again pleading with childlike squeals, "Can I get a yellow puppy?"

"I need to talk to the school, but possibly yes you can."

My enthusiasm is now truly getting out of control as I envision living with a perfect labrador rainbow, a black Spookie, a chocolate Saber and a yellow puppy.

Nancy gets serious as she asks, "Carol Ann, how will it be for you when you have to turn the puppy into advanced training?"

My excitement turns to a very solemn tone, "I have recently endured my toughest challenge, in witnessing my best friend of twenty-three years and husband die of lung cancer. Although I know that giving up the puppy will be traumatic, my heart tells me I have the courage to do this."

I am accepted as a potential puppy raiser and she tells me she will call to advise when this event will happen. Within a day or two the phone call comes. With excitement in her voice characteristic of a devoted puppy raiser, "Carol Ann, I have good news. We have a puppy delivery coming to Phoenix next week."

"It is a yellow litter and your puppy's name starts with the letter L; each litter is alphabetized to track the puppies. Do you want to raise a boy or a girl?" In my excitement this does not matter to me at the time.

"Ok, I will call you when I know the delivery date."

In reality, getting a first puppy can be up to four months or more.

Certainly this is a divinely guided and blessed event. A couple days later Nancy phones again. "The delivery date is March 26 and you are assigned a yellow male lab."

The next day she calls again, "I have bad news about your potential puppy, he is ill and cannot safely be taken on a two day driving trip."

My voice is filled with heartfelt disappointment, "Oh, no, no!"

Her reply to my despair is instantaneous. "Are you willing to raise a female?"

My heart is racing. Without hesitation I plead, "Yes, yes, please, of course."

"Well, the school advised me that there is a yellow lab female that needs a raiser since the potential applicants changed their mind."

Within the short minutes of our phone call my life is being routed down a totally new path. Upon hanging up the phone, I am literally jumping with joy as I run from room to room with Saber and Spookie. The sad energy filling our home is being shifted as the whole house vibrates to elevated frequencies of laughter and happiness.

Over and over again, I yell out to Robert, "Thank you, thank you, thank you, I know you have helped this happen." Both Saber and Spookie join my exhilaration and playfully prance around me as I dance through the house and outside singing whoopee, whoopee. My instincts tell me this is the perfect thing at the perfect time.

I call out to my puppy miracle in the making, "Thank you, Miss L, whoever you are, I so look forward to meeting you. Thank you to all the gods that be who are bringing you into our lives. For whatever reason you must be meant to be with me instead of the couple you were initially assigned to. It certainly is no accident that my Mr. L became sick and I am now to be with you. If I had said I wanted a female when first asked I would have not been assigned to you since you were assigned to the couple who changed their mind. We must be destined to be together. See you soon."

The night of March 25 is very long and filled with anticipation. My mind whirls with endless questions. I have told no one of my plans. In the morning, I phone my Mom and Dad, "You will never guess what I am going to do tonight." Both of them applaud my news with hearty enthusiasm and joyful surprise. Next I telephone Aly and I am met with the loudest squeals of approval. She is as excited as I am. Thank Godness for Aly.

In the evening with Saber and Spook and a host of butterflies in my tummy I drive to the Tempe library for a guide dog puppy orientation meeting. The car seems to drive itself. I am in a complete daze of disbelief. Over and over my mind repeats, how can you do this? What do you think you are doing? This is complete madness! How will you ever turn over this puppy after 14 months?

Yet somewhere within me calmness resides and I listen to my inner wisdom reminding me that I have already survived the impossible. I came through giving up our son for adoption and now am surviving the death of my beloved Robert. If the strength was in me then for that then it must still be in there, right?

I sit through the meeting learning the rules of raising a guide dog puppy, fidgeting impatiently. The wait is truly unbearable. Finally, it is time. "Ok, everybody let's go get your puppies."

There is a white truck with the guide dog logo on its side parked in the lot outside the library. The back door is open and a crowd is gathered around. Inside on both sides are crates double high. I cannot control myself and silently sneak my way inside to peek. The puppies are all yellow, each one as cuddly and adorable as the next.

"Where are you Miss L? I am waiting." I jump out of the truck and drool as puppy after puppy is passed by me into the arms of squealing adults.

The moment arrives, "Carol Ann Arnim, are you here?"

I jump to the head of the line, "Yes, I am Carol Ann."

In that moment I am handed my bundle of miracles, "This is Laverne."

"Laverne, her name is Laverne?"

"Yes, you will get used to it."

I slowly walk to the car with her bundled close to my heart as I whisper in her big velvet soft lab ears, "Laverne, that is an awful name for such a beauty, but never mind. My name is Carol Ann and I thank you for rescuing me."

She receives lots of sniffs from her big dog buddies, Saber and

60

Spookie. "Welcome to your new family Laverne, for now you are an Arnim."

I chuckle with glee as she stays curled in my lap as I drive home. "Well, Laverne, I cannot tell you how utterly thrilled I am to meet you. You and I have much to do little puppy." My earlier heartache and anxiety are replaced with a sense of relief and the highest gratitude. The butterflies in my tummy have flown the coop.

I have no idea what this bundle of puppy is about to do for me yet I trust in her completely. I have nicknamed her Bobby Magic Angel.

I have moved Saber's dog crate used for the Montana flight into the corner of our bedroom. This shall be her sleeping quarters during housebreaking. I am up a couple times in the night with her little woofs. Her leash is attached and I walk her into the backyard. "Ok, Laverne it is time for you to learn the command, "Do your business." She is rewarded with pets of good puppy the moment she squats to my words.

In the morning I now have good reason to get up faster and my first chore is to have her do her business. "Ok, my labrador rainbow let's get some breakfast."

I have arranged with Aly to take our young girl to the movies. Laverne is met with joyful glee at the entrance to the movie and receives lots of snuggles. It is indeed a most memorable day for all three of us.

The next day I take Laverne for her first official walk with big dogs, Saber and Spookie. We are quite the comical sight as within minutes the leashes get tangled up. It would be great movie material for America's Funniest Videos. I capture a couple great photos of my pesky puppy annoying Saber getting his leash all wrapped around his legs and another of her pulling with all of her puppy might on his leash as he rolls on his back.

Guide Dogs for the Blind enjoy a few of my photos and I open the next guide dog newsletter to see the one of Laverne pulling on Saber.

About a week later Aly joins us for a yummy spaghetti supper and evening with wine. Conversation turns to the day we met as my lovie lay dying. Aly warms my heart as she shares her impression of me and Robert. "From the moment I entered your home I felt a very deep and unique connection between the two of you. It felt like the kind of love that was beyond this earth. Certainly beyond that which most earthly couples experience. It is the kind of love which defies judgement, boundaries or labels. Everything in your home was a symbol of your love for each other. The specially designed saltillo tiles on the floor which I knew had meaning of your love."

"I remember sensing your desperation, not just because it was so clear that Robert was in his final hours, but because you expressed feeling at a loss for how to care for his physical body in its final stage. I remember how showing you a few techniques changed your face and softened the furrow in your brow. Your energy grew more relaxed.

It was clear to me that your love was all around Robert and you just needed to be able to share his last moments with him in peace, free from the anguish of not knowing how to move his body. I remember feeling waves of deep love just in looking at all the photographs. I knew instantly that there was something very special about the both of you together. I was compelled to call you against my superior's advice when I found out about his death. I had to tell you how meaningful meeting you had been for me."

I cannot control my tears in hearing her talk about us. "I could never thank you enough for following your heart in calling me when you heard the news. Robert brought us together. It was destined we meet I reckon."

I am now motivated to go out more and we make our first trip to the grocery store. A few days ago I had talked to the manager explaining that the store is about to be blessed with a four-footed angel puppy in training. Service dogs are legally allowed in all public places. This is one challenge a puppy raiser must deal with in explaining why the pup is with you; usually an explanation will suffice.

Our first time in the Bashas grocery is a grand adventure for both of us. The distractions for a young four legged hoover are endless. I soon discover that it takes more time to shop. Most folks love puppies. Laverne is greeted enthusiastically by the cashiers and soon everyone remembers her name. There is much for a first time raiser to learn so both of us are in training. Once a month we attend training class with the other puppies.

Everyone wants to pet your puppy everywhere you go. Educating the public is a constant part of being a puppy raiser. Laverne is told to sit prior to being petted. A working guide dog in harness is not be to be distracted while working, but when the harness is off then it is ok. Or when the jacket comes off the same applies. Laverne soon learns that her magic green cape means work. From the beginning she seems to understand that her place is to be with me.

Our friend Kristy, is back in town and is overjoyed to meet the new member of the pack. She accompanies us to our first restaurant outing in Scottsdale. We all climb into a comfy booth and Laverne falls asleep after some good attentions from me and Kristy.

The training of a potential guide dog requires taking the puppy to as many different situations as possible. One class we meet at a fire station and all the pups are face to face with men in full fire gear and the sounds of the trucks and the whistles. Another time we meet at the airport. It is becoming good fun for me as well. Wherever there are lots of distractions the pup must learn to stay calm and well mannered.

She becomes popular at my volunteer job at the American Cancer Society. Bob chuckles upon our entrance, "Here comes Laverne. Maybe you could train her to answer the phone, Carol Ann."

There is another volunteer named Mary Kay who squeals with delight in meeting Laverne. We soon become good friends and Laverne becomes quite a shock to her dogs as well. Mary Kay has two pomeranians. She cannot get over how big Laverne is next to them. It is indeed a comical sight. She becomes a regular part of our lives and we enjoy lunches together. Mary Kay proudly introduces Laverne at her favorite Mexican restaurant which we frequent. "This is Carol Ann's guide dog, isn't she beautiful." She makes herself comfortable at my feet as I enjoy a yummy margarita and chicken fajitas. It certainly is a new adventure taking a dog into a restaurant but we all become used to it very quickly.

Puppies need to be exposed to all types of situations and one day I decide to cruise around inside Scottsdale Memorial Hospital. I know it will be a challenge for me due to the time spent there with my ill Robert yet I have my Bobby Magic Angel to assist me. I reflect on the fact that as yet I have had no response from my letter addressed to his oncologist. A few months after his death I was compelled to share my sincere dismay that he had glossed over the harsh realities of chemotherapy. Conversations regarding this decision all addressed buying him more time. However, the quality of his time was not spoken of in honesty. Full disclosure was not made about the impact of chemo to his body and mind. Doctors do want to save lives and yet the harsh reality of our situation was not spoken of to any extent. If my words could change how he addresses any of his patients then it would be worthwhile.

As difficult it will be I know it would be helpful for my aching heart to go up to the oncology ward. Slowly I make my way around and head back to the elevator a few minutes later. As I wait, a man is walking towards me. I cannot believe my eyes. It is his oncologist.

Both of us are startled to see each other and he admires Laverne. My tummy is rumbling as I ponder, what the heck I am going to say to him; yet I cannot let this opportunity go by. I take a deep breath and ask, "Did you receive my letter?"

"Yes and it is still sitting in my inbox. I have not been able to respond."

"I understand yet I had to speak my truth."

He refers to the document Robert signed regarding the clinical trial chemo saying there is language in it referring to my concern. He shares that he had a black lab and he gives Laverne a pet. Our conversation ends and he makes his exit. I regain my composure and slowly walk out to the car. "Hokey mokes, Laverne! I cannot believe what just happened. Thank Godness for your calming presence. I could not have done that without you." Upon getting into the car I snuggle into her soft embrace.

As I drive home I contemplate the other letter I had written to hospice. After long careful deliberation regarding the nursing care with Robert I wrote a letter to advise hospice I wanted to meet with someone to express my concerns. I did receive a phone call and met with a woman who listened attentively. I shared my upset over the experience of the nurse having a hospital bed delivered despite my telling her I did not want one because my husband needed to die in his own big dog bed. She kept insisting also that I get a live-in aide and I refused telling her I needed to care for him. On the driveway one afternoon she had presented me a piece of paper prior to getting into her car. I looked upon it in shock to see that it discussed signs of death. Would it not have been more considerate to share such difficult information in person?

The hospice employee listens as I share my opinions. "There is always room for improvement," she says. She did value what I had to say. I shared with her also that a young nineteen year old aide who came to give me some relief took the extra time to educate me about caring for my hubby. Thank Godness for her. She had asked me to be a reference for a nursing job and on the bottom of the page I said, "Hire her."

And of course I am referring to our dearest friend, nurse Aly.

Upon getting home my thoughts are still on the visit with the doctor and I go find the legal document he referred to which discusses effects of chemo. I read it and re-read it. Yet there is not sufficient language held within which addresses my concerns about the full impact of the chemo drugs. I cannot let him think this is sufficient. He had a black lab so I make a card with a photo of Spookie and compose him another note.

I seal it with the intent that he may in the future be more forthright with his patients and take more time in discussion of treatment. I sense my lovie approves as I hear him whisper, "That's my girl. Thank you."

Bobby Owl

It is eleven months since the death of my Robert Charles. Life is gradually forging a new path, since the arrival of Laverne. I knew she would be of great assistance guiding me through the endless hallways of my grief, but I was unaware of the other magical trails she is sniffing out. I nicknamed her Bobby Magic Angel and indeed she is living up to her name.

I have captured some lovely photos of her and decide to forward more photos to Guide Dogs for the Blind. The angelic pose of her on the bed asleep in her green work coat shall be printed in the 1998 Guide Dogs for the Blind calendar, for the month of October. Synchrodestiny has played its hand. October is the month of our son's birth and our wedding.

This wondrous news is difficult to deal with in his absence. Robert and I used to discuss how we could get my love of photography and writing into the public eye. A couple days later I receive a phone call from the magazine, Bereavement. I had submitted a short story which I wrote shortly after his death. They plan to publish it in an upcoming issue. Shortly after writing it I read it over the phone to my Mom and Dad. My mother shares, "Carol Ann, I think you have found your niche. You need to keep making good notes."

Again I am overcome with excitement. My happiness is overshadowed by the sorrow I cannot share this with him in person.

My love of photography has become a therapeutic part of my life again, thanks to the guide dog pup, Laverne and our two labs, Saber and Spookie. I decide to create photo cards from the many great shots.

One day with my angelic frisky four footer by my side I march into my first bookstore with cards in hand. Serendipity has paved the way! The right lady to make this decision is available and within a few short minutes I am rewarded with my first order.

I leave the store walking out into the desert's oven like heat with an ear to ear grin about to split my face it is so intense; such joy had become a foreign feeling. I yell out to my Bobby sky, "Wow, Robert, did you see us just now?" He had always been my spokesman sharing my photography with great gusto with anyone who walked through our door. He is my biggest fan.

The news of the guide dog school publishing my photos, the magazine publishing my story and now a store purchasing my photo cards has all come within a week's timeframe. I believe that Robert has been helping orchestrate this for me. All of this is not random good fortune or mere coincidence.

Everything is tied together through guide dog puppy, Laverne. She truly is my Bobby Magic Angel. I know Robert is assisting from the other side through this dog.

From the first night of his spirit flight I felt his presence. Every day I tell myself to pay attention. However, there are times I get very frustrated in that I am not able to communicate with him as we did in real life. I can never get enough of his messages from the other side is the reality of my situation because the pain of grieving is too overbearing. There is no respite!

I know he is busy in his new dimension where there is no sense of time. Often it seems like a long while between his messages or feeling his warm presence. Sometimes I think he has completely left me and I call out in desperation, "Where are you, Robert? What are you doing? I want to talk to you. I need to hear from you."

Through my grief I have learned to be open, receptive, patient and interpret signs. Scepticism and human doubt only serve to hamper the process of being able to tune in to him from the other side. I have come to believe he can now talk to me through nature, such as butterflies and rainbows. I do my best to stay alert to my environment and listen to my inner messages. Whenever I am desperate for a sign from him it always arrives in some fashion.

Shortly, after all this incredible news my emotional state is in complete overload. I am overcome with the most profound mixture of emotions. My grief has been like this. The intensity of the feelings I cannot describe nor even truly bear the pain of them. All this news is of a very joyful nature, and yet grief is not a happy path, so this created great inner turmoil. As people we always want to share our happy events with those closest to us and that person for me is no longer of this world.

I communicate my happy news with everyone close to me, and yet it makes me miss Robert even more. My loneliness for him is beyond any pain felt to this point. I miss Robert now more than ever, as my dreams shared with him are starting to come to fruition. This is pain that goes beyond bone deep; it is the worst I have felt since he died many long months ago.

In despair I call aloud to him, "As wondrous a spirit that you are now, I wish with all my heart that you were not a spirit." Grief is definitely a roller coaster ride. Unwillingly my happiness takes a seat on a flying toboggan, downhill all the way. This being a widow is unbearable and by the way, I hate that word with a passion. I hit the bed and remain horizontal unable to move. Breathing alone is a chore. It is not enough that I understand Bobby is helping me from his new role in spirit. I want him with me for real.

I call out to him, "Please talk to me. I need to hear from you, somehow, some way, please."

After the dogs supper, thanks to my training a service dog puppy I force myself outside with Laverne to work on the command, "come".

As we walk slowly onto the road in front of our home, I sense something moving out of the corner of my right eye. I look and to my disbelief it is an owl, swooping low right beside me and Laverne. I have never seen an owl fly so close to humans, particularly with a dog present.

I stand very still in complete awe. In that very moment, the owl stops! He is directly in front of Laverne and me where he hovers for about five seconds at my eye level. Laverne barks excitedly and yet the owl remains in the same position looking right at me. I catch myself by surprise as I exclaim aloud to the owl, "Robert, is that you in there?"

In that very second I hear, "I am right here Possum, just keep going." The message is imparted and off he flies to land in a nearby tree. I am unable to move. What a moment!

Our Carefree, Arizona desert home has many owls. Robert took great delight in talking to them as they landed in our backyard palm trees. He would hoot along with the owl who replied back.

I am filled with a welcome sense of peacefulness. My Robert had heard my tormented cries and swooped down to whisper his love through our friend the owl. He was making sure I got his message without question.

Prior to his death, both of us were in a state of fearful denial. The topic was rarely discussed. The fact that his physical presence is gone makes it very tough to remember that indeed he still exists; yet energy cannot die. It only changes form. In those moments when I am truly in that rut of not believing anymore he gifts me with gentle reminders and encouragement.

The morning after his Bobby owl visitation, I am refreshed and able to face a new day. I stand at our kitchen sink chattering away to him. I am marveling with him about his magical creative message. Again I begin to feel his presence and hear, "Yes, I really am right here, you do know this."

With grateful tears I grin as I wipe my face replying aloud, "Yes, you are, I know and thank you."

The messages received from Robert become my buoy. My story submitted to the grief magazine did not materialize to my knowledge. This is all for the best however. In reality I never actually read the magazines. They were ceremoniously thrown into a clutter pile and forgotten. Grief is now my partner. For seven days a week, in twenty four hour clock it controls my world.

I have received satisfaction that my story was well received, that seems to be all that is needed at the time. And with that I cancel my subscription to the magazine for the bereaved.

My Blue Eyed Labrador

One morning while enjoying my coffee in the bedroom I momentarily place my cup aside. Laverne is next to me and to my surprise leans over for a slurp. Within the next moment I surprise myself by exclaiming aloud, "Robert?"

I am dumbfounded and yet excited at the same time. My other dogs have never shown any interest in my coffee cup. My heart tells me that my deceased husband's presence is here with me. And more than just that, somehow or other his energetic presence has become a part of this puppy before my eyes.

Well, I tell myself, why not! If his energy can enter an owl and bring me a message why can't he enter my dog. Seeing is believing. The warm fuzzies filling my heart confirm it. Almost every morning we now have a new ritual. She comes up beside me to get her sip as I pet her head and feel a connection with Robert. I feel his energetic presence through the dog although I cannot see his spirit.

I know that my dogs are able to witness when his spirit is present. I shall always remember the morning of Robert's death and how our labs responded when I called them to come up on the bed after he died.

Both Saber and Spook lay silently watching and yet would not approach the bed. They never left the bedroom unless I did. They were glued to my side. I realized they both were able to see his spirit hovering over his lifeless form, so why would they want to lay by him.

Spirit is a most affectionate dog with me and wants hugs every day. Often she comes into my lap and positions herself with her front paws placed over both my shoulders. It truly is a full body hug. One day while we are enjoying our daily cuddle I close my eyes and breathe fully into the bliss of our embrace. When I open my eyes I catch a split second of seeing Laverne with blue eyes. I blink and look again in disbelief. They are now brown as they ought to be and yet they had been blue.

In this moment I know in my heart that this beloved magnificent dog is allowing the spirit of my Robert to enter her so I can feel his loving in physical reality. What a gift! I am awed and yet somehow not surprised that he would choose her as a vehicle. My guide dog puppy and my husband's energy become entwined on a regular basis. Instinctively, I know they have formed a partnership and an agreement. This co-mingling of energies must be hard on her yet I trust in their wisdom and am so grateful. Just to look into her eyes and be in her presence is like having part of Robert perpetually by my side.

One day I also discover that she likes wine. I offer her a slurp from my wine glass and thus a new ritual begins. I offer the wine to Saber and yet he turns his nose away after the first sniff. But my lovely Spookie thinks this is quite the treat.

Laverne needs to be exposed to as many diverse situations as possible and must always be at ease. Consistency is very important yet this is my biggest challenge. I must train myself in this regard. With time we do become a team of oneness.

With devoted daily work Laverne learns to ignore food temptations and even tennis balls. Training the retriever out of the retriever is no easy task and yet eventually I can place a ball by her nose and she learns to turn away from it.

I do not know how I have managed to get through these days in my dazed state while training this exuberant pup. I am very much blinded with grief and she has effortlessly guided me through my endless maze.

I have talked to so many people in our months together being forced to overcome my former quiet self. One hears all kinds of responses from people about her future day of recall to advanced training. "It would be like giving up a child." In my mind I acknowledge I know that pain too well.

Yet I have never regarded myself as her Mommy. Laverne, along with Saber and Von Spook are regarded in the highest sense as my companions, my teachers and my healers. I never gave birth to a being with floppy ears and four legs so why would I call myself their Mom. They depend on me for their daily needs and my heart depends on them.

I cannot imagine life without them. They have given me purpose. Laverne shall always be my guide dog no matter what happens with her training. Grief will not let go easily and yet the darkness is not all consuming anymore thanks to her. It is no accident after all, that dog spelled backwards spells, "GOD."

Spirit's Elephant Seal

Guide Dogs for the Blind have another campus in Portland, Oregon. I learn they are having a puppy fun day. I decide it would be neat to attend with my Lollipop girl. All three dogs get themselves packed for the trip and we head to the freeway. We make a stop in Livingston, Montana and spend a long time at the cemetery. We all lie on the green grass of Robert's grave as I chatter quietly with him.

The guide dog event is indeed a lot of fun. There are a lot of new distractions to work amongst. A tired Laverne and I join the big dogs waiting in the car. The next day we head north to the Canadian border. I want to see my brother Roger. He is living with Wendy in an apartment and greets me in the parking lot. "We are not allowed dogs here, CA. But you could take turns putting the green jacket on the other dogs." He is all smiles as we successfully get all three dogs upstairs for a merry visit.

Laverne is maturing quickly and before I know it I am faced with the unpleasant notion of having to say goodbye to her. I decide to visit my sister Valerie in Jacksonville, Florida. It momentarily takes my mind off of this horrific prospect. I am distracted with educating Valerie and Dick about working dogs. Valerie gazes on with pride as she watches Laverne perform. Each evening Laverne climbs into my lap for a Bobby hug and I ask Valerie to take a photo.

Both Laverne and I return home with tails wagging happily. It is a great adventure flying with a puppy in training. The pilot comes out to shake her paw and the stewardesses all make a big fuss. I feel proud of our teamwork but now I must face the harsh reality of her turn in. People around me who have fallen in love with her are all distraught about this day also. "How can you give her up, Carol Ann?"

I knew all along I had to give her up but living with my grief I have trained myself to go only one day at a time. I decide the only way to survive letting her go is to do it all over again. The sad day of departure arrives. The guide dog truck is waiting for her. On the truck is my new puppy. The moment she is taken from me I burst into unstoppable wails. Someone tries to console me, "It will only be a few minutes, Carol Ann. Your new puppy is coming right out."

Laverne is gone from sight and I am now looking into the eyes of a puppy called Terrace, another yellow female lab. My heart is heavy but with my new bundle of love I head homeward to introduce Saber and Spookie to their new recruit. I call this girl, Bobby Sunshine Angel. Grief for Laverne is soothed with this little miracle that grows much faster than I like.

She becomes a phone volunteer also at the American Cancer Society. My volunteer friend Mary Kay's tears over Laverne turn into love for Terrace. I decide I need a change. I become a driver for the cancer society and like the one on one with people better than the phone work. Terrace accompanies me each time and provides her own medicine to our passengers. Time marches on and I become a better puppy raiser, experience is indeed a good teacher.

I learn about a fundraising event for hospice and decide to submit a couple photo enlargements dedicated in memory of Robert. I choose one of the colorful photos of our Baja, Mexico trip and a photo of my labrador rainbow. Terrace keeps me company at the evening event. It is a silent auction. We have a lot of admirers to the photo enlargements and a couple pay extra special attentions to Terrace.

"Our daughter has a guide dog from Guide Dogs for the Blind. Perhaps you would like to meet her."

Thus a friendship is forged with Rosalyn and her yellow lab guide, Razzle. I pick her up and bring her out to our home where she is overcome with my labrador rainbow. We spend time together working in public with Terrace and she becomes a regular guest. Mary Kay sometimes agrees to pick her up. Our home is filled with lots of laughter and everyone leaves happy.

A long ten months after I turn Laverne in for her formal training with Guide Dogs for the Blind I receive a phone call from my guide dog leader. "Carol Ann, I am calling to tell you that Laverne is being released. She had great potential. They certainly kept her a long time. They tried different harness setups on her but she was always too sensitive. Her posture slumped and she was not totally happy in her work."

I instantly become teary eyed. "Do you want to adopt her?" One of the blessings of raising a working puppy is that you can take the puppy back into your life if you so choose.

"Yes, absolutely." Through my shock and tears I continue to listen as I am told that Terrace needs to stay with another leader while I go to California to pick her up. I am disappointed for I truly did want her to succeed. Part of me wanted her for my own and yet that was not why I had become a puppy raiser. If she is not to be a guide dog she could never live a happy life with anyone other than me.

Upon hanging up the phone, I am joined by Saber and Spookie who sense something is up. Terrace joins in also as I huddle with my labrador rainbow, "Well my best buddies, I have miraculous news to share with you. Our Miss Laverne has been released from her guide dog training. I shall drive to California to bust her out of guide dog boot camp and in a few days be back home with her. My sweet sunshine angel girl, Terra, you shall have an adventure of your own because you need to stay with someone while I take this trip. You shall be meeting our first guide dog puppy very soon and you will become great buddies." After a good cry I make some phone calls to share this exciting news.

"Take the car in to get checked out before your trip." I have heard this message more than once.

"Ok, I hear you, thanks." I have learned to listen to my love's guidance from the other side. I advise the corner Shell station I am coming over and out the door I go with my working girl by my side.

"I am planning a drive to San Francisco and would like you to check my tires and see that my car is road worthy."

Terra and I stroll over to the post office and return a short while later. The mechanic shares, "It is a good thing you came in because you would not have got far down that highway. You have two tires with nails."

Later as I drive Terrace into Phoenix for her little sleepover, I am prattling happily to my Robert, "Holy smokes, my love what an incredible wise spirit you are. Thanks for helping with my car. Oh my God, that is it! That is the perfect name for our Laverne puppy. Her new name shall be Spirit."

Since learning she will become my dog I have been meditating on a suitable name for her. That birth name of hers is so ridiculous! Due to that goofy television show called Laverne and Shirley, I cannot tell you of the annoying uncountable times I had to tolerate someone giggling, "So where is Shirley?"

Now she will be blessed with her rightful name, for this miracle dog was a gift from the realm of spirit. She literally has carried the spirit of Robert within her young puppy body.

Terrace arrives at her stay over destination. "Ok, my puppy in training be good for me and I shall be back to pick you up in four days."

I shall miss her but this will be good training. One of the challenges a potential service dog must face is the ability to adapt to all new situations. Also they must bond with more than just a puppy raiser before they are ultimately matched with a blind person.

In the morning a friend arrives at our home to stay with Saber and Spook. Hugs mixed with joy and sorrow to my earth angels and I am off. The only company by my side is a box of Kleenex which is in constant use. I shed tears of gratitude and more tears of gratitude and disbelief that I am about to be reunited with that most beautiful yellow labrador named Laverne, soon to be Spirit.

"I shall not keep you to myself dearest sweet puppy, you are going to become a therapy dog and share that big heart. Saber, Spookie and I need you. You will be a great surrogate Mom to my second puppy Terrace, whom you shall meet very soon."

I arrive too late in the day to get into the school yet I am at their door the minute they open in the morning. "Hello, my name is Carol Ann Arnim, I am a puppy raiser and I am here to pick up my released dog, Laverne."

I am guided to the appropriate place to wait after signing the paperwork of her adoption. Thankfully, it is only a few minutes. The door opens and in walks my beauty. Laverne is a mature well-mannered dog walking in the door and yet seconds later that demeanor switches to pure pandemonium as she rolls and jumps all over me with total abandon. We are both in complete shock to see each other.

"She certainly knows who you are." The women watching are all smiles at our reunion.

"Could I be introduced to her trainers please, I want to thank them and get photos."

Laverne sprints joyfully by my side as I find the two women responsible for her training. The one woman picks her up. "My God, you have discovered her love of being picked up."

"Yes, she is such a huggable girl."

I capture shots of their farewell. It is very obvious the close bond she shared with the one woman as human and canine kiss. I express my profound gratitude for the release of my potential guide dog now a career change dog. "Is there somewhere nearby I could witness some dogs in training?"

I am given directions into the nearby neighborhood. I spend time observing and taking photos. It is such a thrill to watch them strut along in their guide dog harness. In my mind I am envisioning my own Laverne working on these very same streets. I imagine some people would be looking out their windows commenting on the dogs in training parading by their home.

I stop in a grocery store for a bag of carrots, the one human food treat she had been allowed. Her excitement is too much for her and they remain uneaten. "Come up on the seat beside me big girl, you can now ride like a human passenger and put your head out the window if you desire, isn't that wonderful." I roll down the window for her and she sniffs the air with great delight.

"No more lying on the car floor for you, some blind person will have to find another dog for themselves; you and I are meant to be together, right my girl. You are now officially my guide dog."

I plan to stay the night and have supper with a friend. I ask at the inn's restaurant if I can have Laverne with me during supper explaining that she is just released from guide dog training. The staff are familiar with the nearby guide dogs and happily agree to their four-footed guest. She settles quietly by my side without any instruction.

After a lovely evening chatting about dogs and life, my career change puppy and I have our first night together. What a heavenly treat to have her back by my side. Both of us snuggle on the bed in a cocoon of bliss. "Laverne, the world will now know you as Spirit. I trust this meets with your approval. You can be very goofy yet your birth name, Laverne, does not speak to your true nature." She thumps her big tail approvingly.

In the morning we say our farewells to lovely San Francisco and joyfully head south. A rendezvous with my friend has been cancelled due to her unavailability so it is time to hit the open road.

As we drive I chatter nonstop with my arm resting on her. "What a sight you are, I never envisioned having you for my own but here you are for real. Hallelujah! I shall find us a safe beach for you to have your first run of total freedom as soon as I can, ok."

Our first full day together we spend enjoying the coast highway. Marveling in the view of the sea and Spirit by my side again I chat away to her like old times. "So, Spirit, how does it feel to be with me, just you and I?"

I am eager to find a quiet beach for her first run of total off leash freedom. She cannot contain her excitement as I park the car alongside an open beach. I walk her down to the water on her leash. The anticipation for both of us is too much. She is beside herself unable to control her exuberance. It is time to let her go. Off comes the leash. "Ok, Laverne Spirit, time for you to fly free."

She needs no encouragement. Boy oh boy, what a beautiful beyond words sight it is to watch her fly through the sand to the water. She brings tears to my eyes. "Go Spirit."

After a good run and time in the surf she happily trots back to the car and falls fast asleep with her magnificent head resting on my thigh.

After a couple hours I decide to find another beach before we head inland. There is another perfect looking spot without any people nearby. Off she charges at break neck speed leaving me far behind. Occasionally, she runs back towards me running big circles around me and then takes off again. Both of us are ecstatic yet still in a state of disbelief at being together. "It is ok, go run. I am right here, go have fun."

Spirit frolics in and out of the waves as she continues her sprint down the beach. I see something in the distance which she is running towards. I am not sure what it is and call her back to me. The closer I get I see it is definitely a large animal.

Spirit is more interested in this creature than coming back to me. She begins to bark at him. I run toward her and put her back on leash. In astonishment, I am looking down at a sea creature which for some unknown reason has come in with the tide. I assume him to be a seal. He has been stranded there in the sun for hours and is in distress. The water level is far from reaching him.

Timidly, I approach him as close as I dare to find out if he is still alive. Thankfully, there is life in his eyes. I am at a loss to know what to do. There is no one in sight and it will be a couple hours or more before the tide comes in.

It seems the only option is to connect with him. I begin to talk to him and Spirit barks. He raises his head attempting to flop around. He lets us know his discomfort through loud cries as he thrashes about. He changes his position. I cheer him on. "Ok, Mr. Seal, that is great, keep going. You must get up and head toward the water. Get going."

As I look at my watch I know we need to head down the highway soon or we will not make our halfway point back to Phoenix. Yet I cannot pull myself away from this forlorn seal that is in desperate need of help. The best and only thing to do is for both Spirit and I to continue our vocal encouragement. Her barking definitely is rousing the seal to move.

The tide is slowly coming in yet the seal really needs to be wet to get relief. After about an hour and a half of flopping around growling at us both, he starts to position himself to head to the water. "Ok, that is great, you can do it, flop yourself out to the sea." Once he gets a taste of the incoming water on his nose, this is the encouragement he needs. "Yeah, keep going. You need to go home. I am sure someone is looking for you."

Even though he has been able to move himself forward enough to have the incoming tide hit him, the actual sea is still several feet away.

With disappointment I watch the ripples hit him and fall back into the ocean. The tide is coming but is taking forever.

I yell at him over and over. Spirit and I continue to circle around him. Suddenly, he makes his biggest effort yet, starting to flop to the water. "Yeah, keep going!"

Finally, he hits the incoming waves, proceeding slowly into his ocean home. With the greatest relief I holler as loud as I can, "Be safe, Mr. Seal and stay in the water." I hope he is not injured from his long stay in the sun.

And then, just before he is about to disappear from our sight, he stops. He raises his head for a few seconds looking at his whereabouts. I am mesmerized, waiting to see what he is going to do. To my total delight, he turns his head back to look at Spirit and myself. I sense he is saying, "Thank you and good bye."

I feel an incredible sense of awe as I observe this creature of the deep returning to his sea. His acknowledgement of us has made the whole experience truly magical. It is hopefully his only encounter with a human and her canine friend. "Take care; I trust you are alright now, Mr. Seal. Thank you for our meeting."

"Well, big girl, this is one time that the intelligent disobedience of a potential guide dog came to play. You disobeyed my command to come and yet it resulted in us helping this distressed creature. So good work my guide dog puppy extraordinaire!"

As Spirit and I walk back to the car I marvel in this blessing we shared with a sea creature. I believe it was due to her barking the seal became motivated to start moving. Certainly, without her running ahead so far on the beach I would not have walked that far on my own. So, it is because of her that we met this seal in need of our help.

Back at the parking lot there is a sign which I had not seen earlier. "WARNING. Stay clear away from the elephant seals."

Our seal adventure would not have happened if I had met my friend that day. I thanked the gods that be for our being able to share our eye to eye encounter with this seal.

Maybe, I give us too much credit in him returning to the sea. Perhaps, we did not really save him. Yet Spirit and I had a marvelous experience for our first day back together.

I take it as a sign that great magic and more miracles are coming our way with my guide dog partner by my side where she is meant to be. My Bobby love in spirit and my angelics had guided her into my life and now have gifted her back to me. Our future lives together can only herald the highest good!

Why Did God Invent Anger

Anyone familiar with grief knows that anger is a part of the journey. Prior to the death of my Bobby, I swore silently to myself that I could never allow myself to engage in anger. Wishful thinking that turns out to be. It is a couple years after his spirit flight that I find myself waking up one day mad at the world. This catches me by surprise and yet this undesired anger holds me in a firm grip.

To be angry at someone who is no longer around is a challenge because he certainly is not here to respond. Reckon it is for his best that he is dead because he would be black and blue from me pummeling him in my anger!

Every day of being angry is most intolerable and unpleasant. Anything can set me off. I have become my own guru in my grief and know that I must somehow express this in an appropriate manner. Often I am merely yelling aloud to the sky but it still helps.

Only God knows how much I have suppressed and he becomes a target for my anger. "God, they say you know everything and are the driving force behind everything. So then it seems to me that the scourge of a disease called cancer must be of your making also. What is your relationship to cancer? Do the two of you conspire as to whom will be the next target?"

On a day I am overwhelmed by my rage I decide to take a walk with Terrace. Being outdoors always has a calming impact and better not to express too much of my anger while inside our own living space.

"Terra, let's go for a walk. I must warn you that my mood is stormy.

Close your lovely labby ears to my ranting. My anger in this moment is at God and not you."

We head down our quiet road. The silence is soon shattered by me shouting and shaking my fists at the sky. "What the hell good is anger anyway? It only makes me feel worse and certainly getting mad at my husband at this point is useless, although I am madder than hell at him right now!"

"By the way God, why did you have to invent such an unhealthy emotion as anger? Why in bloody tarnation did you create anger? I hate being angry. I do not want to be angry at my Robert or at you; but as you can see and hear I am very irate. What possible benefit can come from this intense anger? I could explode right here on the spot. And then what would happen with Terrace and my dogs? What would you do about them?"

My voice gets louder and my pace quickens as my one free arm flails about beating the air. My heart is racing and Terra has to quicken her pace to keep up with her enraged companion.

I turn onto another road marching along consumed with my venting. I come to an abrupt halt. I am dumbstruck by what my eyes are registering. Somehow I find the words, "Puppy, stay. Good girl, Terrace, sit stay."

A short distance between us stands a bobcat. This is the first time I have ever seen such a creature. Certainly, he would have heard me coming with my hollering aloud to the sky and yet he stands as calm as can be just looking at me. All three of us are immobilized staring at each other. I am caught up in the splendor and the wonder of this magical moment.

Only seconds ago I was ranting, asking why God invented anger and then the universe sends me a bobcat directly in my path. We continue to admire each other as my mind is abuzz. Ok, so you got my attention now, thank you. What are you telling me, Mr. Bobcat? I certainly believe this is no fluke of timing. The uncanny reality also, is that this creature happens to have the name of Bob within its name.

Then ever so slowly and gracefully he begins to move away. I stand transfixed and watch as he climbs amongst the huge boulders of his desert home. And then he is gone.

I am startled back to the reality of the tremendous anger which had been spewing out of me uncontrollably minutes earlier. Again I feel the intensity of my question I had posed to God. As I feel the anger rising within me, I take some calming breaths. I know the answer is here. It is suspended in the energy around me just waiting for me to grasp it. Then it hits me.

"Why did God invent anger?"

"So I can learn to heal myself." I repeat these words again very slowly, "So I can learn to heal myself?" The truth of these words register within my being.

I smile with relief saying aloud, "Yes, that works for me and thanks for listening."

A bobcat crossing my path at such a divinely perfect moment is encouraging me to not suppress my anger and to be true to my innermost pains. He had graced me with his steady gaze looking intently into my troubled heart, telling me patience.

Symbolically, a bobcat crossing one's path has a lot to share; but only provided one is ready to hear the message. The universe knew I was ready and Mr. Bobcat helps me to turn a corner that day. I allow myself to more fully surrender to my anger and with time it passes.

Bobby Adorable Angel, Maggie

While raising Terrace, I come upon a puppy in training with a yellow coat. The young recruit is with Canine Companions for Independence who trains dogs for the deaf and wheelchair and therapy dogs. It is an opportunity for a good visit and we spend several minutes comparing notes about the differences of raising a guide dog versus a CCI puppy. I walk away with a lot to think about and the process of perhaps changing schools begins.

This just may be a new path which is meant to be. Thanks to Robert and I being in Anacortes, Washington our kitchen was graced with CCI calendars since 1995. This had planted the seed about puppy raising. The prospect of training one of their puppies becomes very alluring and I contact their school.

Terrace is over a year now and my time remaining with her is counting down. During our last week together we are out on the golf course taking photos. I capture a magical moment between the two guide puppies. Terrace has her head held high looking towards her destiny and Spirit's head is turned downward in sorrow that her playmate and puppy will be leaving her. Afterwards they enjoy a good long run since there are no golfers anywhere in sight.

Again I have been guided to the right place at the right time in crossing paths with a CCI working girl. I know I am destined for this. Magically everything falls into place and I am accepted with them and put on their list for a female pup. Excitedly, I ponder who this next

Bobby angel is awaiting on the other side to come into a lovely lab body destined for me.

The sad day of my farewell with Terrace arrives and instead of going on the truck to California she is sent by airplane. I place her nylabone in the crate but she has no interest and sadly stares. "Be a brave soul, my dearest Bobby Sunshine Angel. Remember what Spirit whispered in your labby ears about school and you will be well taken care of, trust in this. We shall all miss you."

Our market sells marrow bones and I occasionally treat the dogs to a bone in the evening. Spirit is extra fond of these and to my horror I discover that she has a bone lodged in her lower jaw. I call my friend Karen who arrives with her husband and a couple tools. Despite his efforts it cannot be removed. We have to take her to the emergency clinic in Paradise Valley. The husband goes home and Karen drives my car while Spirit lies in my lap.

She is taken into a back room and less than five minutes later emerges with a big grin. She is her happy self once again her lovely smile returned. I am handed the bone which is triangular in shape and just perfectly fitted over her lower jawline. The bill is printed off and I am sixty dollars less in pocket for a job that took two minutes. Karen returns home as Spirit is greeted with big sniffs by her pack.

Thankfully, my wait for the CCI puppy is short. Within a few days I am off to the airport with my friend, Karina that I met while raising Terrace. Both Karina and I squeal with delight as we look inside the crate to see my eight week old yellow puppy. I need to lean inside to pull her out. Her name is Maggie and she is adorable. This becomes the name of my third girl, Bobby Adorable Angel.

Saber, Spookie and Spirit are waiting at my neighbour's for the introduction to their new student. Fran and George's kitchen is filled with childlike delight as each dog takes turns sniffing and inspecting this young pup. Awhile later we all pile into our Labaru as they watch from the patio. "We shall see you soon, Fran and George. Maggie shall come say hello to you in a couple days."

The next time they see us I am greeted with big chuckles. "Look Fran, what she has the baby pup inside."

"Oh what a sweet baby you have Carol Ann. How funny, but a grand idea."

"Yes, I decided that this baby carrier was just what we both needed. They get so tired working during the first month and this will be good fun." We do catch people by surprise over and over when they realize it is a puppy in the baby snuggler.

Soon after her arrival I catch her imprinting teeth marks into a paperback. I get my camera right away and capture an extraordinary image. The book she has chosen to chew on is a tiny book on grief entitled, "How to Survive the Loss of a Love, by Melba Colgrove, Harold H. Bloomfield and Peter McWilliams. How positively magical and indicative of what she is doing and going to do for me.

Raising and training any kind of a potential working dog is extremely rewarding and fun although there are big differences depending on the type of working dog. Unlike a guide dog puppy, Maggie is able to take food treats from the hand and playing with balls is allowed. Retrieving can be a large part of a wheelchair dog's future life so it is a big change for me to remember that I am allowed to throw a tennis ball now.

My brother Mark comes for a long visit and is beside himself with the prospect of going everywhere with our little bundle of joy. His love of dogs oozes from every pore of him. He affectionately calls himself laughing labby. He is quite the sight in the grocery store for the first time trying to steer the cart and manage the puppy. It is great fun but he soon gets the hang of it and our pupil has another person to work beside. We take a camping trip up into the trees near Flagstaff to enjoy the cooler temperatures. This is a most memorable time sharing a tent with my two legged lab, three big dogs and a rambunctious young hooligan flying around the tent.

Mark loves vintage airplanes and we make a trip to the air museum. Maggie is very well received and is gifted a pin which reads, "I love to fly." It is especially memorable for us to climb up into a B24 plane which is the bomber which Robert piloted. There is a great Mexican restaurant nearby and we share a festive lunch as Mark and I toast our Robert with the clink of his corona and my margarita. I imitate my hubby's song he used to sing, "Fours, fours, they sent me to war in a B24."

Mark adds to our silliness with a beer fart. Next I sing the Roberto song, "The moon is coming soon my boys, the moon is coming soon. Hey Mark, you know there is a biplane at the Carefree airport which gives people short rides. Would you like to go up in a biplane?"

His face lights up in disbelief and he responds, "Would I ever, yes."

A couple days later with Maggie by our side both of us are standing next to a yellow biplane. "Ok, you take charge of our puppy girl while I take a ride first." I am very afraid of heights yet find myself forgetting this until the plane rumbles along taking flight and then I gasp in fear. I grab on to whatever is in sight and close my eyes momentarily. Alright now, you can do this Carol Ann I tell myself.

The pilot had asked me if I wanted any rolls or any zippydo flying. I promptly responded in the negative. It is very noisy and of course very windy. I have been able to calm myself somewhat but am most relieved that the flight is short. "Ok brother, your turn. Hang on."

And off he goes. A few minutes later a wide eyed Mark greets me. "Now that was a white knuckle ride."

"Yes, I know for sure me too, I was quite terrified. But it was neat eh!"

Maggie gets some extra cuddles from both of us as we head home to share our adventures with the rest of the pack. Sadly, the day arrives Mark has to return home. He is missed by all.

One day upon entering the post office a white haired lady walking slowly becomes all smiles asking, "Can I please pet your puppy?"

Her face lights up as she leans over. "Oh you are a sight for sore crying eyes, you angel. I just lost my golden retriever, Brandy and my heart is broken in a million pieces."

A few days later I see this same woman in Walgreens and again I have Maggie sit for a visit. My heart tells me I need to see her again so I ask for her phone number. Her name is Margaret and she lives alone a few minutes from our home. We agree to visit the next day. She is grieving the loss of Brandy so our company is just what she needs. We share an instant rapport and our love of dogs quickly draws us close together.

Once Maggie is big enough she learns the lap command, which entails her putting her front paws over the lap of a person. This is one of the favorite commands for someone with a wheelchair dog. It proves to be a fun thing to teach. My student is very willing and happily gets an edible treat and a big hug. My adorable Bobby angel is indeed a great responsive pup.

Margaret loves to accommodate teaching the lap command and Maggie is well rewarded with a tight embrace. She next has the pleasure of meeting my other three dogs. "Margaret would you like me to leave my dogs with you while I drive a cancer patient tomorrow?"

"Really, you would let me watch your big puppies?" she squeals with girlish delight.

"Yes, it would be great fun for all of you. I can bring them in the morning and be back after lunch."

"Ok, Carol Ann. That sounds wonderful." We share big hugs and this soon becomes a great ritual. "Oh boy, you are the best hugger."

"I miss my Bobby hugs so enjoy receiving hugs myself and you certainly are very huggable." We both giggle.

The next day Margaret has her first adventure in sharing the morning with my labrador rainbow. Upon returning I am greeted with happy tail wags and an earful from her. She is full of happy tales of what dog did what and when and where. As I get up to leave she chuckles asking, "So which of your beauties are you going to leave with me?" This becomes a routine question every time I have all the dogs over.

"Margaret I have something very special to share with you. The guide dog school has used a photo of Laverne for the cover of their millennium calendar plus she is also the puppy featured for the month of June."

"Your Laverne Spirit is a calendar girl?" Margaret is beside herself with excitement.

"Yes, the cover shot is a lovely photo of her taken shortly after her arrival in her oversized green cape. She is sitting on a grassy knoll of the

Legend Trails golf course looking out at her world. It is a memorable place for me because for a short period of time during Robert's illness we walked around there with Saber and Spookie. There was no one around back then since the development was still being built."

Shortly after Spirit's transition to being a career change dog and pet she becomes a certified therapy dog. She had been used to working all of her life yet now had to stay home a lot. However she is well suited for her new role as a therapy dog and I begin to take her into hospice units. On such days Maggie stays home with her buddies Saber and Spookie. A potential working puppy also has to learn to stay home unsupervised.

I ponder a lot about how Terrace is doing in advanced training at Guide Dogs for the Blind. After turn in the puppies are evaluated for the breeding program. I receive the most amazing news that she has been chosen to be a future guide dog Mom. I am invited to come to the school on July 17 to present her as a breeder. This is most exciting since out of the many hundreds of puppies turned in only a select few are chosen. What an honor! I share this tremendous news with everyone that my Bobby Sunshine Angel shall be bringing sunshine light into the lives of many blind. Bow wow wowsers!

I make the trip to San Rafael with my CCI puppy by my side and she waits in the kennels during the ceremony. It is a bouncy reunion with Terrace and I get to meet her new family. The breeder keepers are a couple named Robert and Michael. How perfect is that!

Taking a working puppy everywhere is unbelievable fun and can make certain experiences even more special. While doing my bachelor's degree I was exposed to the works of renowned Elisabeth Kubler-Ross. Her book, "On Death and Dying," gives one a whole new perspective. At some point in my travels I learn about a talk she is giving at the Scottsdale library. The topic is, "Being versus Doing" shared with a man named Joseph. I cannot ignore this opportunity.

Maggie makes herself comfortable at my feet as I am spellbound listening to the wisdom of these two wise souls. Joseph addresses the subject of doing and Elisabeth that of being. Since her stroke she has been in a wheelchair and has learned to live more from the mindset of being versus doing. Her words become imprinted on my own beingness. With one of her books in hand I am blessed to have a brief face to face.

She signs my book. She has her finger outstretched and I place my finger to hers. It is an ET greeting. My heart is full to bursting as I walk away with adorable Maggie.

Somehow I learn of the Tibetan Buddhist gatherings in Phoenix and I attend the next event. We have a great aisle seat with full view of the many monks performing. Maggie is exposed to the chanting and the long horns and the clashing of cymbals. She sits perfectly quiet her eyes fixated on the stage. Afterwards she is blessed with the pats from several of the smiling monks.

I receive a welcome phone call from Aly who has returned from her nursing sojourn in Africa. We arrange for her to visit. Later we settle into the comfy wicker chairs of our living room with a glass of chardonnay. Aly exclaims, "Oh my God, Carol Ann, I can still feel the energy of Robert around this chair. It is years since he sat here yet I feel the deep good energy still surrounding this corner."

I smile in delight with my young friend's wisdom always so right and spot on. "I must admit Aly that I do prefer to sit in that corner chair. No doubt you have given him some good chuckles. We both thank you."

Aly has returned a changed young woman sporting a full head of dreadlocks which took many a long hour to braid. She shares tales of her time in Zambia studying HIV and nurses' risk of infection. She also worked in the TB ward and neonatal intensive care. She taught contraception to the bush women outside of the capitol, Lusaka. "It was quite the adventure to be the only white woman these people had ever encountered. I shall never forget it."

Maggie is proving to be a tremendous working puppy and my heart tells me that she will succeed. There is something extraordinarily special about this four legged angel. My grieving heart is beginning to shift into healing. To my surprise I awaken one day with gratitude about being alive. The desire to die has left me. Maggie has rebirthed Carol Ann.

I am startled by this new mindset and look into the mirror to gaze upon myself. Who are you becoming now Mrs. Carol Ann Joy Arnim I ponder. Maggie sits lovingly looking up at me. I sweep her into my arms whispering thank you. All of my dogs have helped me on this journey more than I could say in words yet I know in my soul that this remarkable little puppy has truly imprinted her own paw of healing on my heart. We have most definitely been soul contracted to work together.

Serendipity somehow leads me to an energy healer named Linda. Maggie drops into a deep snooze underneath the table as she works on me. Cranial sacral therapy proves to be of great benefit along with her compassionate ear as she works. During one session she shares, "Carol Ann, I believe you shall meet a man at some point in the future."

"Wow, that is amazing and I thank you for telling me. It seems impossible for me to be so blessed yet I must admit that I have had the same feeling."

I hear about a class in animal communication and spend an enlightening afternoon learning how to connect with my dogs. The woman offers to read photos of pets and when she looks at a photo of Spookie she says the dog is very depressed. I am shocked to hear these words and feel badly for my dog. Yet Spookie was with me from the beginning and I have learned about the concept of animals being mirrors to their people to assist in their life journey. I realize that I must change in order for her to do so.

A woman in the class I have a rapport with is a reiki master. Her name is Christina and this workshop is being held at the reiki centre operated by a woman named Carlyn. I am intrigued with everything she shares and she comes to our home to allow me to experience reiki. There is a class in reiki one just starting and I eagerly sign up. It is a couple days and very much an awakening experience. Maggie receives the reiki attunements as well so now she is more extraordinary than before. The reiki affirmation, I am whole, complete and perfect becomes a daily mantra. Every day I do my reiki positions and with time begin to feel anew.

It opens up a fascinating world to learn that everything is energy. Carlyn gifted her students the Louise Hay book, "Heal Your Body." This leads me to the bookstore where I discover another by Louise Hay, "You Can Heal Your Life." I snuggle on the couch with my labrador rainbow and soon my world is opened up in a whole new way as I read her powerful life changing words.

With Maggie by my side I spend more time at the bookstore

scanning for more new friends. Carolynn Myss goes home with me and soon I am developing a great library of eye opening healing books. Doreen Virtue's, "The Lightworker's Way" leaps into my welcome hands on another visit to the bookstore which leads to more of her works. I am longing to be whole, complete and perfect. I am learning about the amazing influential impact of our feelings, thoughts and spoken word. My guidance is certainly leading me to the right tools.

A quote by Pierre Teilhard de Chardin becomes my favorite. "We are not humans having a spiritual experience, but spiritual beings having a human experience." This casts a whole new look on life when you live this as truth.

I have discovered the healing powers of Aura Soma and purchased a few of these vibrant bottles which combine the healing energies of color, plants and crystals. A blind British woman, Vicky Wall created this tool of vibrational healing through prayer and meditation. Color has a huge impact on our body and mind and I make full use of wearing the colors of the rainbow. It is great fun as well.

My reiki master, Carlyn and I have a personal session together. After turning in Laverne I developed a sensation below by ribs on both sides. I know it is tied to the immense grief over her departure on top of the Bobby grief. Maggie is asleep by my side as Carlyn teaches me to talk to my body and visualize what the discomfort looks like. I tell her it feels like rocks. Our time together is very empowering and I am most grateful to this wise woman. We have discussed my Robert love during the session. As she hugs me she says, "You have special work to do. He loved you so much he died to get out of your way. He had to get out of your way."

I am speechless yet somewhere within the depth of my being I sense her words are truth. I also know that I must have been ready to hear this profound message. When the student is ready, the teacher appears. I drive home in deep contemplation with a whole new perspective on myself and my Robert love. What a gift. What could all this be leading toward?

Maggie is maturing quickly and I realize that turning in this puppy will be most excruciating. The turn in of Laverne had been extremely painful. It was reliving the death of my Robert all over again through her departure for school. And then the second pup, Terrace was difficult. However, due to the horrific pains of missing Laverne I never fully bonded with all of my heart and soul with Terra. I stumbled through the raising of her, as I did with Laverne and I truly do not know how I had been able to accomplish such in my state of immense grief.

Again I realize that the best way to survive her turn in will be to continue with my puppy raising. It has become my passion and I love it with all my heart despite its challenges. These little four legged angels in training along with Saber and Spook have been my salvation.

Tammy's Four Legged Angel Therapy

Spirit and I are at the hospital doing therapy work. I have placed an angel halo on her beautiful head and adorn her with angel wings.

"Did you just see that dog in angel wings?" I turn and see a woman approaching us. The excited woman comes up to me asking, "Do you go to patients' rooms?"

"Yes we do, this is my therapy dog, Spirit."

Something tells me this is going to be special. I follow the woman back up to the hospital's third floor. At the doorway of a room she welcomes us with a huge secretive grin. "Tammy, look at your visitor."

A pretty young woman props herself up in the bed as her eyes get big with disbelief. Total astonishment and joy light up her face. "It is an angel, oh how beautiful you are."

I already know how Tammy will respond but need to ask, "Do you want her on the bed with you?"

"Oh yes, please, can I?"

"Absolutely, she would love it. Her name is Spirit." I position her carefully next to Tammy with the angel wings so they will not be in the way of the intravenous line in her arm.

"My husband Dave and I have a yellow labrador named Faith and I absolutely adore and love angels. Spirit, you and those angel wings are magnificent. What a most lovely name you have also."

"I am so glad your Mom found us. Spirit is a career change puppy for Guide Dogs for the Blind. When she was released from training she became a therapy dog. I am now raising a puppy for Canine

Companions for Independence. I have a nine month old yellow lab girl named Maggie who could come see you next time."

"Wow, two heavenly labs to visit me. How perfect, thank you."

I learn that Tammy has metastatic breast cancer which has spread into her spine. She is hospitalized for the duration of her radiation treatments.

A couple days later I return with Maggie. This time Tammy and her husband Dave, get to share my adorable Bobby angel's healing energy. In honor of Maggie meeting an earthly angel named Tammy, I have my puppy wearing her angel halo and wings.

As I place Maggie on the bed she senses Tammy's needs immediately and completely. All of her worries and concerns are transformed through the undivided unconditional love of my four legger. I can feel the shift of energy in the hospital room as both Dave and Tammy become totally present to my bundle of love.

My heart cries and sings at the same time for being able to witness this very personal struggle. I see myself once again as I observe her Mom and Dave caring for her. My mind is playing my own painful movie as I nurse my husband Bobby, during our journey with his advanced lung cancer. It is now three years plus since his death. Thanks to all of my four labradors I am learning to face my own harsh reality of widowhood.

The ways of the universe are a constant marvel to me. My being drawn to someone like Tammy who truly appreciates my dogs is very gratifying. People such as Tammy unknowingly pass on rewards imprinting my heart with much needed healing.

For the next three weeks I go to see Tammy as often as I can knowing each time she will be transformed by my dog. Even though our presence gives only a brief respite from her illness my heart knows it is very much needed.

On one visit, Tammy is asleep with her Mom by her bedside. She welcomes us in and we share our stories. "How do you know so much about cancer, Carol Ann?"

I briefly share about the death of Robert. I learn that part of Tammy's long struggle included a visit to a Mexican cancer clinic.

Tammy awakens all smiles to see Maggie by her side as she reaches out to pet her. To my delight shares, "I saw you in my dreams pretty girl. You and Spirit were both here."

"Thank you for sharing Tammy, that is very special."

Each time we visit she sits up eagerly as I enter her room inquiring, "So which dog do you have with you today, Carol Ann?"

My beloved Spirit gets very goofy when someone makes funny noises with her. One day Dave is visiting while she is with me. He begins to make strange noises thus getting her into a playful, exuberant mood. "Dave, if you make an oink pig noise she will really respond. That always guarantees the goofiest response from her." Dave imitates a pig and instantly all of us are in hysterics. He is on the floor with her and she eagerly climbs all over him. White fur is flying everywhere as he happily wipes his face clean from her affectionate slurps.

A couple days later I awake sensing I need to go see Tammy. This time her door is closed with a sign on it which says, "NO VISITORS ALLOWED, CHECK WITH THE NURSE. NEUTROPENIC CONDITION." My heart becomes heavy with sorrowful memories of Robert's neutropenic condition which led to his nighttime emergency visit and hospital stay.

I go check at the nurses' station. I know if she could just see Maggie, it would be beneficial. The nurses discuss my ability to visit with a dog. "She could mask her dog." I listen as they discuss what to do. They reach an agreement.

"She can wear a mask and allow the dog in provided Tammy does not touch the puppy."

I don a mask pausing for a few seconds before opening the door. My heart is racing. I am remembering my masked visit with Robert.

Tammy's smiles become a frown when she learns she cannot pet Maggie, yet she is glad to see her. I have to restrain my puppy's enthusiasm as she recognizes Tammy. Maggie is placed in a down and stay command next to her side. Our visit is short because she is about to leave for her radiation.

Saying goodbye, Maggie and I go to visit other patients. Awhile later, I see a woman being wheeled on a hospital bed towards the elevator. To our mutual surprise it is Tammy. She is being taken back to her room. "Glad to see you again, I shall return again soon."

Two days later I sense I must go see her and decide to telephone first. Dave answers her phone, "We are so glad you called, she goes home today but wants to see you with both your dogs."

I chuckle in reply, "I would love to bring them both, but I can only do one at a time."

"Tammy had me write a message on her neutrepenic door sign. I wrote, "Maggie and Spirit please come in.""

I hang up the telephone in tears as I visualize this loving sentiment written for my angelic working dogs. Again I flash back to Robert's unexpected hospital stay, knowing what it would have meant to him to have a therapy dog visitor. Tammy is anxiously waiting to see them again and had written this wonderful message for them. My tears of sorrow become smiles. I thank Bobby for blessing me with meeting Tammy.

As I drive to the hospital I ask God and Bobby to get me there in time before she leaves. As I approach her room her Mom is in the hallway looking out for us. She anxiously exclaims, "Oh good, please hurry, she is leaving."

Maggie and I are greeted by a very cheery spry Tammy, sitting on the side of the bed eagerly waiting her departure for home. Her Mom tells me she had hoped we would come yesterday because Tammy kept asking all day long, "Are the dogs here yet?"

I put Maggie beside her on the bed. I take a few photos as Tammy gingerly kisses my puppy. She is being driven home by a medical service and has to move herself from the bed to the stretcher. This is not an easy task. Her mobility is severely restricted from the cancer which has eaten into her back.

I offer to follow her down in the elevator. As she is taken outside I watch to see where her van is parked and walk towards it. "Perfect timing again Carol Ann."

I place Maggie on the pavement by her side. Tammy reaches down to pet her on the head prior to being placed into the ambulance. We squeeze each other's hands as she thanks me for visiting.

"Maggie and Spirit could come to your home when you are up for visitors. I would love to meet a dog named Faith."

I watch in silence as she is safely secured in the back of the van.

Memories of Robert come to me as I remember the day I went to bring him home from his emergency stay.

As Maggie and I start walking down the road to the parking lot I sense a vehicle following us. To my surprise it is Tammy's van driving slowly past us. Through the back window I see her arm uplifted to us in farewell. Quickly I stretch out both my arms waving wildly in return. "I send you God's strength and good wishes to your family, Tammy."

With a silent heartfelt prayer I envision Tammy in her true Godlike wholeness and perfection without a diseased physical body.

Tammy's struggle on this earthly plane ends a few weeks later. I receive a phone call from her Mom sharing the news of her death. "We know how much Tammy dearly loved those two working dogs of yours and we would like you to come to her funeral service with both Spirit and Maggie."

"We would be honored to be there for you, I am very sad for your news but most grateful for your invitation and phone call."

After the phone call I flash back to memories of the other funerals my service dog puppies have attended of cancer patients they had assisted. My mind replays the movie of my own Bobby's funeral with our labs, Saber and Von Spook by my side.

Tammy's life is well celebrated by a church filled with family and friends. Both Spirit and Maggie are greeted by Tammy's Mom and Dave and many others. The minister welcomes us warmly. During the service the minister speaks of the dogs visiting Tammy. "It is wonderful to see the working dogs here today, as we know that this is giving Tammy great smiles to see them at her celebration of life." Tammy had indeed been a very special person as I listen to people share how she touched their lives.

After the church service I am preparing to leave when her Mom stops me. "Carol Ann you must stay for all of Tammy's service, she would want you here for the entire service and reception, please stay."

Both the dogs are very welcomed fitting in quietly to a somber group gathering at the gravesite. At the reception Dave comes to shake my hand and pet the dogs, thanking us for being there. Her Mom invites us to sit at their table as the dogs get a lot of attention along with treats.

We leave that day with my steps feeling a little lighter. My angel dogs had truly made a difference. Any bit helps during such a painful time. I feel very privileged that my puppies and I were included within their circle of personal sorrow.

I sense a vision of Tammy's face graced with the most magnificent beautiful smiles as she witnessed my dogs at her tribute. She is now indeed whole, complete and perfect in her disease free light spirit form.

Constance

A cancer patient named Constance, Maggie and I are assigned to drive makes an indelible imprint on my heart. The two of us are welcomed into her apartment as she disappears calling out, "Please be patient with me, I am not quite ready but I shall be in a jiff." The scent of urine soaked clothes and bedding greets me. My observant eye catches sight of a book by Louise Hay entitled, "You Can Heal Your Life" and another book on healing by Carolyn Myss. Both books have become friends with me as well. I smile a silent thank you as I sense I am about to be blessed with the potential friendship of a like-minded soul.

"Ok, I am finally ready but first I must sit down to meet this lovely angel dog of yours. What is her name?"

"Constance, this is Maggie. She is in training to be a future service dog for someone in a wheelchair."

We slowly make our way to the car. She has a bad limp and walks with the aid of a cane. My heart's instincts are correct as we make instant connections in our conversation. She also has a love of pretty long skirts. "It is nice to meet another who likes to wear something that flows."

"Oh yes, it is much more comfortable in my mind than always wearing pants."

Constance is very open about her situation and thus I never hesitate to share my truth with her. I do believe this is one of the toughest challenges for terminally ill patients, for most folk will not comfortably discuss such issues, thus making their paths lonelier than need be.

I wait while she has her cat scan. Our compatibility opens the door to sharing lunch together. I enjoy this unique woman and offer, "Constance, I would be happy to continue taking you to any appointments and would like to help you in any way possible. It is refreshing to be with someone so open to talking about their journey. I know from personal experience how difficult it is to talk about these issues." She happily agrees to this arrangement.

A few days later the cancer society requests my availability to drive her to the oncologist. As my angel puppy and I drive to meet her I sense she will be confronted with difficult news. It is no accident that this soul has crossed my path and I desire to make the best of this opportunity to the highest good for both of us. We are about the same age.

As we drive to the doctor Constance delights me with asking, "Carol Ann, would you mind coming in with me when I see the doctor?"

"You have read my mind, yes most definitely. You need another pair of ears today, Maggie and I shall be honored to accompany you."

Indeed the news is most unpleasant. The oncologist advises her that the cancer has spread into her bones and she is given medication for the pain. This is her second recurrence. Her spell in remission was short lived. The doctor suggests finding an urologist for her incontinence. While back in the car silence envelops both of us. A few minutes later, in a low whisper she asks, "So Carol Ann, why do you think the cancer came back?"

"Constance, it is not for me to say. Yet from what I have learned your soul is calling to you to unearth the dark secret, that inner wound which manifested the disease to begin with."

"Yes I know what you are talking about and yet I do not know what my soul is saying to me. I do not know what my soul wants."

"I understand. This is a difficult path and I want to help you in any way I possibly can. Have you heard of healing with reiki?"

"Yes I know about it and yet have not experienced it."

I had recently taken my reiki one level class and was eager to share this with my new friend. My busy mind begins to plot a plan to help Constance. "I know a reiki master who may be able to provide you with reiki therapy if you are interested. I would be happy to gift this to you, Constance."

"You are willing to do that for me?"

"Yes, most assuredly. I feel a kinship with you which is drawing me to say this. The reiki treatments would certainly ease some of your emotional stress. We can do it at my home. A trip out into the desert would be a nice treat for you also. I need to chat with Christina, the reiki master who introduced reiki healing to me and I shall let you know."

Christina and I discuss a plan to provide Constance with sessions. "Reiki has been known to assist people with cancer and yet you ought not to attach yourself to any great outcomes from this."

"Yes I fully understand what you are talking about and yet I want to offer this gift to her. She is willing and open to receiving such. To me this speaks to the fact it is a compassionate right move. It can be a lesson for me to give without expectation and attaching to the outcome."

None of us know what is in store for Constance with this offer and yet it is agreed upon by the three of us.

I pick her up from Phoenix and drive her out to our desert home. I can see just by watching her take in the desert saguaros she is enjoying this outing. It takes a few minutes for all of my dogs to settle down again after the arrival of Christina.

Constance lies on the massage table and each dog finds their own quiet spot. Maggie makes herself cozy underneath the table. Certainly, this is good testament to the fact that all the dogs are attuned with the reiki energy. I settle on the couch to enjoy the healing energies permeating our living room. At the conclusion of the session we set up a second appointment with Christina.

After a few minutes of quiet rest Constance sits up with a smile, "That was a most lovely experience, thank you Christina and thank you Carol Ann for your generosity. It has been such fun to see your home and meet all of your beautiful gang." Maggie is by her side ready for a pet and she is well rewarded with snuggles.

"I am so glad we could this for you and we shall see you again next week for your second reiki. Be sure to drink lots of water when you get home. I will get you a glass right now to take before we leave." Christina reappears with a tall glass of water.

After taking her home I ponder this experience and recall a vision prior to meeting her. I had seen a terminally ill person in our back bedroom and I sense it is meant to be Constance. I consider inviting her to stay the night after her next reiki treatment. I ask Robert to give me a sign this will be proper. One of his ways of communicating to me is through the owls which frequent our palm trees in the evening. Shortly after putting my request out to him I am rewarded with the hooting of the owls. I believe this is a soul directed decision and thank my hooter in spirit for validation.

The second session is welcomed and received as well as the first and a third one is set up. As I take her home I share, "Constance if you are willing, for the third session I would love to have you stay the night in our guest bedroom. We can have a quiet evening together and I would take you home after some breakfast together."

"That is a most beautiful idea and one I would regret if I do not say yes. So I agree and thank you."

The reiki session is for late afternoon. Constance enjoys time outside in the backyard with all four dogs that provide lots of entertainment with their exploits in and out of the pool. I make us a supper of spinach salad. She does not eat much of her meal yet the evening is most enjoyable.

We are off to bed and I lay awake keeping an open ear. She is unsteady on her feet. During the night I hear her crying and go check on her. "I am afraid of falling but did not want to wake you up."

"I am here for you, it is alright." She settles back into bed after her trip to the loo.

A sunshine morning greets us and we enjoy more time together. It has proved to be a most memorable experience. I am grateful to have followed my heart to allow this gift to each other. With puppy in training Maggie, the three of us get into our Labaru to take her home.

After one of my trips driving her to an appointment she has a visit from a home care nurse who has come to check in on her. Constance had shared with her about me and the nurse kindly tells me, "Carol

Ann, she needs you. I am so delighted you have met. You have such a good impact on her which no one else is able to reach."

"Thank you for sharing this sentiment. I believe we need each other. In my reaching out to her my heart is opening to much needed healing so we are of great benefit to each other, this is very much a two way street. I feel very connected to her and had no second thought about having her enter my life so intensely."

After her fourth and final reiki treatment during a quiet moment between Christina and myself she shares, "I feel the desire to thank Robert for all of these special moments the three of us have been sharing in your home."

Her truth spoken with such compassion touches me deeply and I feel a tingling as her words resonate from my head to toe as Robert makes his presence known. My heart cries in gratitude for the blessing of this beautiful experience.

After Christina leaves I tell Constance, "Come with me, I want to show you something." I take her by the hand and we walk side by side into the bedroom to stand before the large closet mirrors. "Take a look at yourself, your light is shining."

"I have stopped looking in the mirror, I am afraid of what I will see."

Her face has shifted and the heaviness is gone. She timidly looks in the mirror. "I do feel better since these sessions began. It has been a long time since I have seen myself. Thank you for your kind observations. I know you speak the truth but I have lost touch with myself so must take your word for it."

She does benefit from the reiki with an improvement in her mobility and a lightened heart. Her pains are not so intense. She struggles with manic depression and has a fear of being committed against her will. It is so good to see her laugh and be in her joy during the moments that it lasts.

I continue to drive her to various appointments and always go inside to visit afterwards. She is madly in love with Maggie. It is very rewarding to witness the benefit of my most loving earth angel dog.

After my time with Constance, Maggie always soothes me as well. It is not easy to observe the personal and medical struggles she is enduring. I hold her inner pains in my own heart as if they are my own. This

107

empathetic heart has become attached. Whenever I get home from time with her my beloved Spirit gives me the longest blue eyed Bobby hugs. Without any word from me she drapes her paws over my shoulders. "Thank you Spirit and thank you Robert."

One day I participate in a walk for cancer with both Spirit and Maggie in downtown Phoenix. After the event I stop in to see Constance. She is declining physically and wants to be able to spend time with her estranged daughter, Lisa. "Would you make a call to her and explain I need to see her."

I make the phone call and silently put the intent for good to come of this.

A few days later I make a visit to Constance. "That so called friend of mine has taken my medication." She has a neighbour who is a drug addict and he has stolen her pain meds. Needless to say she is very distraught. I help make arrangements for another prescription.

She is laying on her bed in distress. Maggie cuddles beside her. I sense my friend needs an honest heart to heart. It is evident that her time is becoming short and I silently ask for Robert to help me to know what to say to her so she will stay of fear. I take her hand and gently share my thoughts. I cannot recall my words but she soaks them in slowly responding, "Carol Ann, you are the only one who will talk frankly with me about this."

"Well that is why I am in your life. I am glad I can be of such help to you and shall make a call on your behalf about hospice if that is alright with you."

"Yes, you are right. Thanks for getting the ball rolling. You have been such a good friend."

To my relief she is taken in by hospice and I go to the unit to visit her with my adorable Maggie. The nurse informs me that her daughter Lisa had come in to visit. I am relieved and grateful. I recognize the signs of approaching death as I enter and stand quietly by her bed. Her eyes are closed as I take her hand and whisper, "Constance, it is Carol Ann and Maggie visiting you."

She squeezes my hand. I am grateful we have been able to make a connection one last time. "Constance you are safe here, you will be taken good care of."

Her only response which she repeats over and over is, "Thank you, thank you, thank you."

My final gift to her has been a death in a clean bed with someone looking over her. Her death rattle is the only sound as I part her company for the last time. "Safe journey to you Constance, until we meet again, my friend."

Dave

Slowly his frail hand reaches out to gently caress my face. I lean over the bedrail while his other arm becomes outstretched seeking an embrace. I wrap my arms around him while laying my head on his chest. Emotion overcomes me as tears pour silently and gratefully. This man is a hospice patient named Dave and yet for an instant he becomes my dying husband, Robert.

I first meet Dave with my therapy dog Spirit. Within a minute of our meeting, she eagerly makes herself comfy in Dave's arms on his bed. He has thick wavy graying hair with a full beard. When we talk there is always a twinkle in his eyes which reminds me of Robert. Dave's lung cancer has spread to his bones and he has been paralysed for a long while. Yet he has a marvelous attitude about life and death.

His oncologist comes in and I take my exit to visit with another patient. I overhear him ask his doctor, "So how am I doing, how long?"

A few minutes later I see his doctor leaving and I go stand in his doorway. I do not know if he would want any more visiting yet the instant he sees Spirit at the door his face lights up with a welcoming smile. So in we go and again Spirit makes herself comfortable on his bed. "I am going home soon," he expresses happily as he pets my dog.

"Oh I am glad you will get to go back home, Dave," I reply.

"No Carol Ann, not home of this earth, but home to the Lord."

In that instant I am drawn into his open honest heart. This Dave is welcoming death without any apparent fear or anxiety. I am spellbound! I begin to sense the presence of his many angelics. The room resonates with a heavenly glow. His contentment about his imminent death is inspiring. Prior to leaving I hold his hand as I express, "Dave it has been a true pleasure and honor to meet you. Thank you for allowing me to visit with my Spirit girl."

"Please come again, I would love to see you," he grins.

"Yes, absolutely, I shall return soon, Dave."

Two days later I return with my puppy in training, Maggie. Dave and I enjoy the most memorable wonderful exchange of honesty, laughter, and stories for about two hours. He shares his faith with me and his simple lifestyle.

"Less is more, Carol Ann. I would be content to live in a simple cabin with only a fireplace, bed, table and chair along with my favorite books. A garden with lots of daisies would be a plus. I would spend nights sleeping outside next to the earth with only the stars as my blanket."

Dave points to my husband's wedding ring which I wear on a long chain. "Did that belong to Robert?"

"Yes." I remove it from around my neck and hand it to Dave.

"It is a very unique piece just as he was I imagine. Please tell me about Robert, I would like to hear you share about your life."

Smiling in silence for a moment, I reply, "Robert was and is a very happy soul. He could always find a smile in everyone. It seems to me you have similar traits." Dave's curiosity continues as I slowly tell about my Robert love.

"Well Carol Ann, when I see him soon, I will say hello to him from you, ok."

"That is a most precious sentiment and I am most grateful."

During our visit he tells me about a book he knows I would enjoy, written by the Vietnamese Buddhist monk, Thich Nhat Hanh. The book is, "Peace Is Every Step." He also shares a poem he had written about dying which is truly moving and magnificent. Plus he shares a poem a relative had written to him.

He watches the clock closely, keeping track of thirty minute intervals when he can give himself another dose of morphine. "My only fear, Carol Ann, is to be in pain. I want you to understand what the visits with your dogs means to me. This is the very best thing you are doing. Your hospice work is the best."

He continues to hold my hand in a tight grasp and then quietly says, "I think I need to rest now Carol Ann, please come back again soon."

My next visit is a couple days later with Spirit. A nurse who recognizes us sees me approach his room and she welcomes me along with a forewarning, "There has been a big change, but please go on in." This time there is no cheery hello greeting.

I stand in silence at his bedrail and take his hand, "Dave, it is Carol Ann and I am here with Spirit dog." There is no response of any kind. I talk quietly telling him how glad I am that we met. I remember the poems in his bedside drawer and reach in to find them. I lean over the bedrail slowly reading his death poems. He shows no response. Yet I know somewhere within in his being he hears me reading.

The nurse comes in asking him if he is in any pain. This seems to arouse him a bit. After she leaves I say, "Hello Dave, it is Carol Ann. My dog Spirit is here to see you."

At that point he reaches up to touch my face, caressing me and reaching out for a hug. His lips are moving, yet it is inaudible. Our reaching out to each other overtakes him. He collapses back on to the bed. "I shall be back in a few minutes, ok."

I wander down the hall and find myself drawn into a room with an elderly woman. She is named Helen and is very happy to have a dog visitor. After a few minutes I return to Dave and announce our presence to him.

Spirit is by my side and Dave starts to get restless, trying to move his arm to the bedrail. I know he is attempting to pet her. I position her feet on the bedrail and lead his hand to her head. He strokes her slowly and then to my surprise he lifts his head toward her. I lift Spirit closer to him as his lips touch upon her nose. Dave and Spirit are nose to nose in a goodbye embrace. Dave has been aware of both of us all along. After his struggle to move about to kiss the dog he falls back into his world of dying. He is in that space between life and death, for now untouchable by me; that place all humans ponder and wonder over.

"Thank you Dave for all of our memorable visits and your kind interest in my Robert. I wish you a marvelous spirit journey into the great beyond. I shall always remember you my friend, you have left your imprint on my heart. You are a marvel to behold for both Spirit and myself. You are a magical being."

As I walk out of his room which I know will be for the last time I recall the vision of his happy face on a previous visit. I had paused at his doorway in a wave smiling to him, "See you later alligator."

And his reply had been, "Yes, after a while crocodile."

Godspeed to You Helen

Helen's face lights up as we hug each other. "Carol Ann, isn't it wonderful how God sent you into my life!"

"Yes Helen, you are absolutely right. Our meeting is no accident."

"I shall never forget the day we met. You had your beautiful dog at your side, standing at my door waiting for my welcome. What a marvelous sight!"

"We made a connection immediately and your lovely Spirit dog climbed into my heart as she nestled next to me on my bed. I am so grateful I was in the hospital at that time otherwise we would never have met. You would not be here now visiting me in this private care home thanks to your asking for the address."

"Yes I agree Helen, life certainly can present little miracles if the heart is open and the ears attuned to your angels whisperings."

This is my second time to visit at her private care home since our meeting at the hospital. Spirit is cozy in her favorite visiting position next to Helen on the bed. When lunch arrives Helen marvels at how Spirit takes no notice of her food only inches from her nose. Helen is very knowledgeable about working dogs and it is a frequent topic of our conversations.

She shares lovingly of her two sons, Danny and Jimmy. One son had two rottweilers which both died close together in time and he was heartbroken. "You must go and get another dog I told him. Well, he got two new dogs and trained them as therapy dogs which visit in hospitals as you do with yours."

Helen's age of eighty-six has not dispelled her great wit and spunkiness. Each time we visit we share laughs. She tells me how at home she feels with me. "It feels like I have known you for years, Carol Ann."

The private nursing home she lives in has two twin beds in her room. "It is nice that you have the room to yourself."

"Oh yes, I do like that. Although if I had to have a roommate, I would want it to be you. And of course your dogs would be with us too."

We both share giggles at this vision. Helen is in good spirits sitting up on the bed with Spirit by her side. "Yes, I want you to come with me. We all have to die sometime right." I chuckle in reply to her comment and she says, "You better not laugh, you just might go with me, you never know, right."

Helen has just received a perm in her hair which really pleases her. With all of our hilarity, she makes us both laugh even more saying, "Oh my, I think that perm did something to my head, don't you?"

One day we are brought cake to her room. Spirit is beside her on the bed. I let her lick my plate. With a mischievous grin, "Shall I let her lick my plate also, it will be our secret." Helen offers it to Spirit who happily finishes the crumbs. Quickly she hands me her plate. "I do not want them to see me feeding their cake to the dog."

Just in that moment, guess who walked in to get our plates. As the woman leaves the room, Helen laughs so hard, rolling from side to side. "Oh boy, Spirit knew she had to hurry, she heard her coming and knew what I had just said. Oh boy, how I needed that laugh."

On another visit, CCI puppy in training Maggie, falls asleep beside her. She is wearing her angel halo and wings. Helen talks about Maggie going to her formal training at school. "I shall have to keep track of you, little one. Yes, I shall watch over you from heaven." I thank Helen for such a heartfelt tribute to my working puppy.

"Helen, tell me about your husband, what is his name?"

"Cornelius Joseph O'Neill."

"My goodness, such a name, did you call him Cornelius?"

"Good grief, no, I called him Corny."

I laugh so hard because that is the name that comes to my mind just as she is about to answer me. "I knew from the moment that we met, that I loved him and would marry him."

The next time I see Helen she has just returned from a brief hospital stay. The lung cancer is taking a very heavy toll on her spirit and body. She is so very tiny curled up on the bed with a weight of under eighty pounds. She smiles at seeing me, "So what are you thinking, Carol Ann, I can see those wheels turning."

Smiling in reply, "Yes you are right; you spoke to me just like my husband used to do when he saw me in deep thought. Helen, you are so very thin and fragile." A recent fall has left her right arm immobile which upsets her. "Well, Helen, you are just like Humpty Dumpty."

This makes her laugh and brings that wonderful smile I long to see on her face. "Son of a gun, you make me laugh. I feel so sick and do not want to laugh, even though you try not to make me laugh, you still make me laugh. I am so glad that I met you on my way to heaven. You are a great friend to me."

I often ask her what I could bring her or do for her. In reply always she says, "Just you and a dog."

Over the last ten days of her life, I visit her daily. She loves both the dogs and my photography. Each day I take a different photo enlargement to place beside her on the bed which delights her and creates lots of discussion. She drifts in and out of sleep opening her eyes to look at the dog photo and smiles.

I leave to drive a cancer patient to her radiation treatment. As I sit waiting I watch all the bodies parading in and out of the treatment room. My heart is heavy thinking of Helen. I know her death is coming very soon. She had told me that she refused any treatment for her lung cancer. I admired her decision, a very brave and wise choice.

My heart weeps as I feel the energy of the room. A sense of anticipation, fear, anxiety and hope surrounds everyone. Someone told me recently there is no such thing as false hope. Well, I beg to differ on that statement. Although Robert did not speak of dying, he knew the harsh reality of his illness. I was the one living in false hope until his very last breath. I do not wish anyone to experience false hope, but believe me, it is indeed real.

Observing Helen's strong desire to live and stay with her sons, I see a strong parallel to Robert. Through Helen I see a lot of Robert. The same as him she desperately wants to keep living. She does not want to leave her sons, as Robert did not want to leave me. Hearing her talk so put me into Robert's space of dying. In his last days he was not able to converse verbally in a coherent manner. His eyes talked to me though, eyes of pure sorrow. Helen as Robert, did not eagerly embrace death, they both fought with all their feeble might. But then that time came when the body was truly ready to let go and their spirits started to consciously seek the light.

During one of our heart to heart visits Helen asks me, "When am I going to get better, I know I can get better." I take a moment of silent contemplation as I remember such pleading questions from Robert. Helen still has such hope despite her body's physical wasting away condition.

One of my toughest lessons from Robert's death has taught me honesty in the face of death. So as Helen looks to me for answers, I quietly say, "Helen, you understand what is wrong with your health, right?"

She replies, "Yes, but I keep hoping it is not so. There must be some hope."

As gently as I can muster, I tell her, "Heaven awaits Helen, you are going to heaven soon."

She replies, "Well, I know that, but I was hoping otherwise."

With each day I see Helen there is a change as she gradually lets go of life. It is getting harder to go see her but I know I must not stop. After all I believe we are a gift to each other. Through the help of Helen another layer of deepest repressed grief is being released as it needs to be.

During one visit she tells me I am a powerful woman. I do not feel such a word is appropriate for me. I certainly do not feel like a mighty mouse powerhouse. Her use of the word powerful to describe me seems inappropriate. Yet as I drive home that day I begin to see myself through her eyes. And yes, thankfully, I do have my moments of feeling powerful, as each of us ought to. It can be fleeting, but it is a great sensation to feel the power of the spirit within me and learning to honor it. Life is indeed a great gift to share, I realize now that nothing can rob me of my divine power and make me powerless unless I allow it. I realize through Robert's death, his loving spirit and God, I have been blessed me with a great deal of ongoing power and strength.

The next day she begins to call out to Mary. I know there are beings in the room with her. I sense a presence over my shoulder. In a lucid moment I ask, "Who is Mary?"

"She is my sister who died of brain cancer a couple years ago."

"Helen I believe your sister Mary is here to help. You need to listen to her and follow her. Do you understand?"

She smiles and takes my hand, "Yes." I silently thank Mary. She is not alone, no one dies alone even those without anyone by their side.

In the next moment she slips back into her world of dying. She cannot lie still as she thrashes between this world and the beyond calling her. It is agonizing to witness her restlessness. She opens her eyes saying, "Let's go. Hurry up."

Robert and I were always waving to each other even from across our living room. As I prepare to leave Helen catches my eye and we share a hug. As I stand in the doorway looking back at her she says, "Goodbye, I love you." And she cups her fingers into a small wave in the same manner as my love used to do. My heart skips a beat.

The next morning I get a phone call from her nurse. "It is Helen."

I know what her words are going to be. Helen has died an hour ago.

My sorrow is mixed with relief as I whisper to Helen, "You good brave soul, you let go, you followed Mary. Thank Godness."

I decide to do some yard work to help release my sorrows. It feels good to be outdoors. As I work my thoughts are on Helen. In that moment a whisper of "thank you" comes to me. She has brushed me with a soft loving desert breeze. "I shall not forget you. Godspeed to you Helen."

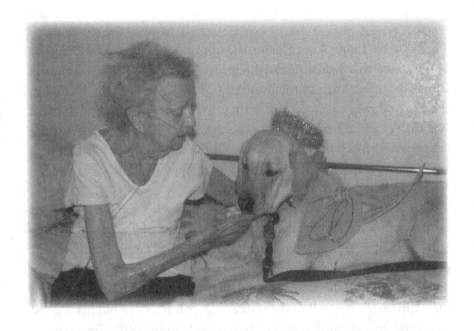

Trust

Thanks to my frequenting a Scottsdale store called, Peace of the Universe I am guided to a woman named Kim who is able to help Maggie and I prepare for her turn in to advanced training. We are now blessed in the use of flower essences. Today there are many sources of such but it was thanks to Edward Bach who discovered that plants carry healing energies and when bottled they can aid human or animal. It will be a very traumatic day to let go of this healing puppy so our flower remedies are put to daily use.

I receive the date of Maggie's recall for May 13 and have arranged for puppy number four. I decide it will be to the highest good to have Spirit go along for the turn in trip. Our hardest farewell is with our dear Margaret. It is thanks to young Maggie that our paths had crossed. There are more of these tender moments with those who have cherished their time with her. All of the staff at the grocery store bid her a good adieu and we get our Labaru ready for our California driving safari.

A friend has come over to dogsit beloved Saber and Spookie. It is time to depart. With a box of Kleenex in constant use and my two healing puppies we arrive in Oceanside, California. It is my first time to this campus and I enjoy a tour. It is time for Spirit and Maggie to part. I know in my heart they shall see each other again and yet it is a difficult moment for the three of us. Spirit stays in a crate of the puppy raising department office and I dress Maggie in her blue turn in cape. "Ok, my sweetest angel girl it is show time. We both need to be very brave."

The CCI turn in ceremony is a real tear jerker. There is a lot of Kleenex in use everywhere. All of the puppy raisers turning in their dogs for advanced training form a line to take turns crossing the stage being introduced. It is a memorable never to forget experience. My face is awash in tears as I make my way across the stage with my Bobby Adorable Angel. She is in perfect form during the whole ceremony. Next there is a line of graduate dogs and their new partners to make their entrance. All of those former rowdy puppies are now in their true glory in their lovely blue working vests each one taking their diploma in their mouths as they make their exit off the stage. Triumphant music accompanies them.

The ceremony is over and now the toughest moment must be faced. My tummy is in turmoil but I keep putting one foot in front of the other. In one of the training rooms a long line has formed of puppy raisers with sorrowful faces, about to let go of the puppies they've been attached to at the hip for the past months. I squat next to Maggie whispering in her ear not wanting to let her go. But she knows her moment has arrived and pulls away from me as the woman waiting to take her leans down to exchange leashes. Off she prances confidently passing through the door out to the kennels without even turning back. My aching heart is buoyed as I know she will succeed.

Thankfully, Spirit awaits me. She joyfully bounces out of the crate and we head back to our motel. After a tiring drive we arrive back in Carefree to the exuberant greetings of Saber and Spookie. "Well my beloved dogs, all of us have done a great job in training Maggie. I do believe there will be a good news phone call from CCI a few months from now. We all need to rest up because our new girl shall be flying into our lives four days from now."

My grieving heart is comforted with the arrival of the new puppy that is flown into Phoenix. I am greeted with the delightful surprise of a black lab pup named Serna. The first three were all yellow labs and interestingly all Aquarians like me. I let out an uncontrollable holler of whoopee joy when I read the name of her birth Dad. It is Bobby! Bow wow wowsers! This Serna puppy is going to be very special indeed. I name her Bobby Precious Angel. Our soul friend Margaret is one of the first people who meet her.

Once again we are all in transition. Saber, Spookie and Spirit are accustomed to this puppy parade by now yet it can be very trying on them especially during the initial growing spurts. Spirit is the surrogate Mom and receives the brunt of the pulls and tugs and chewing. She plays such a huge role in our lives.

Shortly after the arrival of Serna she graces my side at a Tibetan Buddhist gathering. The forever smiling Rinpoche is delighted with his four legged guest and one of my favorite photos is him holding her.

Housebreaking of Serna is behind us thankfully and she is accepting her place in our pack. I enjoy taking the four of them on outings on a quiet desert road so they can have good runs of freedom. Serna loves to run with her big dogs.

It is thanks to Serna that I embark on my conscious growth into higher trust. One day we are out enjoying a desert walk on a dirt road as she happily runs with her big dog family sniffing out new territory. There are no houses or cars anywhere. The air is still except for the sound of the dogs. The majestic saguaros salute us as we stroll past them. In the distance I hear the rumble of a truck. The big dogs come to my calls but Serna is still exploring. The truck is now in sight. I stand in the middle of the road, arms waving madly as I yell, "Slow down, please slow down."

The driver slows as he sees the dogs, but keeps driving. Serna is a good puppy coming when called running towards me, but then to my horror she runs toward the truck. Just as I am about to grab her up she is underneath the moving vehicle. It is a high riding truck.

She is under the middle of the truck as it is moving. "Stop, stop," I scream. Within the split second that fear grips me I hear a loud message of, "Trust, trust." Simultaneously, as the words hit my knowing, I know she will be safe. She is still underneath the moving vehicle when the words come through. She dances a small circle as if telling me, "I am ok, Carol Ann." Indeed she is, as my Bobby puppy safely emerges from under the truck to my side.

I sweep her into my arms with tears of joy and gratitude, "Oh thank you, thank you Serna." She is unaffected by the episode and the driver has stopped.

"Is everyone alright?"

"Yes. Thank you for asking, thank you for stopping."

This is my moment of learning trust. It is merely a few seconds in time but it leaves the impact imprinting strongly within my whole being. Serna becomes my "trust puppy" and I shall always be grateful to her.

During a trip to the bookstore my gaze catches sight of books by world renowned animal communicator, Penelope Smith. Her wisdom touches my heart and I desire to find us a trained communicator. Serendipity somehow guides me to discovering an animal communicator named Leta Worthington. We share a delightful introductory conversation about my dog blessed driven life and she makes an initial brief connection with my dogs and shares her impressions.

Serna is of course still immature. She as yet does not understand her role and is very distractible.

Maggie wants to know if Carol Ann is alright. She really misses her. She feels her messaging to her at school. Her trainer conveys she is progressing nicely and how much she loves people. Leta asks, "Do you understand your job?"

"Yes. I am ready. I see the pictures in the minds of the trainers, they have no idea how much I see."

"Carol Ann misses you so much and is so grateful to you."

"I miss her terribly. I listen for her communications. Her letters nurture me so. She will be very proud of me. I will help someone."

Spookie's session warms my heart to know that she has emerged from the intense heaviness and sadness. "For a long time I wanted to die just as Carol Ann did. Our new girl, Serna I recognized instantly." She shows Leta a vision of two black horses running together in a shared former lifetime.

Her impression of Saber is that of being the king. He lives in a constant state of grace, hanging out in his seventh chakra. He loves everybody living in a state of holy beneficence. He shares for Carol Ann. "The quality of my huge heart is shared with you. All is not lost when we can no longer see our loved ones upon death. Open your eyes in a new way and feel the love all around you. We in this family have been brought together to create a perfect union in love and you are beginning to feel this now. Your understanding is great. This is why you are now slowly beginning to feel better. Yet grief is good for the soul for it provides healing. Bless you, I love you."

The message with Spirit is illuminating. She reveals after her release from guide dog school she was feeling a bit of confusion and guilt over not graduating. Yet she saw the big picture of how Robert and your dog family are part of a large karmic group. She shares that Maggie and her have been together with Carol Ann before. Her role in coming to Carol Ann is to embody Robert to provide a vehicle for him to help her heal.

Again I am in awe of the agreement between my husband and my guide dog.

During one of our trips to the grocery I catch sight of a couple admiring Serna and I at work. The woman has big smiles as I approach them to introduce my Bobby girl.

Her tall husband leans over to greet her. "Are you the woman who sells the photo cards of the lab puppies?" she asks.

"Indeed I am."

She is beside herself with excitement exclaiming, "My husband, Cliff has purchased a couple of your cards recently. I have the one of the puppy with the carrot bundle in her mouth."

"That is marvelous. She is my second puppy for Guide Dogs for the Blind and is now a breeder."

They have two yellow labs, named Augie and Baloo. Their home is in the desert just outside Carefree and we agree to get together in a couple days. Once again I have been blessed to be at the right place at the right time to cross paths with this lab loving couple. Serna and I leave the store with big grins and happy tail wags. "Good work, Bobby girl. We are about to have a couple more big dogs to grace our days and a couple of great two leggers also. Whoopies!"

Our rapport with Linda evolves into frequent time spent at each other's homes. It is a real blessing to have Linda in our lives. Serna has someone else to train with and she even gets to have sleepovers. One evening while at my home fixing all of us supper Cliff stands at the kitchen doorway with a stunned look on his face saying, "Spirit just ate our supper."

"What? You mean she got on the table?"

"Yes, she jumped down when she saw me but she had her big head in the salad bowl and she ate some of the butter too."

All of us are laughing. "It is a good thing I prepared a lot." I open the fridge and pull out another bowl of salad fixings and get more butter. "That reminds me when Spookie was a puppy she jumped on the kitchen counter while Robert and I were eating in the living room. She had her nose stuck inside the Chinese takeout containers eating as fast as she could. Boy oh boy, what noses dogs have, eh."

The next time we are at Linda's I ask her to get some food and come in to the bedroom with me. Both Cliff and her follow with perplexed looks. I get my naughty guide dog and put a leash on her. I place a plate of food on the floor telling her down. She complies with the down command and turns her head away. My friends are amazed.

"This is what you have to teach a working dog and even now years later she still knows once she is told, "Leave it.""

My brother Mark arrives for another month long visit and gets to grocery shop with our Bobby girl. He is still a bit challenged with this task but it is great fun for all of us. One day we head into Target to buy balloons. Saber loves to pop them and I love them myself. We have a grand time as I practice with a balloon blower upper and Mark demonstrates that he has enough hot air of his own. "Hey Mark, blow up another one and put it in front of Serna as you let the air expire." He gladly complies and Serna is startled but does not overreact.

"Good puppy, what a good girl this puppy is, eh Mark. Let's go home and blow up these two bags."

We spend an hour of great hilarity covering our living room floor with balloons. Soon we are hearing the sound of happy Saber making balloons pop. The next day I share, "Mark we have to move these balloons. Linda and Cliff are coming over with Augie and Baloo. Dearest Baloo is afraid of them when you know who pops them."

"Oh no, you mean we have to move all of these?"

"Yup, we better get busy, they will be here soon."

We share lots of giggles moving them into the guest room. Mary Kay arrives also for our little get together. She has picked up Rosalyn and her guide dog Razzle. We all share a lovely afternoon together and when it is time to go I whisper to Mark. "Let's play a little trick on Rosalyn."

I get the guide dog harness and put it on Spirit. Rosalyn commands her, "Forward." Spirit complies and a moment later Rosalyn calls out, "Hey, wait a minute this isn't Razzle Dazzle."

Rosalyn is a great sport and gives Spirit a hug as I help remove the harness. "That was pretty funny but I think your silly girl is better suited to live with you Carol Ann."

Another great dog party is behind us.

A few days later I head to the bookstore, Peace of the Universe to introduce my new puppy. Everyone inquires about the training status of adorable Maggie and nods their encouraging approval for her potential successful match. I have met a gifted woman named Halina who gives readings. The toughest of my grief is behind me as I have embraced life more fully yet something compels me to set up a session with this beautiful being of light and love. I am guided to have Linda accompany me and Serna.

The day is September 23, 2000. I have taken a couple photos of Robert along to share. Within a few minutes I discover why he has led me to see this wise soul. "He wants to come back to you."

"What are you saying?"

"There is a phenomenon called walk-ins. When the time is right this is what he desires to do. It is an agreement made between someone alive here on earth and someone on the other side such as himself. The person on earth desires to leave their present life for whatever reason and the spirit on the other side takes residence in their human vessel."

I am spellbound and naturally Linda is also. "Is this truly possible? That is all quite unbelievable."

"The potential certainly exists and this is what he is telling me."

"So you mean it is like when his energy has entered into an owl or into beloved Spirit?"

"Similar yes, but the life-force of the human he has entered leaves. This is called a walk-out. His spirit would now live within the body of the walk-out who has exited earth."

"Holy jumping Geronimo, what a miraculous feat of engineering. Wowsers, Robert was a petroleum engineer so guess that reference just came from him. He still has his great sense of humor which is dearly missed."

"The two of you certainly share a depth of love rarely experienced in this world."

"Yes indeed, Halina, you got that right. It is why my grief and healing journey have been so excruciating. But thankfully all my four legged angels are paving my way." I lean myself over my Bobby girl hugging her tightly as she does her lap command.

"Serna's Dad is named Bobby, isn't that an amazing perfect miracle that she is the one to bless me with hearing this remarkable news."

After the biggest hugs of gratitude my working pup and I head home with our dearest Linda. Boy oh boy, I am so glad that I followed my guidance to include her for this session. Halina's words will be echoing over and over within her mind also. We are both in quite a state of shock over this incredulous news and agree to have supper at my home.

I shall never forget her genuine sentiments of admiration and love. I meet them outside as they arrive for supper and she presents me with a huge bouquet of beautiful fresh flowers. With a big hug she shares, "I am so happy for you and Robert. I do not know what to say."

"Thank you; yes I know what you mean. Whatever the outcome of this news is time shall tell but it gives me a lot to ponder."

That evening I write in my journal. "As much as I want to be with my Robert again I cannot ask this of you, God. I leave it in your hands. If we are to be so incredibly blessed I thank you, yet I shall not ask it of you." I breathe a sigh of relief for stating my truth and put my trust in an outcome to my highest good.

It is all very far-out information to process let alone accept. Yet I do believe we learn things in appropriate timing. I am ready to hear this and within the depths of my soul it resonates as truth. I reckon it is years into the future. I still have a long way to go on this healing journey.

In my travels I learn about a presentation by a spiritually wise woman who channels higher beings. Again I seem to have been at the right place at the right time and eagerly listen to Sheila give messages from the group callings themselves Theo. She also does private one on one sessions and I set up an appointment.

With Bobby lab Serna, at my feet I have an intriguing session with Theo as she answers my curious mind addressing the news of Robert wanting to come back to me as a walk-in. "Yes, he does desire such, this is a possibility. First he wants you to heal. He is very pleased with what you are doing raising the puppies and your work with cancer patients and hospice. He himself is assisting the dying as they transition to the other side. It takes time to set up the arrangement between the walk-out and him on the other side."

I am most gratified to have been led to another gifted woman to soothe my questioning mind. I purchase a couple of the little paperbacks Halina has referred me to by the author Ruth Montgomery. "Threshold to Tomorrow," is a groundbreaking book to first address this extraordinary otherworldly topic of walk-ins. She has case studies which shock and rock my world.

She has received information through her guides about walk-ins and shares that walk-ins have always been in existence. The walk-in needs to finish up loose ends of the walk-out's life before they can move into beginning their own mission.

I read bits of it and put it on our bookshelf. I am overwhelmed beyond words. I know I am far from ready for such a miracle if indeed it is to be. I do believe and yet have a lot of living to do first. With faith all things are possible. I trust I shall continue to be well guided and live one day at a time.

A week later I am distracted from my Robert walk-in news with the joyful announcement of Terrace's first litter at the guide dog kennels. It is October 20, 1999. As a puppy raiser I am allowed to submit a list of names. When her task as Mom has concluded she will return home to become a pampered pet at her home with Robert and Michael.

Michael and I share our delight. "Can you let me know when you go to pick her up at the school and I shall fly over for the afternoon. I can get to see Terrace and meet all of her little angels prior to their embarking on their lives with puppy raisers."

Dearest Terra Puppies

Happy tail wags and kisses to all nine of you yellow labrador puppies snuggling up to each other and your beloved Mom, Terrace. I have been informed by the school of your names which all start with the letter H since this is how the school tracks all of you beauties. Thus I can address you all individually now, dearest Henna, Happy, Hilly, Hugo, Harold, Hadara, Hanita, Humble and Hayes.

My name is Carol Ann and I am the fortunate puppy raiser who raised your Mom. I recently got to spend time with you at the guide dog school in your playground area. It was the most wondrous time watching you all interact and climb around on the various big plastic slides and tubs and balls. You were all so very busy, exploring and tumbling around. One day in a few weeks all of you shall be assigned a human companion to live with so I want to share this news with you to prepare you. I know that Terrace is imprinting you with her own wisdom and guidance in this matter also.

When you are old enough you shall be separated from your Mom and from each other. There are people already awaiting your arrival though they do not know about you yet. You are not puppies in the normal sense but special beauties that will be raised and trained with special skills. There are many people in the human world that cannot see and your role if you are appropriate will be to become their eyes and guide them.

This is not an easy job and will require a long period of training. Some of you may even become a Mom or a Dad and create more puppies. Each of you will be assigned a human family where you shall stay for about fourteen months. After that you will then go back to the guide dog school and be trained to work in a guide dog harness. Some of you will not succeed in becoming a guide dog and will be adopted as a career change puppy. You would not be considered a failure in this case. Your life shall still be very special for some deserving person.

This all sounds very serious to you right now I know but I can share the best news of what this will mean to you. You will not be considered a pet and will wear a special little green jacket which says Guide Dog Puppy In Training. When this super green cape goes onto your wiggley beautiful little bodies you shall learn that you must be on your best behavior. The good news is that you get to go absolutely everywhere. And this is something a pet cannot do.

I can hear your puppy whimpers wondering why.............well, the human world has a lot of rules and that is just the way it is. Life can be a challenge for a puppy but it is for us humans also. You have been blessed with the miracle of life and I can share that you will have a very good time wearing your capes.

Ok, so you want to know more about what I am talking about now that I have your curiosity piqued?

I shall be brief as I well know that you only want to sleep, eat and play at this stage of the puppy game but listen up as best you can.

I am excited just thinking about your future lives and all of the countless adventures awaiting each of you. You shall meet literally hundreds of people on your travels and will learn to behave appropriately in each new situation you encounter. Being raised as a future guide dog there are a lot of special rules. You shall learn a series of commands which will ultimately help you throughout your whole lives. It is very important you pay attention to these and do your best to master them. Do not take offense if you are compared to another puppy that does something faster or better than you. Each of you is unique and special no matter what.

Some of you will go to a puppy raiser who is a first timer and some will go to an experienced raiser. Every one of these people at some point will be asking the question, do I want to do this again? The bond you share with your human and the journey you share will influence their decision. This is a heavy matter for you to ponder but what is most important for you to understand right now is that you do your best.

It is not a task suitable to all, for after many months of going everywhere with you there will be a goodbye. This will be difficult for both you and your human, but it is necessary. You will be the topic of endless conversation day and night. Everywhere you go people will want to pet you and cuddle you or feed you or play with you. However when the magic cape is on none of this is allowed. You will learn this tough lesson quickly for each of you has been bred for this important task.

Despite the inevitable challenges you will have to face and the fears on your part and your human there will come a day when both of you will walk with your heads held high and confidence in your step. People will admire you with excited jubilation as they exclaim, "Look, there goes a potential guide dog."

This is not all work, when the jacket comes off you can play and frolic and run with other dogs. It goes without saying that you will provide a lot of laughter and joy and silliness. Enjoy these moments and keep them in your hearts for these will be a source of much story telling for years even after you leave this earth plane.

Even during off work times your human will still be keeping an eye on you especially in your early time together. Without a doubt you will be corrected for inappropriate behaviours even when your little green jacket is off. Puppies will be puppies but sometimes your behavior will prove to be exasperating especially to those who are new to the adventuresome world of puppy raising. Despite any moments of frustration, anger, impatience, fear, inconsistency or disgust on the part of your human always know that you are loved.

Depending what illicits these strong reactions from your human, rest assured that looking into your most lovely eyes the feeling will pass. I must advise you however that not all humans possess the endearing trait that dogs are most admired for.

And what is that you may be pondering.

Unconditional love. All of you little lovely beauties naturally give from your hearts without questioning whether it is safe to do so or appropriate. You do not question whether a person will like you or should I do this or do that. You love without question and you never hold a grudge or judge. Your tails do not require batteries and are always at the ready even in your sleep.

It might sound strange to you right now but what you all do so effortlessly humans struggle lifetimes with; learning how to love and even tougher, how to love and accept ourselves.

So you see this is why dog is spelled d..o..g for when it is reversed it spells g..o..d which as you wisely know spells God. Another thing you must be advised about is that many humans tend to think you are not as smart as they are. You will overhear conversations implying such during your many travels out in the big wide world. Some will say you do not understand English and know only a few words. They will imply your memory span is faulty or lacking. Pay no heed to such foolish notions.

Some of you pups may find this all hard to believe at this point in time and yet some of you already know of what I speak. Humans and dogs are very different and yet in my mind we share a lot in common. My life is dog driven and dog blessed. The numerous four footers of my past, present and future life all have my never-ending gratitude and love to each and every one for their special roles.

Well I can see that your attention span has left me so I shall let you dream and ponder my message. Have a marvelous adventure and remember you are loved by your Terrace Mom and myself, Carol Ann, her puppy raiser.

Flyboys

I often pick up Margaret for various reasons. She loves going into the grocery with our Bobby girl. Our favorite cashier Tommy is always thrilled to see us and has known Margaret for years. This makes it extra special.

During one of the countless hours shared with Margaret we learn that our deceased husbands knew each other. Her Arnold was mad about airplanes. Prior to my meeting Robert he spent time at his first Carefree home and went to Kiwanis. Arnie was a member also.

It was expected that the members speak about their careers. Robert was never at a loss for words and loved to share stories. Yet Arnold was not keen on talking to the group. Margaret shares how my future husband got her bashful flyboy to open up to the Kiwanis telling him, "Arnie you are the only commercial pilot in this group and they would love to hear about your job."

"Oh no, I could not do such a thing."

"Yes you can and you will feel better after."

"So one day Arnie comes home from a Kiwanis lunch with a big smile and I asked him, what are you so happy about?"

He replied, "That Bob Arnim is sure a great guy. He convinced me to share about my piloting for TWA so I finally took him up on it today at the lunch. Funny thing once I started to yap about airplanes I could not stop."

"Well that is great Margaret. I have my own story to share about Kiwanis."

"What do you mean? That is for men."

"While I was raising my second guide dog puppy Terrace, someone contacted me and asked if I could come give a talk about raising a service dog. We were the guests."

"That must have been interesting."

"Yes, we were very well received. I also gave a similar talk to a local woman's group with Maggie."

As I listen to her chat on about dogs and flying I marvel quietly how we had been drawn together and share with her, "So what do you think Margaret, isn't it fascinating how we have come to be friends thanks to a dog. It seems to me that our heavenly loves brought us together. I find it amazing."

"Yes, it is a miracle for sure. I think of how much they had in common with their love of flying and now here we are continuing their friendships through our own."

"Robert piloted B24s during the great war as he called it. He shared about flying with a cowboy hat and if he had too much to drink the night before he flew with oxygen. He had a scar on one arm from shrapnel but would never talk about it. He brought a plane in more than once without all engines operational due to it being on fire."

"Well kiddo, it is a miracle they both survived. Many of those bomber pilots and fighters did not come home. Arnold was not a drinker prior to the war and yet he became one after he got home."

"Yes, I have always thanked Robert's angels for keeping him alive so we could meet so many years later."

"Arnie never talked to me about his war days either. I always told him he should write it down but he would say, we were sworn to secrecy."

"Well you can share a bit with me."

"Arnold was a fighter pilot and was shot down in German occupied France. He ejected by parachute to get stuck in a tree. The Germans were flying all around trying to find him since they saw his plane go down. He thankfully was taken in by a French count and countess who sheltered him for a while. He then walked his way out of enemy territory and was awarded, "silver boots.""

"Wow, that is a great story."

"How did you meet Arnie?"

"I was working the nightshift of the Minneapolis airport working as a reservation ticket girl for Northwest Airlines. This guy came up to my counter asking, can I talk to you? Of course you can I had replied. He asked me if I smoked or drank. I told him, nope I do not smoke or drink. And next he says to me, you are the girl I want to marry. I am on my way to Europe right now but I will write to you. And sure enough he did. I got a special delivery letter from him a couple days later."

"Now that is a great story. We both have great stories, thanks for sharing that one."

"Did you wear a little airline uniform?"

"Oh yes, it was navy blue with a little matching hat perched atop my head."

"A man in uniform falling for a woman in uniform, how neat is that."

"Thanks to my work for the airline I got a lot of passes and flew around the United States. After marrying Arnie our children, Joanie and Don got to go many places, it was wonderful. He was one of the first TWA pilots to travel overseas. When he started to fly the ocean

I always asked him, aren't you scared to fly so far without getting any gas?"

"His reply was always the same. Of course not. There are no gas stations in the ocean. I will get gas upon landing in Europe." We always had a good giggle. "He only flew the overseas flights; that was his passion."

"He was my second husband. My first true love was a Canadian flyboy named Art. I was a very young eighteen when we married on Sept. 10, 1942. One night I dreamt he had died in a plane crash and shared it with my dearest Mom."

"My Mom would not hear of this talk responding, no, it is only a dream."

"Well it was a dream alright and yet it did happen just as I saw it. He was doing a test flight and his plane crashed." She is all tears. "Oh boy, I can never tell that without crying."

My dogs love ice cream and sometimes we take bowls of it onto her back porch watching them slurp it up. One day I bring a big bundle of colorful balloons which I tie to a chair and we happily watch them dance in the wind. Before I leave I release them over her backyard. A few minutes later a rainbow appears.

"Margaret, look at the rainbow. I have come to believe rainbows are a heavenly message for me from Robert. Often they come to me at the most auspicious times. One of my favorite rainbow stories was when I was raising Laverne. My parents had flown to Denver, Colorado for a masonic meeting my Dad was participating in and I drove with the three dogs to meet them. We all drove into the mountains to stay at a lovely little cabin outside of Steamboat Springs. Robert had a condo there and often we would take weekend trips. As I am giving a tour for my parents about to drive up to the mountain where his home used to be, I looked to the sky. Look over there Mom and Dad. There is a Robert rainbow over Mt. Werner, above his former condo. It is positioned right where we are going."

"The rainbow is right over his old house?" squeals Margaret.

"Yes, it appeared just as I was about to make the turn heading up to the mountain village. All three of us were amazed with the timing."

"Oh boy, so rainbows are sure connected with your Robert."

"Yes over the years I have seen so many and sometimes doubles."

Our bond has been strengthened through our common ground of widowhood and our flyboys knowing each other. "I would like to share a special story with you now about my Robert love and myself."

"Go on, I am all ears." I walk through the tale of Robert and our son Jade.

Margaret listens raptly and aptly says, "That Robert and you were definitely a match made in heaven. I have never heard of a couple who were so much in love. I hope your son comes to Carefree so I get to meet this handsome boy of yours."

One day Margaret phones me. "Carol Ann, I have a friend named Vivian who is bedbound. She has a dog that needs to be walked and she is having trouble finding enough people to help. You are so good with dogs, could you possibly help?"

"Give me her phone number and I will arrange to meet her."

The next day Serna and I find her home tucked off the road in the desert. She gets my attention immediately with her opinioned sharp tongue and no mincing of words. Her dog is a shock to my eyes. "What kind of a dog is she and where did you get her?"

"Her name is Amber and she is a keeshond. I fell in love with her instantly when I saw her at the pound."

I confess that I have only eyes for labrador retrievers. Vivian encourages her, "Go on with Carol Ann, she is here to give you walks." We chat awhile more upon our return and arrange for another day to come. It seems to me the two of them are quite a pair and I contemplate what is coming next in this new arrangement. Soon Serna and I become a regular part of their lives. She calls when no one else will show up. We come to an agreement for a schedule.

Vivian is a serious animal lover and I hear many a tale about dogs and raccoons and the wild pig of the desert, the javelina. She feeds them and this becomes one of my duties also. Often when we approach her front door there are javelina nearby which is a good distraction for my working girl.

My sentiments of being a lab lover only are gone with the desert winds. Amber has won my heart. Her feisty two legged companion and I forge a strong connection in no time. We talk almost every day by phone. We discover our shared belief in reincarnation. "I eagerly await coming back to life to do it all over again. Death will be welcomed because I know I shall cross the rainbow bridge to reunite with a long line of creatures. This alone comforts me so I do not feel badly about death."

One day I take Margaret with me to visit. I have a pair of big bright sunglasses which I pass to each of them. "Ok, my funny beauties smile for the camera." We all enjoy a festive conversation and girlish giggles.

Margaret shares, "My Arnie and Carol Ann's husband knew each other, isn't that amazing. Both of them were flyboys during the war and both flew after also."

"I think it is wonderful she still talks to him. Your love continues even in his death. Spirits must need that connection also. God certainly gave them both a big stamp of approval in my mind. It is one of the best love stories I have heard."

Margaret chimes in, "Has she told you about her son?"

Vivian replies, "Oh yes, that is a wonderful story. My goodness what a blessing that the three of you could be together before your Robert became so ill. I want to meet that boy."

"Vivian the puppy before Serna is named Maggie. She just had her birthday at school and her trainer phoned me with a good report. Maggie was with her during the call and I got to sing her happy birthday."

"You got to sing to our Maggie?" Margaret is beside herself. "Oh, she must miss you so much but you know she is going to be a success Carol Ann, that puppy is so special. She must find her match. I cried my heart out when she left that awful day." Margaret gets teary just thinking of my Bobby Adorable Angel.

"Oh boy, I do not know how you do it kiddo."

Maggie Retrieves Her Joy Girl

At a Tibetan Buddhist gathering I am mesmerized to witness a monk lean over Serna and whisper, "Thank you for your good work." He offers me a gracious knowing smile as I nod my gratitude. Speaking of good works my adorable Bobby angel Maggie has been chosen as one of the potential working dogs for an upcoming class of new applicants. The phone calls from CCI have been very encouraging and I sense her success.

My intuition is right on track when I receive the phone call announcing her match. "Whoopies, I knew she could do it, thank you."

"Yes, I remember you telling me and you were right Carol Ann. She is a skilled companion to a young girl named Joy with a single Mom named Annie. They live in Littleton, Colorado. The Dad is named Bob."

I am beside myself with jubilation unable to control the emotions overwhelming me. "You are kidding me, her name is Annie and the girl is Joy? I am Carol Ann Joy. And she lives in Littleton? I lived in Denver ten years prior to coming to Arizona."

"Really, now that is amazing. She works at a lab in lung cancer research."

"Well now I cannot believe my ears. My beloved husband Robert died of lung cancer a few years ago."

The puppy raising coordinator and I are both in a state of heightened good shock. "The graduation ceremony is on March 17 and your puppy in training Serna is invited along by your side."

"Thank you so very much for this exciting news and most definitely the two of us shall be there with bells on. Boy oh boy, I have a lot of people who will be whooping with joy over this unbelievable story."

Our home is rocking with my exuberance and all of the dogs prancing around me. "Holy cows Maggie, you sure have outdone yourself my sweetest Bobby angel pup. Guide dog breeder Terrace has a Robert connection and now also you, with Joy's Dad named Bob." I immediately pick up the phone to share this jolly news with family and friends. Everyone shares the same overwhelming response. The timing of this is most propitious since my parents are coming then.

Linda cannot contain her enthusiasm. "I am going with you and Serna for this glorious celebration. Congratulations, I so look forward to meeting this angel Maggie."

"Yes, you will be blown away by the whole experience witnessing the turn in of puppies and the graduating dogs. And I get to walk across that stage to formally present Maggie to her new family. Wowsers, this is going to take time to sink in, glad we have time to prepare."

That evening I come up with a grandiose plan as I am about to share the news with our son, Jade. We enjoy many a phone call together. Yet due to my immense grief over the loss of his birth Dad, we have not seen each other since his trip to us in January, 1996. It has been too unbearably painful. It is now over five years since we have seen each other. Grief makes no logical sense that is for sure.

Thankfully, he answers the phone in his ever jolly tone. "Hey there, Carol Ann."

"Jade, I have the most wonderful news. My working puppy Maggie is graduating on March 17 and I want to fly you down to be here. You can go with me and my friend Linda to California for the ceremony and meet her. We shall all travel together with my working pup, Serna. And more good news, my Mom and Dad are going to be here during that timeframe so you shall get to meet your birth grandparents."

"Wow, that all sounds awesome, thank you. I really look forward to this."

The arrival of my parents comes and my Dad bends down to shake paws with Serna. They have blessed me with their company during the raising of each of my puppies thus far. How great is that! They are most excited and pleased with the Maggie news and being able to meet Jade.

One day we drive up to the beautiful area of Sedona. I treat the three of us to a helicopter ride. Both my parents are beaming with delight as they admire the lovely red canyons and formations before their eyes.

Margaret wants to meet my parents and invites us to share a lovely lunch on the outdoor patio of the Carefree Inn. "I also want to meet that Bobby boy of yours, Carol Ann."

"Yes, indeed you shall after Maggie's graduation. My parents leave the next day so perhaps after that, ok."

Saber, Spookie and Spirit are left in my parents' loving care for the day as my Bobby puppy Serna and my Bobby boy Jade, meet Linda to fly to Oceanside, California. I am already off the ground so it is good that my working girl is by my side. Thankfully, Linda is able to navigate and drive our rental car.

After a beach run for Serna we all arrive safely at the CCI campus and find our way into the training room. There is a row of crates with puppies awaiting their reunions with their puppy raisers. It has been ten months since we have seen each other. The moment arrives and in the instant she hears my voice chaos ensues. I collapse onto the floor as the two of us are literally rolling around in uncontrollable abandon. Jade cannot believe his eyes and laughs good heartedly as Linda films this momentous event. "Oh Maggie, how beautiful you are," she repeats.

This behavior between Maggie and me continues for several minutes before the two of us calm down. Finally, we both get up and shake ourselves off. She walks calmly over to meet my Bobby boy. "Maggie, lap." She proudly drapes her magnificent self over our son's knees and receives his affections.

Next we all meet in another room set up with long tables. It is filled with the smiling faces of the two leggers who have been matched with the graduate four leggers. There are framed photos of each graduate dog with their team. I recognize my Maggie's photo next to a lovely blonde girl in a wheelchair and a beaming black haired woman who must be my Maggie's new Annie. She greets me warmly, "You must be Carol Ann." We both hug and laugh at the same time. Serna is introduced along with Jade and Linda and we all sit to enjoy listening to the trainers present each puppy raiser. The room is overflowing with happiness beyond measure.

It is time to head over to the ceremony. More photos and moviemaking continues. I cannot believe my eyes as I sit with my blue vested graduate puppy Maggie, and yellow vested puppy in training Serna, lying side by side. They both turn their head upwards adoringly at the same time and I capture a memorable photo. The time arrives for me to present my girl to her waiting family.

There are no butterflies in my tummy this time but only a heart brimming over with joy and gratitude. Maggie does her perfect lap command with Joy and I stand with an ear to ear grin beside them. After the ceremony we go for a walk along a pier and all enjoy chattering away. I am pushing Joy's chair with Maggie in work mode. How glorious! This is what puppy raising is all about. I am so honored. Soon the time comes for us to catch our plane.

My joy is overturned and I have the toughest time pulling myself away from Maggie. What heartache! I climb into the back of the rental car pulling Serna in a tight embrace. I am numb and silent. I have been very privileged to be in the company of my angel puppy spending time with her family. It is very bittersweet. I know Maggie faces her own challenges as she settles into her new life in Littleton and allows her heart to bond with her beautiful Joy and Annie. But for now my heart is very heavy.

Upon arrival back into Phoenix we decide to have a celebratory late meal at Denny's Restaurant. I listen to Jade and Linda talk on about the day and my heart is buoyed. My labs at home get the biggest hugs and are busy with lots of sniffs. My Mom and Dad patiently listen to my endless chattering. What an incredible day. Now we sit sharing it with my two legger Bobby boy and my parents.

I am overcome with exhaustion on all levels of my being the next day and spend a long time just hanging out in the backyard hammock quietly contemplating all these miracles. Mom and Dad depart.

Jade is thrilled with the offer of a biplane ride so we head out to the little airport and a while later I am greeted with an ear to ear grinned son. "That was awesome Carol Ann, thank you."

"Would you like to go up in a glider? When I raised Maggie I took a ride in a glider and it was marvelous after I got over my fear. I felt so close to Robert being up in the blue sky with clouds and no sound."

"Gees, yes. When will we do that?"

"I reckon we could go right now. Tomorrow I will take you to the air museum Mark has been to and then lunch at a Mexican place which we both loved."

Jade seems to have more of his Robert Dad's love of the air and is without any fear for either the biplane or glider rides. We have had a marvelous time together. Linda invites us over to their place. She has developed a fondness for my two legged Bobby boy.

It is time for him to depart. He has worked a bit with Serna and at the airport when he walks away she cries. She is mirroring my own sadness. It is so touching to hear her sorrowful whimpers. "Serna, you truly are my Bobby Precious Angel, thank you."

Serna's birthday is now upon us a few days later and I raise our rooftop with a wondrous dog party in honor of both Serna and Maggie. Margaret and Don join the festivities, along with guide dog Razzle and her partner Rosalyn as well as Mary Kay. Naturally, Linda and Cliff bring their Augs and Baloo. Fran and George from up the street join in blowing my party horns and dogs are charging every which way. It is utter mayhem as my beloved brother Mark loves to say about my dog parties.

The premonition I had received at some point after Robert's death has manifested. One day I received a vision of our home with lots of laughter and people everywhere. It stopped me in my tracks and I was dumbfounded, questioning what the heck am I seeing in my mind. Who are all these people I am foreseeing and what the heck are they doing here?

Maggie's Annie and I have corresponded with letters and phone calls. Joy now sleeps through the night better with her skilled companion dog by her side. This is a huge relief for Annie. She invites us to come visit her in Littleton prior to the turn in of Serna. This sounds great and we make our plans.

We all receive the rowdiest exuberant greetings upon arrival at her doorstep. Joy loves the extra dogs under foot. It is such fun to be together again with Maggie. Spirit is in her full joy to once again be with her puppy she raised. Maggie is a cross between a golden retriever and a labrador. Annie takes delight in stroking her beautiful body starting at the top saying, lab and goes down the body repeating lab and when she gets to her tail says, golden, golden. Indeed she does have an extra fluffy tail.

I gift Annie with several movies of Maggie's puppyhood. Many hoots of laughter and toasts to our graduate are shared as we enjoy the movies. In Annie's bedroom, Spookie announces the discovery of her cat snuggled in her little bedside cocoon. Big woofs and more hilarity. "That is a cat, Von Spookers, she must be your first one." She snorts disapprovingly and returns to the living room to join the festivities. Eventually we all wear ourselves out from our celebrating.

"Would you like to come to the lab with me tomorrow?"

"That would be wonderful, yes."

Annie happily introduces me to a fellow employee and I find myself following her into the lab with Serna and Spirit by my side. Maggie is in her glory, as am I. What a treat for us to be together again. "I am studying a lung at the moment if you want to take a peek."

I am not sure this is what I really want to be doing, gazing at a cancerous lung and yet that is what I find myself doing. Annie chatters on about the lung while I am doing my best to just stay upright. Roberto succumbed to lung cancer. Spirit dog is close by my side and I give her a tender pat. She knows I am distressed. I take a breath and step away quietly. Wowsers!

Thankfully, the lab tour is over and we make a drive outside of the city to play with the dogs. She takes us to a park with a stream nearby. Joy is perched on a rock and throws the tennis ball to her canine friends. We all enjoy getting splashed on by the happy labs running to and fro in and out of the stream. Happy times.

One of Joy's favorite places is the city zoo. This is a great work outing for Serna. We exchange dogs so Annie can work my Serna and I get to work Maggie. Such joy. "Serna is doing great, Carol Ann, I think you have another winner here."

"Thanks, and yes I agree. I have a very good feeling about her future success."

The best part of raising puppies is always in the last month. The dog has matured and marches confidently by your side. She knows what to do. The bond of team work between you is obvious and those who know us cannot help but notice the difference. It is great fun!

Shortly after our arrival home I have care of Augie and Baloo while Linda and Cliff are on a trip. Cliff flies in alone while Linda is off for work somewhere. I take my four dogs and their two labs with me to the airport. Cliff meets us at the curbside arrivals pickup and looks in the car with a startled look. "Carol Ann, you nut, where am I going to sit?"

I chuckle with delight telling him to throw his bag in the back and climb in up front with Saber. I move the front seat all the way back to accommodate Cliffie's long legs. Sabe settles on the floor while Cliff gives him an approving grateful pet.

Augie, Baloo, Spirit, Saber, Spook, Serna

A dear friend named Liz, from the days of life with Robert is still in our lives thankfully. Her husband Jim is a lover of old corvettes. Robert enjoyed many a corvette club meeting and gathering with all the cars. I used to attend some of the functions. Liz and I check in with each other by phone often and we agree to meet for another lunch. I always welcome my time spent with her since she is now the only nearby person who knew me from my life with Robert.

I marvel in her words as she speaks of her observations of me. "Carol Ann, I have to tell you what a joy it is to see you. Compared to how you were when we first met through the corvette gang you have become such a different person. You used to be so shy and quiet, but look at you now. You are like a flower blossoming. It gives me such happiness to witness you as you unfold and open more and more all the time."

I welcome her truth as my body resonates with goose bumps. I recall the words spoken to my parents on the night of Robert's burial. I sense he is smiling in full agreement with Liz. I am so grateful to have Liz in my life.

I am now gearing my mindset for turning in my Bobby lab. The phone call comes. Her date of turn in is set for July 28. I want to have animal communicator Leta, do a session with her in preparation.

I share with Leta about the wondrous trip for all of my pack to reunite with Maggie in her new home. Serna has benefited from the use of Aura Soma and flower essences to prepare her for leaving us. Recently I learned about a form of therapeutic bodywork called Tellington Touch or T Touch which is repetitions of simple circular touch. It can work wonders on behavioral issues and health. Leta confirms this when she connects with Serna acknowledging that she now feels more confident and grounded. "I can sense a big difference in her from our last chat with Serna. She had not understood why she was with you and was very distractible. The physic energy she picked up from someone during your outings has cleared."

"Yes, I used one of my Aura Soma bottles on her and I could tell a difference in her."

Leta asks Serna how she is doing and she replies, "I am very happy now. That orange Aura Soma magic potion was great. I have my balance buddy in place and he directs me most of the time now. I know my job and I am ready."

"What created this awareness?"

"It was going to Maggie's graduation in California. Also the trip to Littleton where I witnessed her in action with her new family. It was inspiring. I feel someone is waiting for me. I know I will succeed."

Leta continues, "Yes, Carol Ann senses this also and that you are aware of this. You do understand how much she loves you and how proud she is of you?"

"Yes. We have become in awe of each other. We share wondrous moments feeling palpable waves of awe radiating between us. Our bond is very deep."

"Carol Ann has a lot of emotion about your leaving for school and it makes her very sad. She is concerned about your being affected by this."

Serna shows Leta her own sorrows and bit of confusion over saying goodbye.

Leta asks her, "Do you think you are in heat?"

Serna replies, "It feels like it is coming on."

Leta then explains to her that her being in heat will mean she will be unable to be at the turn in ceremony. Both Leta and I thank her for our chat and we turn next to Spirit.

Spirit shares with us, "It warmed my heart to see Maggie in action and to be able to be with her again." She heaves a sigh filled with great happiness and speaks to being so comforted with the presence of Robert around us all the time.

Leta asks, "Can you tell us about the time being in the cancer lab when Carol Ann was being shown the cancerous lung. How was that for you?"

She says, "Robert was there leaning over her shoulder to look at it as he was holding her up. He did not enter my body that day. I was very concerned for her but Robert could literally do more for her through his spirit body than through me at that moment."

Leta asks Robert, "Do you actually get in Carol Ann's body sometimes?"

"Absolutely. She has given me permission and I can help her."

"Carol Ann has told me that sometimes she feels that you are the one driving her car."

He chuckles in reply, "Yes, sometimes she needs a little help. And I love the feeling! I am her constant companion."

"Carol Ann feels she has grown a lot since your death, can you speak to her about this? What are your thoughts of her calling your first wife, Marion?"

"My dearest love Carol Ann, I watch you study your predicaments and am so proud of how you are handling things. You are forgiving. You are healing the greatest things that can be healed for your own spiritual progress and direction. These things are essential. I see people all the time whose hearts are totally shut down. They are living like automatons and cannot feel as they were truly meant to feel. Yours became closed when you and I were not able to be together early on. You are now reopening. That's my girl."

"Robert, can you speak of my writing?"

"It is your truth and it opens eyes and hearts. You must keep it up. It is your calling. I am seeing a book with a collection of stories. It is our soul's path, do not let anything discourage you."

"Robert, Carol Ann knows you are with her always and is very grateful. The Serna turn in will be very hard for her to do without Serna."

"I will hold her up."

Next we touch base with Maggie. "When are you coming back, it was so great to see all my family again."

"Carol Ann shares how it breaks her heart to have to leave you again yet she will always continue to send you strength."

"Yes, I am most grateful; Carol Ann has been my touchstone and is helping me to grow into grace about my new life. I know my job is to spread the light and sometimes I soak up emotions like a sponge and get very heavy."

"You must choose not to do that, angel pup. Taking on others sorrows is not your job. You must learn to shed that energy like a duck so you can keep spreading the light. Pretend it is water and you are shaking it off. Do you understand?"

"Yes. I love the duck image."

"Good. This is a way to protect you. Carol Ann says you love to shake."

"Yes, thanks. I keep good track of Joy's energy. She slips away a lot out of her body and I help draw her back. I am very committed to my job and need to go be with Joy now."

I thank Leta and all of my puppies for our great chat. A few minutes later the phone rings. It is Terrace's breeder keeper Michael. I receive the happy news that guide dog breeder Terrace has birthed her second litter of puppies. They are named Pepper, Pharaoh, Pluto, Phillipa, P.J., Paradise and Paragon. Soon there will be seven puppy raisers welcoming them into their lives and homes. Such fun for me to contemplate.

Walking Through My Past

As I contemplate the approaching turn in day for Serna my thoughts turn to my two legged Bobby boy. I have always envisioned meeting his adoptive parents, or as I affectionately call them his puppy raisers, with Robert by my side. Yet his soul called him home to the light so it is up to me. The phone call I have been anticipating comes. It is CCI. "Carol Ann, the date for Serna's recall is July 28. We shall see you then."

I have been driving a feisty woman named Bernice with lung cancer for a few weeks. We have shared several lunches together and I always get invited inside upon returning her home. She loves to chat about whatever comes to mind. "I refused the chemotherapy they suggested."

"That was a wise choice Bernice. I walked that path with Robert and it imprinted me very strongly. He never enjoyed his food again after that and his quality of life was nonexistent. It did not really buy us any time."

"Yes, I am glad for my decision. I have lived a good long life."

I am scheduled to drive Bernice in a couple days. After her appointment we share a happy lunch together with our Serna for the last time. She is very tired when we get her back home and I help her into bed. Serna is by her side and she affectionately gives her a special long hug. "Study hard, Serna."

Everyone is notified of her departure date and I plan a party. I find an enormous card of congratulations which goes everywhere with us.

I request the Tibetan Rinpoche who met her as a puppy to come to our home for a Tibetan Buddhist blessing prior to her turn in. It is a heartwarming time as I witness Serna on the couch next to him as he performs his rituals with water and bells. He happily signs her card in Tibetan with a translation which reads, "May you always be auspicious, happy and perfect."

I have found a source for Tibetan Buddhist prayer flags and joyfully string a couple lines of them in our backyard tree. They are such a lovely sight. It warms my heart to be doing this just prior to the turn in of Serna. Every time I gaze at them I will be sending out the best and highest good for her and all of us.

All of her fans and friends sign her card wishing her success. Her celebration is a grand event. People from the city arrive connected with the Arizona Service Dog Brushup I became involved with recently. There are a couple graduate CCI dogs with their wheelchair bound companions and of course guide dog Razzle and Rosalyn arrive with Mary Kay. The lady with the seizure alert dogs also arrives and a couple more working dogs with their partners. Margaret and Don are busy watching and petting all the dogs.

Kyoko arrives with her joyful Sakura, a golden retriever who flies out the back door to hit the pool. I met Kyoko, who is from Tokyo, Japan on a shopping day with Maggie. "Hello Ms. Tokyo, welcome to our party."

"Thank you Ms. Canada." She continues with her standard greeting to my home. "This is not reality. Your life is not reality, Carol Ann."

All the people with working dogs share their optimism for Serna's graduation. I have congratulatory balloons and a big pin with number one graduate on it. Serna along with everyone enjoys the festivities in her honor.

Our last visit with Serna to Vivian is tough on all of us. A few days ago on our last Serna outing with Don and Margaret I had found a big lab cuddley. I instantly grabbed it up. My little girl self is thrilled. This is what I can carry with me at the ceremony.

Vivian greets us with a big smile when she sees me walk in with the big lab under my arm. "She is in heat so I plan to walk across the stage with this under my arm instead of her. She has to stay in the kennel."

"Oh the poor baby, she won't like that."

"I know. Linda and Cliff are joining us for her big day so that will help."

Serna assumes her regular position as close to Vivian as possible and receives lots of extra attentions. "Ok big girl, we all believe in you, make us proud. Be brave and know you shall be forever missed. I do wish there were two of you. One could go off to school to graduate and the other one of you could stay here with Carol Ann and keep coming to see us."

"Vivian, that is the nicest thing anyone could say to us, right Serna girl. I do not think you shall be blessed with her presence again because she has turned into such a great working girl."

"Yes, I think so too. Ok, you girls go for your last walk with Amber and let me have a good cry."

Amber happily jumps off the bed when she hears the word walk. We enjoy a leisurely stroll around the neighborhood returning awhile later for the last farewell. Serna jumps back on the bed for her last big embrace and we head down the hall. Vivian's cries follow us to the front door. She will be only one of many who have tears when this black beauty leaves us.

The day arrives to fly to California. I am quite the sight on the plane with my big soft cuddley and my four legger. She receives the extra attentions of the flight crew. "It is time for her to head off to advanced training today. We are going to her turn in ceremony at the school." The stewardess gives her an extra pat and wishes her well.

Upon arrival to the CCI campus we spend time in the side yard lavishing our Bobby girl with great affections. It is now time to let her go. I have the permission of the kennel staff to walk Serna into her new home myself. I remove her bright yellow CCI scarf and put it around my own neck. I pick her up for our last long tender embrace and open the kennel door. I place a nylabone on the floor next to her. I whisper, "Be brave my Bobby Precious Angel pup, I shall see you again." I turn and tearfully head outside.

Linda, Cliff and I are a very forlorn threesome standing at the fence line gazing into the kennels. Serna is now barking and howling without restraint. Cliff wraps his arm around me, gently guiding me away. "Come on Carol Ann, we must go." Serna's cries continue to fill our ears as we turn the corner out of sight.

When my turn to cross the stage arrives they announce that Serna is in heat. I am awash in tears with my big soft cuddle lab as I cross the stage. My Robert has bolstered me. I somehow make it back to my seat and collapse with sorrow. We head home to Arizona and I wait the arrival of our new puppy. Thankfully, it is only a few days. I decide to fly over to pick her up. Her name starts with a T.

The moment I catch sight of a woman approaching me with a small bundle of puppy I hurry towards her. I hold the puppy up before me and exclaim excitedly, "Oh my goodness, how totally perfect she is. I love her color. This is a good change for me." She is fox red and her name is Treya. She becomes my Bobby Perfect Angel. She travels under the airline seat in front of me in a soft blue carrier. Our eyes are fixated on each other for the whole trip.

Linda picks us up in Phoenix and Treya receives nonstop oohs and ahs from her new admirer. "She is so beautiful."

She is welcomed into her new pack and the parade of eager people waiting to see her begins. Our first time with Vivian is most exciting. She lifts up her lab ears and cooes her giggles of delight. "Oh boy oh boy, I do miss Serna but I reckon you can help me recover from that trauma, my beautiful girl." Amber is not too enthused to take her walk with this young hooligan but we manage.

Within only a week she has jumped into the pool and I stand at the steps to help her out. Her legs are still too short to climb out on her own so I make extra steps. This girl is a real water dog. She reminds me of Spookie. Right away she had wanted to get into the pool and yet whenever she tried her Saber Dad had been right beside her and nudged her away. We had a huge bucket for their drinking water and Spookie climbed inside it. Robert assisted in her desires to swim by going into the pool with her as Saber looked on intently.

A few weeks later while at Linda's I share my thoughts of wanting to go see Jade and meet his adoptive parents. I have my perfect Bobby angel girl now so feel confident the timing will be right for this mission of the heart and soul. "You know CA, I have to make a trip to Edmonton in October."

"Really, wowers!"

"Yes, we could fly to Edmonton together and then you go off on your adventure from there."

So the plan is set in motion for October 17. Leta has a session with the dogs prior to our trip. Terra has had another litter of puppies and the school has determined this shall be her last. The pups are born on September 11. Leta shares she will be retired from being a breeder and have a spaying surgery. She also shares that I will be coming to see her soon. Terrace is pleased with this news of my coming visit.

Leta helps an upset Spirit to understand that she will have to stay home while Treya and I go to Canada. "But you could put a working coat on me." Leta explains it does not fit anymore and she is not a puppy.

Spirit suggests flying in the cargo hold and Leta inquires, "Why do you think your presence is so necessary?"

"Because when I am with her she can feel Bobby better. And she will need a lot of support while going through this journey of walking through her past."

Leta conveys, "You must trust she can get through this. Bobby can go with her in spirit."

Spirit responds, "Yeah in spirit, as in me!"

Leta responds, "One reason Carol Ann feels prepared to do this difficult journey now is thanks in large part to you. She has always considered you her guide dog even though she is not blind. She believes this is why you came into her life."

"Yes, we have a full understanding of this between us."

Leta checks in with Serna at school. "I miss home terribly and I feel Carol Ann's feelings. I hear her messages and letters."

"You do understand why you are there at school?"

"Yes, Carol Ann showed me all the time what I was getting into. The people here do not do that. Being with Maggie was such an inspiration to me so now I know I shall be on the team. I want a child to work with instead of an adult. I know now that this is my calling."

"That is great, hold that thought. Carol Ann will continue to show you every day your role."

Next we turn to Maggie who conveys her adjustments to her new life are going good. She appreciates the messaging from Carol Ann and still feeling connected to her soul family.

Leta shares, "Maggie, that is so wonderful. You always will be so, you know!"

"Yes, I see that now. We are like spokes on a wheel with Carol Ann at its centre. We go out and carry the light but we come off of her. Carol Ann's rituals and intents and communications fuel the wheel. They are essential."

Next Leta conveys that Robert makes an appearance. He is upbeat as always but sobers and places his arm over Carol Ann. "In terms of being a survivor you are really stubborn and you shall be ok through this trip. Your strength will carry you through."

As the session ends I bring my devoted Bobby Magic Angel Spirit into my lap for a long hug and cuddle whispering, "You know I am strong enough to do this now, otherwise it would not be happening, my beloved guide dog. You shall see upon our return a different Carol Ann, trust in this as I do."

With ever joyful Treya in her little yellow jacket by my side Linda and I board a plane from Phoenix, Arizona to Edmonton, Alberta. We spend a great evening in high spirits literally. Treya entertains us as she flies to and fro between the two beds. As usual her love of tubs requires her inspection. In the morning the three of us share big hugs of farewell.

"Ok, my sweet angel puppy, you and I are off on our saga together heading north to Peace River. It is a very special place for me and will open my heart to long held pains, so it is very good that you are by my side." She snuggles into a tight ball and falls asleep as I drive back into my past.

Coming down the hill toward picturesque Peace River I can feel my tummy tighten and I know my decision to come here has been a heavenly orchestrated plan. "Ok my Bobby love, I am going to need your shoulder. Stay close to me please."

My plan is to retrace as closely as possible all of the places that were a part of my life during my pregnancy and after when I moved to Peace River. I desire to recapture the lost parts of me that were left in the hills of this lovely valley and Prince George, the birth place of Jade. I pull into the parking lot of the Travellers Motel, a familiar place for me. This is where Robert spent many a night. I believe this is where he was on the night of our son's birth. So this is most appropriate.

Treya makes her customary inspection of the bathtub by jumping in and sniffing everywhere. I do not know if she will be home but I would love to see my old friend Erna from my days of working at the nursing home. I ring her number and she answers. Her voice sounds the same. I have lost touch with her since leaving here in 1977 and it is now 2001.

She cannot believe that I am actually only a few minutes from her home. I explain about my four-footed shadow and within minutes we have an invitation. But first I want to explore my old haunts. I drive to the two places that were my home and also go to the Sutherland Nursing Home.

"Ok, Treya, let's get your supergirl yellow cape on and go give someone a smile." We both prance confidently through the front door of my former employer.

Someone wonders who we are and why we are there. "My name is Carol Ann and I worked here many years ago. This is my puppy in training." We wander around for a while and Treya receives lots of attention. It is great fun for both of us. "Good work Treya, thank you. That was awesome."

I spend time driving around town and head up to the twelve foot Davis hill which I hiked many a time. The view from here is spectacular and I reflect on the countless hours spent hiking these hills taking photos. It is time to get ready to see Erna so we head back to the motel to get ready.

Sometimes when Erna was on night shift I would go visit the nursing home and we would share great chats. I had opened my heart to her about Robert and the baby. Amazingly, she shared that she had adopted two babies. This was a truly wondrous connection between us.

Needless to say the evening is filled with much hilarity and reminiscing. Her hubby, Pete takes great delight in Treya. "This girl is too funny, how can she ever become a serious worker. I just cannot imagine it." Her jacket is off and she is having a great time. Their small dog is really getting a work out trying to stay out of her way. Our visit carries long past midnight but finally my exhaustion tells me it is time to get back to the motel. Erna and I plan to meet in the morning. After big hugs I am down the road.

With all of the festiveness I have tipped back more wine that I ought to have and my driving is somewhat impaired. I see the whirling lights of a police car just as I pull into the motel. The policeman approaches. I take a deep breath and stay calm as I get my rental car papers and license ready. I ask for angelic assistance to keep us safe. Treya awakens sticking her head out the window and is greeted by a friendly pat.

"Have you been drinking Ms. Arnim?"

"Yes, indeed I have had a couple glasses of wine. My puppy and I have been having a great reunion with a friend whom I have not seen in over twenty years."

Miraculously, he requires nothing further and tells me to go slow and have a good night. "Treya my perfect puppy, I think you saved the day by showing your beautiful self right away. And always thank you to Robert." I hastily park the car. My perfect hooligan and I hit the bed with the highest gratitude.

In the morning I share with Erna this story and she cannot believe her ears. "I should have had you stay with us last night."

"Well, I was watched over so all is well."

Erna and I meet each other at the top of the twelve foot Davis hill and take photos. It is time to hit the road.

I head north. Outside of Manning I turn off the main highway and just drive where my heart leads me. I find a large field and let Treya out to run. As I am standing taking photos of a huge array of hay bales, a truck slows down and stops. "Do you need help? What are you doing out here alone?"

I am jubilant at being outside in the fresh air with my puppy and not far from the rig country. I tell this kind stranger the truth. "My husband who died a few years ago worked the rigs out here. I know I cannot find the same place as where we met but I am out here exploring and walking down memory lane. Could you please take a photo of me with my puppy?"

He kindly obliges and then takes off leaving Treya and I behind in a whirl of dust. I am all smiles as my pup and I continue down the road. I head back out to the highway driving further north until I see a sign for a drilling operation. I make the turn. I do not have any idea of where I am or where I am going but trust I shall find my way.

My heart is singing as I explore and see a rig tower in the distance. I follow the signs and turn into a road heading towards the tower. There is no actual camp but it is not winter yet.

I stop my car and wander closer with my camera in one hand and Treya on her leash. Soon I am met by a rig crew man in his dirty overalls and helmet with a most perplexed look. I give him the same story as I had the friendly young man on the dirt road awhile earlier.

He asks questions about when this was and what company, etc. He is understanding of my story and suggests that I be safe.

I head back out to the dirt road and explore some more. I find another tower and drive in to take photos there. This time I am told I ought to leave the area. "Where did you come from and what are you doing here? You cannot be here. And what are you doing with that dog?"

Every time I encounter someone I share the Robert story. A guy in a truck pauses beside us inquiring where I am going. After a couple hours of this adventure I decide I ought to head back to the motel. Then the sky blesses us with white stuff. "Oh how fun, look Treya, it is starting to snow."

I am all smiles as I head back to civilization. "Wow, Robert that was amazing, thanks for helping keep us safe."

I feel his loving presence and hear him whispering, "Possum dearest, you never cease to amaze me."

The next destination of our journey is Chetwynd, the home of Jade. I telephone him about an hour outside of town and we agree to meet somewhere. We share big hugs and smiles and an evening supper at a local restaurant. People are not familiar with what a working dog is and I am told that Treya cannot be in the restaurant. I explain she is not a pet yet the employee is most belligerent. Magically, a man overhears our conversation with the waitress and comes to my aid. He is aware of service dogs and informs the management that indeed it is legal that my working pup be allowed to stay. I thank him for his intervention.

The next day Jade takes me to the home of his adoptive parents. I meet Norm and Mary Jo and his brother Shale. It is all quite formal but thanks to having my Treya the atmosphere becomes a little lighter. I sit beside his Mom on the couch as she shares photo albums with me. I am doing my best to keep my heart pains to myself and a smile on my face, but boy oh boy it is not easy. When she shares the photos of his hospital stay after his near fatal car accident and time in coma I begin to fidget restlessly. Thankfully Treya is by my side.

All of us are feeling the tension. We have supper together and take some photos.

Back at Jade's I slump into his couch and drink some wine. I climb into his daughter's little bed with my Treya nestled in close and attempt to sleep. Yet I lay wide awake despite my exhaustion. Physically, I am tired but my emotional self is keeping me alert. Walking through my past is requiring all of my attentions. It is a long night.

In the morning a cheerful Jade asks, "Would you like to go into the bush with me Carol Ann? I need to get some firewood. Jeremy will join us also."

"Yes, I would love to."

We head off to pick up his son and are soon tumbling down a long back road into the thick of the bush. He finds his spot and soon the quiet is filled with the whirl of his chainsaw and then the loud thump of a tree as it hits the ground. I am in a state of high disbelief. Here I am sitting on a huge fallen tree with my grandson Jeremy, watching my son fell trees. I sense Robert with a big grin and his arm around my shoulder. If only he were here for real, this little grove of trees would be enjoying the guffaws of many a shared joke with birth father and son.

Jeremy, Treya and Jade

Young Jeremy climbs onto another fallen tree watching me with little boy grins. I capture a beautiful shot of my grandson.

That evening Jeremy, Jade and I along with my working girl have a happy meal in a little restaurant. This time there is no dispute about my puppy thankfully and she receives many a pet.

It is another sleepless night as I toss and turn. Morning arrives and it is time to say farewell.

My next destination is Prince George, the birthplace of our son. I intend to go into the hospital where I gave birth.

As I park the car my heart is filled with emotion and I have to concentrate on putting one foot in front of the other. Ok, Carol Ann, you can do this. Robert called you a brick for good reason. You have come this far and you can do this also. Thank you Robert and my angels for being with us. Treya happily pants by my side and in we go. The maternity ward has been moved from where it was in 1974. This bothered me but then I think that is ok, the point is that I step inside the energy of a maternity ward and place myself back in that timeframe.

Someone sees me with the dog and tells me that I am not allowed. I take a moment of polite instruction about the fact that she is not a pet and it is within our right to be there. This silences the person and we carry on our way.

The maternity ward is ahead of us. I find a couch and sit with Treya in a down command. I allow my mind to play the movies of seeing my baby through the window of the nursery. I recall seeing the label boarder instead of a real name. I recall walking out of the hospital and seeing him for the last time. He was my baby and yet he was not. I am fully present in October of 1974.

I am sure my face is portraying some anxiety as someone approaches me. "Can I help you?"

"No, I am fine, thank you."

"What are you doing here, is there someone you are looking for?"

"I am not lost. This is a trip down memory lane for me. I gave birth to my son in this hospital many years ago and gave him up for adoption."

She is at a loss for words and leaves me alone. I feel it is time for us to leave. I have come for what I needed and it is ok to go now. I merge myself consciously back fully into the present.

A few minutes later Treya and I find our way out of the hospital. My steps are much lighter than when we entered so this is all good work. My next stop is to drive up to the hilltop park where Vivian took me after leaving the hospital empty handed.

I find the park and let my puppy out for a run. It begins to snow and my heart is filled with joy. I take a self-portrait with snowflakes falling on my teary eyed face. I did it....I did it....I did it. Wowsers. I have done it all, making all the stops of my past, hitting all the places of my former life. I stood as close as I knew possible to the scene where Robert and I had co-created our bundle of love.

I drive next to Jasper and treat myself to a higher end place to stay the night. Treya inspects the tub and rolls on the bed with approval. We are celebrating a Rocky mountain high with the snowy peaks in view out our window. I am very tired but sleep still eludes me.

We continue our journey into Calgary with lots more rigs in view saluting us. Robert certainly is paving our way every step of this blessed healing trip.

On the plane Treya and I have a window seat at the bulkhead. She gets lots of attention from the flight crew and many a smile from the woman in the aisle seat next to us. We make a stopover in Denver to see Maggie and family. It is such a blessing for Maggie and I to be together again. What a treat!

Both Treya and I receive the heartiest welcome home from the rest of the Arnim pack. Spirit in particular is overjoyed to see me arrive all intact. "Yes, my dearest guide dog, I am safe. Treya did an excellent job and everything was perfect, Spirit." She continues to sniff just to make sure I am all there.

The next few days are spent in rest and integrating all of the inner work which transpired over the trip. I had not been able to sleep during the whole trip and now I collapse into rest, reassembling all of my lost pieces which I had put into my pocket over the last several days.

With time I do feel more complete, more whole and more perfect. My pains over giving up our son are lessened and I am filled with healing joy for all of my choices. I know that my husband in spirit is also benefiting from my work. "Well done wife of mine, love of mine, well done."

It is time for a grand celebration for our Saber who is now fourteen. It is another glorious party with lots of two leggers and four leggers.

Communications

I have learned from CCI they plan to do Serna's spaying on November 15. I set up another session with Leta so Serna will completely understand about this. "Hi Serna girl. Tomorrow is your surgery to prevent you from having babies. You will be off work for about ten days and will be well taken care of. Your trainer Todd has given a great report about you. It sounds like your calmness during work has greatly improved. You are performing like an angel."

"Yes, I am calmer. I am thinking all the time in class."

"That is fabulous, keep up the good work. Do you still feel the same about all this?"

"Absolutely, I want to succeed. Thanks for telling me about the surgery. I am fine with it."

"Wonderful. Carol Ann will be checking in again."

"Yes, I feel her. She does it all the time."

Next dog we chat with is Terrace. "Carol Ann will be coming to see you soon."

"That is great. I always love to see her."

"Soon after that you will be going back to the school for your spaying surgery. Remember you had your last litter of puppies. Sometime in the next few weeks this will happen. Enjoy your retirement. Carol Ann thanks you for being such a good Mom for all of your puppies. They have gone out into the world making a big difference in lives. You have made a major contribution to the world."

Terrace feels very proud and thanks us for the visit.

On November 9 Saber had a party for this fourteenth birthday. Leta asks him about this.

"Thanks for my party. I had a ball."

"Are you doing alright?"

"Yes. Tell Carol Ann not to worry about me. My quality of life right now is very good and I am very happy."

"Carol Ann is really glad to be home after her trip to Canada. Do you or Spookie have anything you would like to say about her trip?"

Spookie pipes in, "I really missed her. I thought she was never coming home."

"I know she missed all of you dogs as well. Didn't you understand she was coming back?"

"Oh yes, but I just missed her. I need her a lot you know. She thinks I am more independent than I am."

"How do you feel since she has returned?"

"More solid. I feel like we are better glued together."

"That is an interesting picture, why do think that is?"

"She is more grounded and happier."

"Saber, how do you feel about her?"

"Tell Carol Ann she did a wonderful thing for herself. I tracked her the whole time and always knew what was going on. I felt all of her highs and lows. She was amazing."

"Thank you. Do you think Spookie's description about the glue is apt?"

"Absolutely. That is a good way to put it. She is all here now having integrated parts which had been left behind. She got her balance buddy back as Serna would say."

"She wants both you and Spookie to know how grateful she is to you. She loves you each so uniquely for how you have improved her life. Saber if you had not come into the family, Carol Ann would not be who she is today. So thank you for your part in coming together with Robert."

"It was meant to be. Thank you."

Next dog to share is Spirit. "What were your impressions when Carol Ann got home?"

"I was so relieved and overjoyed to see her. I checked her out very carefully."

"What were you afraid of?"

"When one goes through a regathering of oneself sometimes it does not work too well without the right support. One can fly apart more than they were before and lose parts of themselves they had not lost before. So I was not sure who would be coming back. Doing what she did alone is not always advisable. That is why I wanted to go. Little Treya did a great job providing comfort but I knew she could not help if she got in trouble."

"You know the special place you hold in Carol Ann's heart. Is there anything she can do to ensure your happiness?"

"Just be at peace. When she is happy and at peace, I am. This has not been our path together much so far, but I feel we are headed toward that now."

"Do you recognize that she has changed and is happier than when you first came into her life?"

"Yes for sure. But there have always been backslides of grief. I do not say this negatively, but her life has remained under a pall ever since I met her. I feel this is lifting now."

"What created this pall?"

"All the events she has just gone to clear out and then the death of Robert to cap it off. No one could come out of all that and stand in a place of joy and lightness."

"Do you enjoy the therapy work with her?"

"Part of me wants to stay home and rest but I want to be with her."

"She will take a break from that for a bit. She wants to stay home and rest with you. Carol Ann wants you to know that she would not be in the positive mental state if you had not come into her life. You are her successful guide dog who guides her through life. You know this, right?"

"Yes, I could be with no one else."

"Thank you dearest girl, we will talk again soon."

On December 27 I receive a training report from Todd at CCI. Unfortunately kennel cough has entered the kennels and Serna has it. She is on antibiotics. It is a stressful time with her being in advanced training scheduled for the upcoming class the end of January. Todd shares that she is doing excellent work. They went on their first official field trip with a wheelchair. She was tentative at first with her tail down yet became more confident wagging her tail. She held the positions and was responsive waiting for guidance from Todd. I decide a session with Leta would be beneficial for Serna.

Leta senses her discouragement due to the cough and the stress. She explains she will feel better with time.

"I hope so; all I want to do is sleep."

"Your energy will return. Todd gave Carol Ann a great report on your progress. We know you are feeling the concerns of the staff but you need to trust everything is being handled correctly."

"Ok, that is good. When will I see Carol Ann?"

"About six weeks from now." Serna gets very excited wagging her tail. "Remember you can talk to your balance buddy to help bring in good energy."

"Thanks for reminding me. That will help."

"Great to talk with you, we will do it again very soon. Rest up."

Recently I took Saber and Spirit for jin shin jitsu treatments. The therapist named Linda loved working with both dogs. I ask Leta to check in with them.

"Saber, how did you like the session?"

"Oh, these creaky old bones cannot take much. She needs to be gentler or else do a shorter session. Toxins get released which go into the joints and make me sore."

"What can we do for you?"

"It has cleared out now, I am fine."

"Carol Ann says you will not go to any more sessions. Thanks for talking with us."

Leta checks in with Spirit. "How was your session with Linda?"

"It kind of felt like I was in a different body."

"Is that a good thing?"

"I think so, I am still fitting into it."

"Carol Ann says you have had a couple scary episodes in the night with breathing abnormally. Can you share about this?"

"I don't really understand it myself."

Leta senses pressure in her chest and a feeling that things do not always fit well inside her body. Perhaps the coming and going of Robert energy has created a misalignment. "Can you tell us what your sense is of Robert? What is the situation with him being in and with you?"

"He is staying outside my body most of the time now. He will come very close but he has not come in lately."

"Do you think this adjustment was beneficial?"

"Very. I am still adjusting but would like to go again."

"Linda told Carol Ann that you are the most balanced entity she has ever worked on."

Spirit becomes very humble. I silently ponder that indeed she would have to be so in order to have my lovie's energies coming and going since she was a young pup.

"Do you feel ok?"

"Yes, a lot of the heaviness has lifted."

Leta has the impression from Robert standing in the background that he will not be entering Spirit anymore. This phase is over. I share with her that my trip to Canada has affected all of us positively and this is why he will no longer need to enter Spirit.

Leta shares that Robert is standing a few feet away from me being very quiet. His energy is not so ebullient.

I ask Leta to convey my message to him. "Robert, I feel I have gone through huge shifts since my return from Canada and desire your input regarding such. I sense I am no longer in a space of fear like I was for years even prior to your death. Over the last year with Serna and now after my trip I have been lifting away from that. I have questioned my higher self why I have certain behavior patterns such as overspending. The answers I get refer to feeling unworthy and undeserving. I felt not worthy enough to be the mother of our son, or to be your wife. I felt not good enough. Since your death it has emerged more strongly creating patterns of overspending and overindulging in food and wine. I am now beginning to feel worthy of living in our beautiful home. Such a burden is lifting off me. I just had an amazing visit with Aly. She felt the change in my voice sensing my shift. She said I am the bravest person she has ever known. Her comments caught me by surprise yet lifted my spirits. I suppose that is part of my euphoria. What do you feel?"

Robert replies through Leta, "The glorious part of all this, my love, is that you no longer need me to confirm these things. You know the truth in your own heart now. You and I were brought together to bring this lesson to fruition. My death at the time it occurred was key to this whole process. I want you to know I am no wiser than you. I have a broader perspective from this vantage point. I am continuing to work on my own issues yet I have not been elevated to an all knowing state. That is a continual process requiring lifetimes. You are beginning to process independently of me now for the first time since we met. It is a wonderful development and I am crying with joy. I did not want to stray far from your side until I knew you could take care of yourself without me. Now that I know that I will be pursuing other directions as well as visiting with you. My love for you will never change. It grows stronger all the time. But in our own soul strengthening we become more strongly entwined in essence. I will not be getting in Spirit now because I do not need to anymore."

"When you are ready you ought to take my voice off our answering machine and put your own strong voice on your telephone. Do the same with other records and materials. I belong in a different place in your physical life now. This will be a culminating experience for you in the process you have just gone through."

Leta continues to share for me. "Carol Ann wants to work toward channeling you more directly. It is too difficult for her to put you out of her life altogether. She says that is impossible."

He replies as he moves closer placing his hand on Carol Ann's shoulder, "Yes, this is a big step distancing from me a bit. Yet there is no soul distance. I may or may not be able to talk to you. I am being bidden to go do some healing work on myself. Touching down into the earth plane is very hard on the spirit. I have had great help in staying by your side. Great help and support. I know you can and will have direct communication with myself and others. A change is approaching for me now my love. My spirit needs some rest."

Our session ends and I thank Leta and all of my messengers. Upon hanging up the phone I envision my Roberto surrounded with angelic beings lifting him into his temple of healing.

Guide Dog Breeder Reunion and Spirit Flight

In the beginning of January, Treya and I fly to San Francisco to visit Terrace at her home with Michael and Robert. She is now retired since having her third and last litter of puppies. Their names are Farina, Freddy, Fenton, Flint, Falstaff, Fresco, Florence and Fanette. They were born on September 11, 2001. As the rest of the world was reeling with the horror of the twin towers tragedy in New York City, my Terrace was birthing her eight bundles of sunshine light. Wherever I went after this when someone talked about this tragedy I shared that something beautiful happened on that same day. The face of the person became more relaxed as I told them about the birth of Terra's guide dog puppies that would be spreading much light into the world. It helped me feel better and usually the person walked away a bit lighter upon hearing of my puppy miracle.

A smiling Michael pulls up to the curb as we wait at the arrivals. Both the puppies share an exuberant greeting as I climb into the car. After a few minutes the puppies settle back. I am greeted with a big welcome hug from Robert upon arrival to their home.

The next day she has to go into the city so puppy girl and I get to spend some time in downtown San Francisco. Magically she has let me out near the Huntington Hotel. Roberto and I had a couple stays at this lovely old hotel. This time with Treya I am walking through pleasant memories. She receives many an appreciative glance and some good pets.

Across the street is a lovely majestic old church. Treya takes advantage of her down time and falls into a deep slumber as I savor the peaceful energies surrounding me. We walk across to a clearing with benches and sit to admire the busyness around us. There are lots of birds flying all around which is a good distraction for working girl. It has been a most pleasant time and we meet up with Michael heading back to the house. Terrace gives working puppy lots of good sniffs and the two of them have a good romp in their lovely large backyard.

In the morning we head north to meet up with Pam, the breeder keeper with CCI. I am eager to see her setup for the puppies.

Treya is snoozing on the back seat while I am being treated to special cuddles with Terrace. My arm is wrapped around her as we drive. I witness the meeting of Michael, the guide dog breeder keeper; meeting Pam, the CCI breeder keeper. Pam walks us over to the garage where the home of the puppies is. How divinely perfect that my trip is timed with a new CCI litter on the floor. Farewells are made with Michael and my lovely breeder girl Terrace.

Treya exalts in rowdy time with her Dad, Packer and the other dogs of Pam's home. I enjoy every moment of entertainment with the puppies. Pam has a great setup for them. A background tape plays of various noises of the human world acclimatizing the young recruits at an early age.

The next day I am in for a special meeting. Pam has arranged for the breeder keeper of Bobby to come to the CCI campus. She takes a memorable photo of me with Treya and Bobby. He is the Dad of precious Serna. The woman presents me with a small black lab snuggley with a CCI tag.

About two weeks later I receive a phone call from a weepy Michael. "Carol Ann, I have the most awful news to tell you. Terrace died from her spaying surgery."

I am at a loss for words and cannot believe it. "She went through the surgery fine, yet in the night someone went to check on her in the kennel and found her deceased. They believe she was bleeding internally."

Certainly guide dogs would have the best of medical attentions so this is an unusual case for them. She would have been four years old on February 4. Her death is on January 18, 2002. I am so grateful for my trip to see her.

I silently call upon all twenty-four of Terra's puppies envisioning them all huddled around listening to my message. "Dearest puppies, wherever you all are I send you sad news of your beloved Mom, Terrace. She has died in the night a few hours after her spaying surgery at the guide dog school kennel. She trusts you shall all continue in your great work and is very proud of you. I know she has been honored to nurse and guide you. Be happy." The puppies all silently put one paw up in salute.

The next week on the birthday of Spirit my brother Mark arrives. On that weekend we have a visit from Maggie and family. I truly am not up to all the company. Yet of course it is always a most welcome sight to see my adorable angel Maggie enjoying the pool with her canine family.

A few days later I arrange for a session with Leta advising her of Terra's death. Saber has just had a few bothersome cysts removed and she tunes into him first. "How are you feeling now Saber?"

"Back to my old self. I did not like the stupor from the drugs yet I am glad that the source of my need to lick is removed. That was very bothersome."

"Carol Ann is glad to hear this. We are going to talk to Terrace now, do you have anything else to add first?"

"Only that I hope we can come through this in an easier way."

"Can you elaborate?"

"Life and death are all around us being constant reminders for those we grieve. I think as a family we are growing through the impact of the waves. It does not shake the foundation quite so much when better understanding is achieved."

"Thank you for your wisdom."

Terrace enters as Leta asks, "Are you aware of being out of your body?"

"Yes, I knew immediately. I hovered for a while and soared away. I came right back home here to Carol Ann."

"Are you aware there is another place for you to go once we leave our body?"

She is not concerned with such as yet. "Well, you are safe here with Carol Ann." I have become weepy listening to my sunshine girl puppy.

Terra asks Leta, "Why is she crying?"

"Because we humans so miss the physical form of those we love once they leave us."

"Oh me too. I loved seeing her again. I am so grateful to her."

"Can you speak to this?"

"I was allowed to blossom." Terrace shows Leta the petals of a flower opening and each one is a puppy. Her blossoming was through her puppies.

Leta says Terra is not traumatized but because of the anesthesia she needs the time to savor the aura of love with her family. "Carol Ann thanks you for the time together in California. She feels it was a total culmination for her as a puppy raiser. Seeing you in your new role in your new home was very special for her. How you sat in her lap on that last day was very moving for her since you were being so demonstrative. Can you tell us why you were always a little detached emotionally?"

"I came into this life with detachment. My role as a Mom demanded me to give up so many. Yet as my end neared I could give up the detachment."

"Were you happy in your life with Robert and Michael?"

"It was perfect. It helped me stay detached."

"Do you hang out with Michael?"

"Right now I just want to be here. Thank you to Carol Ann for providing a safe place for so many souls."

"Thank you Terrace, Carol Ann is most grateful. We will check in again with you in a few days."

Leta makes a quick connection with Serna at school. It seems she is busy working and is very happy. She gives Carol Ann a big lick on the face. "We will check back with you in a few days, it looks like you may start working with people soon."

A week later I set up another session with Leta to tune into my puppies. She connects first with Terrace. "How are you feeling now?"

"I am doing great. I know I have other work to do now with puppy spirits getting ready to enter earth lives."

"That is exciting. So you are ready to go on and know where you are going."

"Yes, I have just been waiting to say farewell. I am sure Carol Ann and I will meet again. I want her to realize what a tremendous gift her work is since I have a totally different perspective of it now. Keep lighting my candle."

"Carol Ann wishes you a safe journey." Leta sees Terrace surrounded in a huge light with angels ready to take her.

I ask Leta to check in with Maggie. "Hello puppy girl. I hear you went to see Carol Ann."

"Yes, it was wonderful to be home again, I miss it a lot."

"Were you aware of Terrace being around?"

"Yes. She was giving me a lot of information about how things work from her new point of view. I know some of this on some level but she helped me to keep everything in perspective." Maggie shows Leta visions of Terrace constantly praising her. She knows she can draw on her as Carol Ann described. It is very anchoring for her.

"Thank you. Carol Ann wants to tell you that when you first arrived it was tough because she was not her usual joyful self with you."

"She was in grief. I understand. It was no accident that I came to see her at that time."

Next puppy Leta talks to is Serna. I have been told by CCI that she is being held back for the next class because all the applicants did not show up. She will be in the upcoming class for May. She tunes in to Serna who is feeling confused.

"I can feel the confusion of the trainers so I am little dejected. My routine has been broken."

"You will be back to working fulltime again soon."

"Yes, I see that now. I can gain more self-confidence working in public. Tell Carol Ann I rely on her messages, keep the letters coming."

"Thanks Serna, you know she will."

"I am glad we talked, thanks."

A couple weeks later I receive another training report on Serna. She has been working well with Todd and is now with a new trainer, Megan. Leta connects with her and tells me Serna is feeling anxious. She inquires, "What is your anxiety about puppy girl?"

"I feel like I have lost my purpose. I feel concern all around me and it is hard to work in that atmosphere."

"How can we help you? Do you remember the purpose you are headed towards?"

"Yes. But I do not know if I can transfer allegiance yet again. I think I am a one person dog type. I just want to go home to Carol Ann."

"You know you would be transferring allegiance to someone who needs your help very badly."

"Yes, but I feel they have lost faith in me here. So I have lost faith in myself."

"Serna, we are all going to hold the trust that your purpose will be fulfilled. Your purpose here is great and it will be fulfilled. Carol Ann has full confidence and trust in this."

Leta says she is grateful but still wishes she could go home.

"Working with your new trainer perhaps will prepare you for whatever is going to happen. Do you see what we mean?"

"Yes, I can get stronger in my accomplishments. I need faith in me from others."

"Can you keep going? Carol Ann's heart aches for you. She is so proud of you no matter what happens. She has always trusted you. Remember you are the dog who taught her about trust in life and in herself."

Serna brightens with this recall and replies, "I want to help others do that."

"Hold that vision. Do you have anything else to tell us?"

"I just want Carol Ann to hold me."

"You can visualize her doing this. Hang in there sweet girl."

As Leta wraps it up with the dogs I share another question which I would like her to query the girls.

"Carol Ann would like to ask Spirit and Maggie, from your perspective what do you think about raising service dogs?"

"We are both in total accord," responds Maggie. "We both know from our own experiences that there are very few dogs that are perfectly suited to the rigors of the emotional preparation required for this work."

"How do you mean?"

"It is what Serna is experiencing right now. It is not normal for most dogs to transfer allegiance several times in their lives. It is not that different than it is for humans but this is not equated with dogs. There are a few who can do so seemingly unharmed but for most of us it leaves deep emotional wounds and scars. It is very, very hard."

"Would you like to add to this Spirit?"

"Yes. There is such a sense of expectation surrounding you all the time when you are in training and even in the later stages of puppyhood. That creates an atmosphere that makes it difficult to feel successful for just being who you are. You must be able to put part of yourself away and conform to those expectations in order to succeed."

"I think we understand. Carol Ann would like to interject that is how you must behave in public but that is your work mode. You can be who you are when not in work mode and be at ease with yourself."

"Yes we understand. That is not exactly what we are talking about here. It is more about going through stages where you are expected to be able to put aside your own cares and desires and follow the direction that is laid out for you."

"What do you think of the overall focus of such programs?"

"We think they are very noble. Anything that can further our species unifying is to be honored. We do our part but not all can succeed."

"Do you think Carol Ann should continue to raise puppies?"

"Oh by all means! That is part of why she is here. She is one who can help the unification and help bridge the gaps and ease the emotional processes involved."

"Do you have any suggestions as to practical steps that would make things easier for you puppies? Maggie?"

Adorable angel girl responds, "No, not really except that her model of communication and frequent visits should be followed. I think it should be made mandatory."

"And you Spirit?"

"I think Carol Ann knows what she is doing. I know it is very hard for her because she hurts in her heart every time one of us does. But she must realize that is what the unifying element is. There are others involved in this work that have this also."

"Carol Ann says she goes off the deep end with this so to speak. She wonders if her excessive amount of love and spoiling makes it harder for you overall."

"Yes, possibly. But what is life without that. It is why we are here. And if the pups do not know love, how can they bring it to another?"

"I see what you mean. But would it not be easier on them if they did not connect so strongly so they did not have to experience such a tremendous change in their lives. Let us use Terrace as an example. Are you here with us Terrace?"

Leta feels her presence come in. "Thank you for coming Terrace. You would like to speak to this?"

"Yes. I was very clear about my job from the start. But that is not usual. That is why I went the way I did. I knew I was to breed babies for this purpose. I knew I was best suited for that. I could have served one person but then my true contribution would have been lost. Even though I did not become a service dog, I am one of the few who is perfectly suited to the work. I always kept a damper on my emotions. It was not hard for me. But that is unusual."

"So do you think Carol Ann should lavish all the love and attention she does on her puppies?"

"Puppies cannot be raised without it. They would become very neurotic. So it is the only true way. If she can stand it, she must continue. Treya would be much more clingy if Carol Ann did not give her the high quality of attention."

"I see what you are saying. This is very helpful, thank you."

"Don't forget I am here Carol Ann to help you."

Leta shares, "She thinks of you every day and lights your candle. She thanks you for everything. Can you share more about what you are doing now?"

Terrace responds, "I am helping the puppy spirits come in who will be training for service dogs." Leta sees a beautiful picture of her launching a small blonde service puppy out of her hands.

"Carol Ann is so immensely grateful for the time you had during your last visit and the extra special cuddles in the car."

"Yes, it was time for me to drop the shields and allow the connection. It was time. I wanted her to see the true depth of my spirit."

"Were you aware you were going to be leaving this earth plane?"

"Yes, of course. I need to go now. There are puppies waiting."

As always I share my thanks to Leta and my messengers for another awesome visit. After hanging up the phone I contemplate Terra's message. I realize that she was the most appropriate dog for me after the turn in of Laverne. She was detached which was perfect because I was grieving the absence of Laverne Spirit on top of my Robert grief.

Spirit Flights

Treya gets to become acquainted with my friend Bernice when we take her to an appointment. She effortlessly wiggles her way into Bernice's heart. Her small dog has someone more his size to chase now. He looks on disapprovingly when she rolls around on his kitchen bed. Bernice chuckles with delight. She is a very spunky soul and we share many a memorable visit at her kitchen table and over lunches. The cancer is taking its toll on her as she grows frailer with each visit.

On February 15 she telephones me. "I want to wish you a happy birthday a little early." I am pleasantly surprised to hear from her. My birthday is on February 17. "I am not feeling so great and wanted to hear your voice again."

"It is so neat you telephoned. Thank you so much Bernice."

"How is that lovely puppy of yours and what do you hear about our beautiful black lab?"

"Treya is doing great. She is always joyful no matter what. Serna is receiving great training reports and I believe she will be graduating in the near future."

"I shall hold that vision for her."

"Thank you Bernice. Serna appreciates your support."

On my birthday I receive a call from her son Walter advising me of the death of his Mom. "You are invited with Treya to her funeral home reception."

"Thank you so much for the call. For sure we both shall be there. I shall miss Bernice very much and never forget her."

My perfect Bobby angel girl and I are greeted warmly as we enter the funeral home. Walter shares, "This is Carol Ann and her new working puppy, Treya. She is a volunteer for the cancer society and drove my Mom a lot."

It touches my heart to see a couple photos of Bernice with Serna on display amongst the other family photos.

During this same timeframe I am witnessing the decline of unforgettable Vivian. She is currently hospitalized. I have her dog Amber at our home with her canine friends. I go visit with both Amber and working girl, Treya. "What a sight you are. Oh thank you so much for bringing her with Treya."

"I could not leave her home while visiting with you dear Vivian. I brought you a treat from McDonald's."

"Oh good, I will enjoy that, thank you." She happily devours the hamburger while asking, "So how is my girl doing with your pack?"

"Vivian, she knows all my dogs so it is not a challenge of any kind. However she is so devoted to you I am sure it is tough emotionally. I have a formula of flower essences I am giving her to help her adjust."

Amber is close by my side. "Come on over her close to Mommy." She pleads and yet Amber continues to lean on me. "Well Carol Ann, it looks like you have gained a dogger. How do you feel about that?"

"I am happy to take care of her. We have formed a close bond over our time walking together since we met so don't you worry about her."

"That is great, thank you."

Vivian goes home but her time there is becoming a challenge with her daily needs requiring more hands on nursing care. She has always wanted to stay in her own home and yet it is looking like a change is necessary. I am able to convince her to be evaluated for hospice care and thankfully she agrees. A weakened Vivian is taken from her home for the last time.

I go to visit her yet there is no response. She is more than ready for her magic carpet ride into the light. She puts up no resistance. She knows the rainbow bridge awaits her with all of her reunions. Recently I had read her the beautiful sentiment called the "Rainbow Bridge" which was very comforting. I am relieved to see her years of suffering finally end.

"The Rainbow Bridge" inspired by a Norse legend.
Steve and Diane Bodofsky

By the edge of a woods, at the foot of a hill,
Is a lush, green meadow where time stands still.
Where the friends of man and woman do run,
When their time on earth is over and done.
For here, between this world and the next,
Is a place where each beloved creature finds rest.
On this golden land, they wait and they play,
Til the rainbow bridge they cross over one day.
No more do they suffer, in pain or in sadness,
For they are whole, their lives filled with gladness.
Their limbs are restored, their health renewed,
Their bodies have healed, with strength imbued.
They romp through the grass, without even a care,
Until one day they stop, and sniff at the air.
All ears prick forward, eyes dart front and back,
Then all of a sudden, one breaks from the pack.
For just at that instant, their eyes have met;
Together again, both person and pet.
So they run to each other, these friends from long past,
The time of their parting is over at last.
The sadness they felt while they were apart,
Has turned into joy once more in each heart.
They embrace with a love that will last forever,
And then side-by-side, they cross over...together.

A couple days later I take Amber over to their home for the last time. She stands by my side as I release a bouquet of balloons with rosebuds attached and a love note. I tell the javelina they need to fend for themselves. "Your friend, Vivian, has left this world. There is no one here to feed you now."

Amber and I enjoy good cuddles. She loves to come over to me and she places her nose under my hand telling me to pet her. I am very much in love.

It is a week later that I receive a message from Vivian. She had told me she would send me a sign from the other side. Somewhere in my collection of countless photographs I have a photo she gave to me. She is with a family of pigs and one of them is giving her a kiss.

One morning as I pass our open front door I happen to look outside. To my delight there on our walkway is a family of javelina munching happily on my plants. I do not feed them because of having the dogs and have never seen them by this door. I chuckle with amusement thanking Vivian. She has found the perfect vehicle for her messaging me from the other side.

Serna's Ariana

On March 6, I receive a training report from Megan at CCI. Serna is showing the same pattern when first working with Todd which is stress. Megan says she is in a regression period yet they do feel she will work out. Serna is receiving lots and lots of praise. She does not require any corrections at this point but nudging to be responsive. They plan to place her on the floor for the upcoming May class. A phone call to Leta will be good for Serna and we get a session set up right away.

I convey to Leta that Serna just needs to believe in herself again. "She would have been released by now if they did not have hopes for her. We need to encourage her to work on her bond with Megan."

Leta tunes into my Bobby precious angel puppy asking, "Do you sense that Megan believes in you?"

"Sometimes, yes."

"Megan told Carol Ann that she believes you can succeed. What are you feeling now Serna?"

"I am sad and torn. I still want to go back to Carol Ann. I do feel I could do this but it might only be halfway and my heart might not ever be in it. I don't know if I can get close again, I am not stoic like Maggie."

"We do understand. Carol Ann feels the same way, she is aware of how you feel. She feels that both of you just now need to do your best and let things play out. Trust that it will lead to the right outcome."

Serna shows Leta she is really torn in trying to do right. She would like to just opt out and knows she can control that to some extent. "I am still holding on because Carol Ann tells me to do so."

"Carol Ann is in heartache for you and hopes you can feel some relief from her love sent your way. She cuddles the soft snuggley lab she walked across the stage with at turn in since you were in heat. She envisions you while doing this."

"Yes, I feel it. I am so connected to her which is why it is hard for me to let go."

"You do not have to think of it as letting go; Carol Ann will always be with you in spirit no matter what. Think of Maggie."

"Yes, but think of how she feels without her Robert present. It is different and that is the part I am talking about."

"She knows this and feels the same way. We must keep going; it is all we can do. Be patient and trust."

I am grateful for our session through Leta. If my Bobby girl can just keep hanging on I know she will make it. I hug the big lab cuddley envisioning her with me.

About the end of April we have a grand weekend when Maggie and family come home to visit. On the Sunday we go to the little desert chapel church and later have a festive party with more dogs. Annie is joyous over the prospect of Serna graduating. There is many a happy salute to our Bobby girl wishing her well and a great match in team training. Saber and Treya are busy popping balloons. I go out to the airport to send Maggie off with my love and watch as she walks away with her Joy girl.

On May 3, I receive the awaited news about Serna. She has been matched as a skilled companion with an eleven year old wheelchair bound girl, named Ariana. There is no other information provided as yet. Whoopies. I always envisioned this happening and call everyone to share the fabulous news. I want to check in with her for a bit and call Leta for a quick session.

Serna bounces in exuberantly when hearing Leta communicating with her. "I think I am doing it."

"Yes, indeed you are. Carol Ann and everyone are so very happy."

"Do you like the person you are matched with?"

"I love her and the family. I feel a lot of good energy in them, there is no depression."

"Is she who you wanted?"

"Absolutely. There were others, but she is perfect for me."

"Do you get to sleep with Ariana on her bed?"

"Yes, sometimes. I want to do that all the time. Already I am feeling possessive with her."

"Do you see yourself now as an important spoke on the wheel which stems out from Carol Ann and the pack?"

"Yes, I am very happy. I feel like I am a very strong spoke." She shows herself on a wheel with Maggie at nine, Terrace at five and herself about two. Carol Ann and her canine family make up the middle all synthesized together.

"That is a lovely vision. Thank you. In a few days Carol Ann and Treya will be seeing you and Linda is also coming. You will get to play with Treya. Carol Ann wants to share that it is going to be hard for her to walk away from you. If you can remember the process at Maggie's graduation this might help you."

"It will be very hard for me also but I understand. I hope she will remain in my life and we can see each other."

Serna shares she has already seen the pictures of her home in the heads of her family so this is helping. She can feel how proud they are of her already. She also reminds Carol Ann that she will be reflecting her feelings and hopes both of them can be stronger than when she was left at school. She does not want to relive that pain.

"Carol Ann does not want that either. This will be a more joyful reunion and the parting tough but without such turmoil on both of your parts. She is so happy you endured for so long and hung in there. You have done a great job. In her eyes you are the number one graduate girl."

"She will continue to light your candle and write to you. Her focus will turn more to working with Treya in her last months of training with her."

"Yes, that is how it is supposed to happen. I can't wait to see her."

I have Leta talk with Spirit next. "Carol Ann will be going to see Serna graduate and you will be staying home this time."

"I understand. It is not my place to go on this trip. I am at peace since she is."

"Can you tell us your impressions of Carol Ann now?"

"She is a different person and much stronger. I still take a lot of waves of energy off her when she dips low and I ground them out. Overall she is much smoother in her emotional body."

"How are you feeling physically?"

"Much lighter. This raw diet is a great improvement for all of us dogs. It certainly agrees with me."

"Is there anything else you want to share with Carol Ann?"

Spirit shows a vision to Leta. "We are like one being connected in all ways."

"Carol Ann agrees. The two of you have always been like one being. That is lovely. She thanks you for being her guide dog and being so good with Treya."

Leta tunes in with Treya. "She is rather a wild child. She is very reactive when I tune into her. She feels unpredictable, with erratic energy and is still immature."

"She will be a year old next month, definitely you are right. She is my wild girl and very goofy."

Leta asks her, "Do you like balloons?"

"Yes, but they scare me."

"Carol Ann will get some for your birthday. She says you like to pop them with Saber. Do they really scare you?"

"Yes, that is why I like them so much. I get a big scarey rush of adrenaline. They really get me going."

"Ok funny girl, you shall have balloons. Do you understand when Carol Ann talks to you and gives commands?"

"I usually tune out half through what she is saying."

"Do you understand your job?"

"I do understand the trained behaviours and love people but I get confused sometimes. There is no goal in this for me."

"Do your best with her and listen."

"I forget and get distracted."

"It is ok, she loves you. With time you will understand better. On Saturday you will be going on a plane with her and Linda. Serna is graduating. It will be a special trip. You will have some time to play together. But there will be lots of time you need to be on your best behavior."

Leta shares Treya does not really care what anything is leading to. She seems to be a very blithe spirit. She would prefer to play with Serna and says it will be hard to be serious.

"Carol Ann loves your sense of humor and funniness. You are very special. She wants both of you to be patient with each other. She thanks you for being in her life. You are her joy puppy."

"Thanks for the visit. I just love being with Carol Ann."

The happy day of Serna's graduation arrives. Linda and I drive to the airport with my perfect puppy, Treya. The rest of the pack are left with Cliff. Linda drives the rental car and we arrive at the CCI campus. The air is electric with excitement everywhere as we await the arrival of the dogs from the kennels. We are standing outside as the parade enters the building.

Linda excitedly says, "Oh here she comes." I silently admire my bravest girl as she passes.

Her trainer Todd gives me a smile as they walk by, "She knows who you are." Serna continues in her best behavior until she is released. She flies across the floor landing in my arms. She has matured so much.

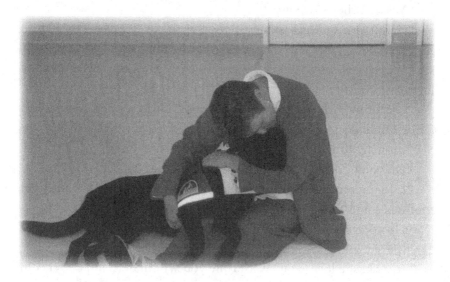

"Serna you look magnificent," Linda keeps repeating cooing in her big ears.

It is time to enjoy meeting her new family. Treya joins the festivities as I get to meet a very smiley Ariana with her Mom, Tamara and stepdad named Robert. Oh boy, perfection again, there is another Robert tied to my working girl. Her Dad, Vinny touches my heart with his words. "Without you puppy raisers we could not be here today, you have our gratitude."

It is Ariana's birthday. When she learned about getting a potential CCI dog she wished for a black lab and she got Serna. Dreams do come true.

Treya sits with Linda as I get to walk across the stage presenting Serna to her Ariana. They certainly are a very happy team.

Afterwards Tamara and Robert drive them to a restaurant where we enjoy a memorable lunch. Both Serna and Treya jump up onto the bench seat beside me and pose side by side. I capture a great shot of the two of them. Treya has a very goofy look on her face while Serna looks at her saying, "You better shape up kid if you plan to be a working dog. You cannot want to just play all the time."

I present Ariana with Serna's first yellow vest, her baby jacket, along with a couple of her favorite toys and photos. As Serna had conveyed during a Leta session, they are all very happy folk. I am most grateful. Ariana seems to be smiling all the time and certainly loves Serna. She is not shy about giving her dog commands. When we finish lunch it is time to say our farewells. Linda holds Treya while I take Serna by the leash and walk aside for a quiet embrace. "Keep up the good work, angel girl. You kept your faith and I shall be forever proud of you and of us. Thank you for your incredible courage."

Ariana is lifted into the back seat and I present her dog back to her. Hugs are shared with the two leggers. Robert is a very jolly soul and a great plus to the day is a hug from a Robert on the eve of Mother's Day. How magically delicious!

The door is pulled shut and they drive away. My heart goes with her. We both faced our moment of goodbye with grace and I know she is in good hands. Linda and I head to the airport. Treya gets extra cuddles.

A couple weeks later I have a grand dog party celebrating the eleventh birthday of Von Spook and graduation of Serna. The fifteen canines outnumber the two leggers for this festive wild pool splashing barking mayhem.

Elisabeth

During July our friend Diane who drives for Federal Express surprises us with a visit. We became acquainted years ago while I was doing the legal work for Robert's estate. She delivered documents which arrived by Fed Ex. She is a dog lover and stops in when in the neighborhood.

"Carol Ann I have a friend Elisabeth who is homebound and could benefit from a dog. You know a lot of people, perhaps you could assist in this."

I somehow sense she is talking about Elisabeth Kubler-Ross who I know lives in the Carefree desert nearby. "Are you talking about Elisabeth Kubler-Ross?"

"Yes."

"Holy jumping Geronimo. I have her books and met her in person at an event in Scottsdale when I was raising Maggie. That is so neat you know her."

"Yes, we met the same way. I deliver packages to her home and we have become friends. I always go by her home to check on her. You could telephone her and arrange a visit."

After Diane leaves I check the phonebook and to my amazement sure enough her number is listed. I take a deep breath and dial the number. A distinctive accent greets my ears with hello. I explain who I am and she tells me to come over tomorrow.

I cannot believe I am going to visit this woman who I have admired and held in the greatest esteem for years regarding her devotion to hospice care. I place Treya's jacket over her wiggley body, "Ok puppy girl we are about to meet a very special woman and you need to be by my side for this memorable moment."

At the entrance to her property is a teepee and a totem pole. Upon entering her home, I hear her voice beckoning me. Since I met her I know her greeting with the ET fingers touching and happily comply with her outstretched finger to mine. She is all smiles especially when her eyes see my Treya. "Now that is the dog for me," she exclaims to my shock.

"Elisabeth, Treya is a service dog in training. She is not my dog."

"Oh no, that cannot be. She must be mine."

We recover from this surprising response and I advise her that I know someone who may be able to find her a dog. I am thrilled to be enjoying her presence in her unique home. "Feel free to explore, you can go see my pool."

I take up her offer and find her indoor lap pool. She has a great collection of unique treasures. I slowly admire her books pausing at the titles of her works. "You may take one with you if you see something you want." I pull a small paperback off the shelf and she nods approvingly adding her autograph.

"After the death of my husband it was a long time before I was able to do any reading. The first book I devoured cover to cover was your "Wheel of Life." I loved your mindset that nothing happens by accident. I have come to be a great believer in synchronicity."

I pause in reflection savoring every moment with this remarkable woman who has done so much for the work of hospice education. My beloved Bobby was able to die in our own bed due to hospice care. She sees my mind awhirling. "What are you thinking now?"

I am pondering the location of her home. "Holy smokes, Elisabeth I am just amazed at how close I live to your home. Awhile ago I started running my dogs in a desert area nearby and I recall seeing this home in the distance. Its unusual shape captured my attention and its white color. I remember an evening drive with the dogs and again I found your home which caught my eye with your Swiss flag and teepee. Now here I am with you."

"As you say, there is no coincidence. We were fated to meet."

A couple days later I do indeed find a four footer. A woman named

Gail who has a small rescue at her desert home just happened to get an older mix named Toot who would be well suited for Elisabeth. "There was a bad fire up north and she just came in. I also have a young black lab puppy if you could possibly foster her until I find a suitable home."

The words lab puppy are always music to my ears and I agree. I have decided that I shall take a break from puppy raising. The coming exit of Saber will take a heavy toll and I think my heart will need to focus more fully on Carol Ann. The next day I greet Elisabeth with Toot and the bundle of puppy in my arms. "We cannot have a dog named Toot, she is a sweetiepie, we shall call her Sweetie."

"Yes, I agree that is much more suitable."

Despite the initial disturbance over not getting Treya she now seems content with the new dog renamed Sweetiepie. We head back home to our pack.

The young puppy seems overly quiet for her age and not very active. I have fallen in love with her without any effort and cuddle her admiring the lovely white patch on her chest. She does enjoy some playtime with Treya. By the next day however I know she is not well. I discover vomit by the bedroom closet and during the night she is in distress with loose poops.

I telephone Gail and she recommends a clinic that will check her without any expense. The little girl and I head out the door. We have a long wait in the room and by the time someone arrives she has left a foul stinky mess on the floor. I hand her over to the person whispering in her ear, "I hope you will be safe and feel better soon. I love you."

However, I sense she will not be bouncing back into my arms and after some waiting I am advised, "She may have parvo and it does not look good for her recovery. The front desk will want to know your plans in case she does not pull through this."

"What do you want us to do with her remains in case of death?"

I am in shock yet respond, "I shall take care of her cremation." She had come into my life for a reason and I wanted to honor that.

In the morning I receive the call that she has not survived the night. Oh sweetest puppy girl, have a safe spirit journey. I am glad I knew you for only our brief time, thank you.

I am very saddened with this news and go over to visit with

Elisabeth. "I could see you had formed a bond with the little one, you were going to keep her weren't you?"

"Yes, I planned to name her Mystic. It is thanks to you that we met so it is no accident as you know."

"Yes of course. She was meant to be with you."

I telephone Leta to share our recent news. She checks in with the departed girl Mystic puppy. Leta senses the pup is very calm asking, "Can we talk with you?"

"Of course, that is why I am here."

"Carol Ann fell in love with you. She was really drawn to you and planned to keep you. It was very disturbing that you were so ill and died."

"I know, yet it was meant to be so."

"Did you feel her connection?"

"Yes for sure. But it was the wrong time. I feel I was supposed to be a puppy with Carol Ann to train for work. Somehow it was not set up properly before my entry."

"Can you tell us anything about what happened to you before meeting Carol Ann?"

Leta sees a little girl in a backyard. Somehow she got loose and her curiosity led her astray.

"Carol Ann thanks you for coming into her life."

The puppy shows Leta that she will be back again. Next she sees the young pup in the arms of Robert which is the vision she received when first connecting with her.

The next evening I invite Gail for supper with Linda and Cliff. "I have decided to get another puppy. This time I want a boy since our beloved Saber will not be of this world for much longer and I want the new one to get to know him."

Gail suggests, "Check the labrador rescue site for the valley and you may find what you desire."

The next day the dogs and I hover over Linda's computer admiring the various photos. There are a couple young labs available and one is a boy. When I discover the location I know that this must the answer. "Linda I need to go right away and check out this puppy. He is at the vet office that did the knee ligament surgery on Spookie."

195

"You are kidding!"

"Nope. I am off and shall return." I head out the door by myself and drive with the determination of sensing my mission is about to be realized.

As I enter the clinic explaining why I am there, the woman points to a lone puppy in a crate. "He is the last of the litter left and no one has shown any interest in him for some reason. He has been living here for a month." She pulls him out and places him in my open arms.

He is four months old and very gangly with a long body and legs. "What is your name little guy?"

The woman looks on his paperwork replying, "He is named Little Devil."

"Well now, that is a most inappropriate name. How would you like to come live with me? You will have a large family awaiting your arrival. Your new name shall be Mystic." It is July 17, 2002.

We drive to Linda's for the full introductions to all of his new family. Awhile later all of us pile into the Labaru and head home. I soon discover that my new pup has challenges. He has not been exposed to much living in a crate at a vet office. The television frightens him and any loud noise puts him in unease. A puppy needs constant affections and attentions to develop without phobias and my little guy certainly is fearful.

Treya is not totally approving of having a younger four legger intervering with my attentions and gives him some grief.

One day I am blessed with a visit from Elisabeth. Her healing friend Joseph agrees to bring her over. He wheels her around our home and we sit out in the backyard surrounded with all the dogs. "I like your home. It is very comfortable." Her stay is brief yet I am so pleased with her visit.

While seeing Elisabeth next I am surprised to see the Tibetan Buddhist Rinpoche in her kitchen fixing her lunch. He is attired in a Hawaiian shirt and shorts sporting his customary smile. As he hands Elisabeth her food, she notices our ease with each other. "You guys have already met?"

"Yes, when Serna was a young pup she went with me to a Buddhist gathering with the Rinpoche and prior to her turn in to school he came to our home to bless her. Your blessing was most beneficial. She graduated in May working for a young girl in Pomona, California."

"I am pleased to hear this. Congratulations."

When he departs Elisabeth talks about her ties with the Dalai Lama and the fact she has been in his personal presence more than once. We share some heart to heart conversation as she inquires about my Roberto. She notices his ring hanging around my neck and inspects it up close with great curiosity. "You have been well blessed in love I see. He is still around you."

"Yes, I know and thank you for your wisdom. Our love is a one of a kind. Have you experimented with penduluming?"

"Of course." She takes his ring on the chain and allows it to respond to a query. She then shares a most extraordinary story with me. "Your beautiful chocolate lab Saber came to visit me last night."

I am at a loss for words. Elisabeth is well versed in experiences considered unusual or farout. I have read about astral travel so I assume he left his body and came to check on her. "Did he say anything?"

"Not really. It was a meeting of hearts which required no spoken language between us. He is a very special dog you have there."

"Yes, I am well aware. He is a most remarkable evolved being within a glorious dog body. Robert was well guided in his discovery."

At some point I realize that the dog Toot will not be well suited to live with her because she lives alone and the dog cannot be adequately provided for. I do not know what I had been thinking in agreeing to do this for her but my excitement had clouded my judgment. I bravely tell her that Toot will not be coming to live with her and I shall find her another home.

Smoke comes out her ears as I am enveloped in the wrath of an upset Elisabeth. This woman does not take kindly to not getting her way yet neither do I, so I understand. I listen to her rage on at me and leave her alone. The next couple visits she is subdued and barely speaks to me yet I will not stop seeing her. Finally she does come back around and is more sociable with me.

Our Mexican pool man Chano has taken a genuine liking to Toot. Each week he gives her extra attentions saying, "This is a really nice dog."

"She needs to find a good home. Would you be interested?"

"I need to check with my family and bring my son to meet her."

"Of course, you could come anytime."

The next day he arrives with the young boy and I witness a perfect match for this rescue dog. They agree to adopt her and I sigh with relief that she has gone to a home with a young boy who can help heal her ailing heart. I know she misses her home and her person. Gail told me that the woman had to go live in assisted living and the dog was not allowed.

Sometime later I learn from Diane that Elisabeth has been hospitalized and she shares where she has gone. With Treya by my side I go to see her. I am greeted with big smiles when we enter her room. My perfect puppy lies on the bed beside her and the two of us listen as Elisabeth shares many a tale about this and that. She has a box of Swiss chocolate by her bedside and encourages me to help myself.

Thankfully I have my camera friend and I capture a series of shots with Treya in different positions. The two of them certainly seem to have an instantaneous rapport and bond.

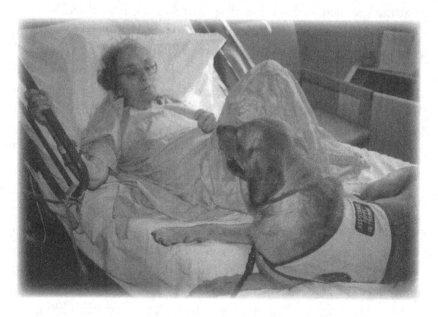

I now have another guest dog in our home. While out recently I ran into a woman who shared that her son has a skilled companion dog from CCI. We chatted a long time and she asked if I would be willing to take care of his dog while they went on vacation. I agree to do so and pick up some extra money in doing this. Our home is now becoming overrun with four legged angels since the rescue lady has asked me to take in a couple more dogs. She is pleased that Toot has gone to a great home and trusts in my abilities of finding homes for dogs. She has a beautiful black lab without a tail. Some dreadful human had removed its tail as a pup. The dog had been in the pound for a long time and was scheduled for euthanasia until dear Gail rescued her. I could not say no to fostering her when she told me this story.

I go bring her home and name her Beauty. Also there is another mix which I bring home. This brings the dog count up to nine. I am shocked myself when I see the number of tails gathering around me at suppertime. The next day I receive a surprise pop in visit from my friend Karen. She has one yellow lab of her own. The instant she sees all the dogs she exclaims, "My God, have you lost your mind! Who are all these dogs? Are you having a nervous breakdown, this is crazy."

"Nothing crazy going on here. There is no need for concern. I am extremely happy and have gone a little dog crazed but in a good way. Let me introduce you to our new four leggers. Saber is in his decline so this is a young black lab I just adopted from lab rescue. He is named Mystic.

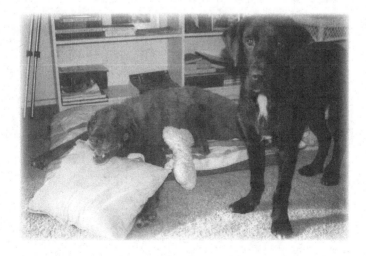

This yellow lab is a working dog whose family is on vacation. This small black mixture is a rescue I am fostering. And this lovely tailless girl is another rescue I have named Beauty."

She chatters away updating me with her news and leaves a few minutes later. I return to my happy tail wagging gang and chuckle to myself over my dog blessed life.

Shortly after the arrival of Beauty I am visiting with a store employee at a grocery I frequent. The woman is a real dog lover and talks about wanting to find one. I have a good sense about her and tell her about Beauty. A day later she arrives with her roommate to our doorstep and it is love at first sight. Beauty is now where she belongs. Gail has found a home for the other young mix so the dog count is now dropped by two. The family of the CCI dog has returned from vacation and I witness a happy reunion. I am now back to my own pack of six dogs.

Saber and Robert Reunite

The dogs have been enjoying their new raw food which resulted from Saber's refusing to eat the commercial dry kibble. Saber being the oldest has been the most challenged with detoxification. It has finally settled down thankfully. The discharges around his eyes have stopped and his poops are firm again. He has thinned significantly and is becoming challenged with getting up. He cannot always make it outside before he has to poop and I often have a surprise to clean up. He has exceeded the normal lifespan of a large breed dog since he is now approaching his fifteenth year.

On September 9, I happen to notice him squatting getting ready to poop next to our kitchen entry. To my horror I notice something foreign slowly coming from his bowels. He is straining to release it and I know he needs my help. I wrap my hand in something and pull. Whatever it is keeps coming. I have heard of dogs swallowing strange things but what the heck is this? I finally have hold of it and decide to throw it in the washing machine for a couple cycles.

He has swallowed over two feet of rope. During one of my many outings with puppy girl Saber decided to occupy himself. I have a toy dangling from a long rope hung in a tree for the pups so perhaps he chewed part off. Hard to know.

The vet is quite shocked when I share this tale with her the next day. This could account for the challenges with his food. It is a miracle that the rope did not get tangled up inside him. There is no way of knowing how long this has been inside him either. What a boy! Robert must be keeping a good eye on him is all that I can surmise with this blessed evacuation.

Saber loves to retrieve anything which I throw into the pool. He loves to carry his bowl around and one day it falls in the pool. It floats around and he catches sight of it and goes to get it out. I go inside the house and put all the bowls into the pool. I watch with delight as he patiently retrieves every one of them. Even in his weakened state he is still obsessed with getting the bowls.

The prospect of Saber's death is very hard for me to deal with and brings the pains of Robert's decline and death to the forefront. As I witness the decline of my dog I am reliving those memories. He will be my first dog to assist in death and I cannot bear the thought.

Thankfully, the vet is available to come to our home. I could never endure the agony of taking my dog to a sterile, cold, vet table to have them exit this world. They deserve the best of tender loving care in their own environment surrounded with all their family.

Saber is now unable to get up on his own. I resort to putting a bath towel under his belly and hoisting him up. He staggers outside and even stumbles in and out of the pool for brief swims. I keep a close eye on him. His weakened legs somehow get him up to the pool step and

I help him out. He shakes happily and comes inside on his bed for a well-deserved nap and a treat.

We live with this new routine for a few days until I finally realize he needs to be released from his frail body. I sit quietly with him and tell him I shall set up a time for the vet to assist him. I am teary eyed calling Linda with the plan. "Can you come over tomorrow? The vet is coming to assist Saber around two. I want us to give him a special last treat. We can drive up the road to the little golf course hill. It ought to be quiet that time of day. We can have a picnic with Saber for his last treat."

"I shall be there and bring him something."

"We thank you friend, see you then."

I help my tired dog into the car and carry him up to the top of the grassy knoll. He happily devours everything placed before him. Linda captures some great photos of our Saber and me. It is a very special time shared between the three of us. I know that Roberto is by our side.

We arrive home and I help him onto his bedroom bed. The vet arrives about an hour later. The young puppies make an entrance and all the pack gathers around. The mood is very sombre and quiet as I position myself next to him on his bed. Spirit holds a close position watching my every move. Spookie is next to us as well as she witnesses her Dad and best companion about to leave this world. I lean over him for a last embrace.

The vet inquires, "Are you ready for this Carol Ann?"

"Yes, we are."

With tears streaming down my face I watch the vet check for a pulse and say, "He is gone." It has all happened so fast, I cannot believe it. I lean over him feeling his body which now is silent. Unbelievable! The vet leaves and I am left with my lifeless dog.

I do not want to move his body. The cremation place expects me in early evening so we have the rest of the afternoon to allow his spirit to linger around all of us. I know he has been well received and welcomed by Robert and his canine family. I decide to smoke a cigar.

Linda's Cliff enjoys a good cigar occasionally and sometimes offers one to me as well. Robert smoked big cigars when we first met on the oil rig and I still love their scent. Spirits on the other side can use scent as a message. He has often delighted me with this gift of cigar smoke in unusual places just to let me know of his presence. Linda lights it for me as I sit next to Saber. It is somehow very comforting for me to be smoking a cigar at this traumatic time. Spirit keeps her close vigil over me while Spookie lies next to the body of Saber.

Amber keeps her distance and has fallen into slumber. Treya and Mystic come make their sniffs of his dead form. I am grateful Linda is available and stays with all of us. When the time comes I carry his body out to the car and place him inside. "Come on all of you puppies, we all need to go deliver our Saber boy to the cremation man." Linda offers to drive and I gladly accept. Spookie, Spirit, Amber, Mystic and Treya take their positions in the car as we all drive in silence.

As we drive home without him Linda offers, "Would you like to come to our place? I can fix us some comfort mashed potatoes and chicken for us."

"That would be most welcome, thank you dear friend. Yes, I am not quite ready to face home without Saber."

His birthday is November 9 and I blow up some balloons in his honor. Ever silly Treya takes delight in finding certain ones to pop. I sense Saber and Robert looking on with delight.

Treya Turn In and Serna Reunion

In early November I receive the turn in date for wild girl Treya which is Nov 16. Linda makes her reservation to join us. I want this turn in to be different from the previous four working girls. I want to mark it with a festive ending. "Linda, I am going to call Serna's family and ask if we can see them. They live close to CCI, don't they?"

"Yes, for sure I can drive us. It would not take long to reach their home. How about we rent a convertible and we can pull up to her home in grand style."

"Hey that sounds great. I like that idea of the wind in our hair after turning in Treya. This time it is going to be special. She is my joy puppy and I intend to cross that CCI stage with a smile instead of the torn heart and sobs. I do not have another puppy coming when she leaves."

"We could fly out of the Ontario airport so you could see the Laverne guide dog poster."

"Really, that would be the true icing on the cake after turning in our joy girl and seeing Serna. On the last trip to California with Robert we flew out of that airport."

"Yes, I remember you sharing that story. Well this is meant to be thanks to your Bobby girl."

I recall the day of the call from Linda. I had answered the phone to hear her share, "CA, you will not believe what I am looking at?"

"Where are you and what are you talking about?"

"I am in the Ontario, California airport. The guide dog poster of Laverne is on a wall here. It is magnificent. Somehow you must see this."

I was beside myself and so very grateful that my friend flew for her business otherwise I would not have heard this. I had called my parents upon hanging up the phone with her. Mom and Dad could not believe their ears either when I shared the story. Dad had kindly said, "I hope you are writing all of this down for a story in your future book."

My mind jumps back into the present as I next hear Linda share, "I will get us a bottle of wine. We can toast the joy puppy as we leave the school."

"Oh my yes, that sounds perfect."

Tamara and Robert welcome our plan and invite us to stay the night instead of going home the same day. I am beside myself with jubilation at the prospect of seeing Serna in her home environment and having the prize ending of admiring Laverne on the wall at the Ontario airport.

Mystic and Treya have formed a bond of puppy partnership enjoying the pool together. She has finally stopped jumping on him after he jumps in. She certainly was naughty to dunk him. They do both compete for my affections yet that is ok. She is my perfect puppy with her imperfections, what a girl. Mystic will miss his best playmate.

Linda and I make our last outing with Treya going into a bookstore. She loves to dance with me so I ask Linda to take a photo of pup and I. We are in the music section of the store and I place the headphones on Treya. She happily complies to my commands of forward and back.

Her farewells are made with her pack and it is time to head for the plane. She relishes in the extra attentions from the flight crew as they assist us into our bulkhead seating. We pull into CCI and I receive the blue cape for turn in. We head over to the ceremony and join the many puppies parading around. We find our seats.

I am able to get through the event without a tear while Treya seems to have ants in her pants. Despite the flower essences she has been receiving she cannot sit still. I know she is anxious about having to leave me but it must be done. Our moment comes and I get up to join the long line of puppy raisers waiting to cross the stage. Linda takes my camera and moves to a suitable position to capture us crossing the stage.

Our names are called and we proceed up to the stage. I take my turn in diploma in hand and walk across with a big grin. I am triumphant. I have done it all on my own. Treya is my fifth puppy and this time my heart is filled with joy instead of sorrow. I take my seat again and lift her into my arms for a wiggley cuddle. "Good girl, you will be alright. I love you."

The ceremony is over and it is now time for the real test for both of us. I want to let her go without the tears and feel confident I shall succeed. We let her run in the side yard. I give her more essences and a long last cuddle. Linda holds her close and we go inside to join the lineup of sombre puppy raisers.

Treya is now more subdued and when the man comes to take her by the leash she walks away calmly. My demeanor remains steady focused on staying out of any sorrow. I let her go without shedding a tear. She is gone from sight but not my heart. Linda and I walk outside looking toward the kennels. "Be brave Treya, I will miss you. Be brave perfect girl." I do not hear a whimper from her. Good girl. We turn and head to the parking lot.

Linda retrieves the bottle of chardonnay and raises a toast. "You did it CA. Congratulations."

"Yes indeedy I did, didn't I. Wow. It all felt so good and right. I am so grateful that Treya has been the puppy to allow me to bless her departure with joy. May the right choices be made on her behalf. Let's go see our Bobby precious dog Serna. I want to see where she lives."

"Whooee, yes me too. I am ready." The top is lowered on the convertible and we head north with the wind blowing our smiles ever upward. We pull up to the home of Ariana and are greeted with a boisterous welcome. There is a bottleneck at the door as Serna hears my voice and neither of us can contain our excitement.

Ariana wheels her power chair expertly zipping around the room. "How did your turn in go?"

"Actually this one went very well. Unlike the other four turn ins this time I did it with a smile, right Linda."

"Yup, she sure did. It was amazing."

"Good for you." I receive a welcome hug from Tamara and her Robert. Ariana introduces us to her dogs Mindy and Scamp, proudly displaying their ability to fly into her lap on command. She has a large bunny in a pen in their backyard. Both Linda and I take turns on the floor with the black beauty. How good it is to see her again.

When it is time to feed her I am all chuckles. "Look at that, she still lays down to eat her food."

We spend a very relaxed enjoyable evening together taking photos and sharing photos. My Bobby girl is well loved there is no doubt. I lift her into my lap for a photo. She fills the chair; she certainly is a big girl now.

The next day it is time to say our farewells. They all join us outside and wave as we drive away. "Wow, Linda what an awesome time that was, eh!"

"Oh yes, for sure. I am so very, very glad we came. She has such a great home. Aree is remarkable."

"Yes for sure, she is a very special young girl and now even more blessed with our Bobby pup to share her life."

At the Ontario airport I am most eager to go inside and find the photo of Miss Laverne. "You won't draw security to us with loud squeals when you see it, will you?"

"I will not make too loud a noise for that but certainly I shall not be silent either. Come on let's go, I want to see this."

"Ok, I am coming. I have your camera ready for this grand event."

The airport is very small. Within moments I am standing with my mouth hanging open gazing at the poster of my Bobby Magic Angel reading its wording, "When I grow up I want to be a guide dog."

"This is beyond belief incredible. What a totally perfect ending to the turn in of my perfect puppy. Robert and I flew out of this very airport on our last trip to California."

"Yes I know, it is all quite unbelievable and the fact that Serna lives so close. She is a Bobby girl for sure."

I return home to a boisterous welcome from my four leggers. Our pack has been downsized by two dogs in less than a month. I am joyful about my trip to California yet very much in shock. About a week later we receive a visit from sister Valerie for about five days. The fact that she has come so soon after the death of Saber is most propitious. I recall upon returning home after burying Robert she had offered to visit and I had declined. When I got home from Montana I could not bear to be around anyone for any length of time, wanting only to be alone with the dogs. Here she is now after Sabe's death and the turn in of Treya. I am grateful.

Dearest Treya Treasure

Dec. 20, 2002

Hello to you my silliest puppy. All of your family send their love. It is now five weeks since we parted; so short a time, yet it seems so long. Your fate is yet to be decided. I remind you to trust in what I impart to you energetically. We both need to trust in the people handling you making the right decision regarding your path.

Whatever is to the highest good for both of us we will manifest in perfect form, for you are my Bobby Perfect Angel. All will be well in our world, you will see. You must stay true to yourself, Treya. Be yourself first of all.

From the moment I saw you Treya I knew you were different from my previous four working puppies. Your butterscotch honey color took my breath away. You were exactly what I needed, a change in color and personality. Immediately, I dedicated you as my Bobby Perfect Angel. In reality, you did not always possess the perfect working girl behavior, yet we did our best together as you shall now also.

Gratefully the previous four girls paved the way for you and our work together. Each of them literally walked me through tumultuous shifts rocking me to the very core and helping create my new Carol Ann self. Thanks to all of you I have reinvented myself.

After Robert's death I had named myself Humpty Dumpty. The existence I had created for myself was one of incessant agitation of inner and outer torment. Yet I was divinely blessed with labrador retrievers.

Labs are incessant in the art of retrieving. Each puppy along with Saber and Spookie became loyal to the retrieval of my shattered self, pasting my humpty dumptyness together over and over. You proved to be an excellent retriever. With you by my side, I reclaimed long lost parts of myself allowing Carol Ann to become more complete.

I am forever grateful for our time together, dearest puppy girl. Continue to be brave. Know the best will come for you. Stay true to Treya. Sweet dreams.

P.S. Treya just a couple hours after writing you this letter the phone rang and it was CCI informing me of your release.

Dec. 21, 2002

Dearest angel puppy,

Hi my sweetest girl. I trust you have seen my visions sent to you that you will be coming home soon. I know you have been under serious stress, your training report shows this in my mind. Be patient, you will be back in your fullest joy soon.

Shortly after writing your letter yesterday I went out for a while. I came home to a phone message from Val with CCI. Her message was, "Please call me Carol Ann." My heart skipped a beat when I heard the message. I had just received a training report so I sensed this was news of your release.

I calmed myself and made the call. Her immediate words were, "Treya is being released."

I reply, "I thought perhaps this was so. I had hopes for her yet she was never consistent in her work. This is for our best. She belongs home with all of us. I want to adopt her."

My emotions became an intensity of relief, disappointment, sorrow and joy all in that order. I shared my thoughts with Val who completely understood since she had raised her own puppies. In six years I had become hooked on puppy raising. It is my passion.

You will have your spaying surgery in a couple days and then soon after you will get to come home. She told me to call her in a day or so to discuss how we will bring you home.

Being a puppy raiser is definitely a profoundly bittersweet experience. One needs to personally experience it to understand the wide range of emotions involved in this endeavor of the heart. It is very tough on you puppies. Treya, you must never feel you have failed since your trainers found you unsuited. You are very special to have been born as a service puppy, yet as you know only a small number succeed.

I had three graduates in a row, so I am due for a return puppy. I am ecstatic that it will be you my joy girl, my best retriever of my fragmented soul. It has been a tough year with the deaths of Terrace and Saber. I sense that both those wise labs will agree your place is to be home with us. So, be patient angel girl. Soon we shall be reunited. Your fulltime name will now be Treasure.

A chapter in my life is coming to a close. My decision to take a break from puppy raising has indeed been divinely blessed with your return into my life. You shall become a certified therapy dog allowing Spirit to retire. Your effervescent joy must be shared. It brings tears to my eyes to fully realize this break from puppy raising is official. I am going to need your help in this regard but you are the perfect medicine. The universe has been watching out for us. Thanks to you and all the dogs, my life is blessed beyond imagination compared to where I was six years ago.

Forgive the mixture of emotions you are feeling from me. Know that I am overjoyed you will be home. A physically challenged person has lost the opportunity to have you in their life, yet as you always knew in that wise boundless heart you are to be my partner for life. Remember my ear to ear grin when we walked across the stage at turn in. That was because of you dear puppy. I am responsible for my own joy yet you played a vital role. I am the full joy of my Carol Ann Joy.

I send you patience through our golden cord. From my heart centre I envision a beautiful golden white cord travelling through time and space to your heart there in California. So you see we are attached just as we always were destined to be in this life.

You may not have the service dog temperament but to me you are perfect. Thanks for your imperfections as a future working dog. I am triumphant in knowing we shall be together. I sense new doors are opening for us.

All of your buddies wish you sweet dreams. Mystic will be overjoyed to have his best playmate back by his side. On New Year's Eve you will be home in your own bed and we shall all start the new year together. I picked our reunion day with this intent. Sweet dreams. See you soon.

Always love from your partner and best friend,
Your Joyful Carol Ann

Guardian Angel Dog

On December 12, I receive a training report from CCI. Treya is taking too long to recover when she is startled. They will work with her. I send her my encouragement reminding her to do her best.

I return a phone call message from CCI on Dec. 20. Treya has been released from training. The best news is she will become our dog. I make a phone call to Leta to ensure that my perfect girl understands what is happening.

Leta conveys that Treya shows confusion and puzzlement. Treya says, "My heart was in it and I understood about the program. But I am just not cut out for it despite my efforts."

"It is ok, Carol Ann knows you did your best. You will be going home to her." Treya is euphoric. She cannot believe it, she was not totally sure. "Remember she told you this would be the case if you did not work out."

"Yes, yes, I remember now."

"Carol Ann is also in a state of shock which is why you have been getting mixed messages from her. She says that you will probably continue to be a bit confused until you actually see her at the airport. She is extremely happy you will be coming home. It is also difficult for her because she knows you were put into the program for a purpose and yet like with Spirit she is now finding out that you are actually meant to be hers for life. It will just take some adjustment for all of you."

Treya responds in a subdued manner, "Yes, but I always thought I was hers."

"I understand. You probably had a knowing that was closer to the truth than anyone else did. You will have a major place in her life and the household. Do you know this?"

Treya becomes very humbled. "I know I have problems and wonder if I really deserve this."

"Yes, you do. Things will be quite different as everyone adjusts to knowing that you are part of her life forever. It is a whole different mindset, you will see."

Treya sees what Leta means and responds it will take some time to process this.

"Take your time. Again the reason you are picking up so many signals from Carol Ann is because she also is processing a lot of realizations. But everything is alright. She cannot wait for you to get home. Carol Ann says you will now always be called by your new name, Treasure. Do you like it?"

"Yes." Leta says she is very proud and yet very shy about it also.

"Carol Ann says she has decided you are all going to have your Christmas on the day you come home. There will be balloons for you also and presents." Treya gets really excited with this news.

Leta shares with her about the upcoming spaying surgery and explains she will be a little sore but will recover quickly. "Carol Ann will remind you every day you are coming home soon. Ten days after your surgery you will be taken to the airport and put into a crate to fly home in the cargo hold on a plane. She will be there to get you the instant she sees your crate."

Treya says this sounds scary to her.

"Keep the vision of going home and feel the golden energy cord connecting the two of you."

I am grateful for our communications with perfect puppy and relieved she now fully understands what will happen to her. Christmas is a quiet one without Saber and Treya Treasure. I do not do the normal routine since we will have festivities upon her return. I have talked to CCI again and her surgery is set up for Dec. 27. I share with Val that I will pick her up instead of the plane plan. She does not need the added stress of being in the cargo hold of a plane by herself. I set up another session with Leta to advise our pup.

Leta tunes into Treya who jumps up as the connection is made. "Yes, puppy it is us. We want you to know there is a change in plans. You will have the surgery tomorrow and then guess what. A couple days later Carol Ann and Spirit will come pick you up at school to bring you home."

Treya goes totally bananas. "You mean I do not have to wait? Can I go in the pool?"

"That is right. She understands your fear of the plane and wants you home as soon as possible. You will still have stitches in you so need to be a little careful. You will be able to go in the pool soon. Carol Ann wants you to share how your time there at school has been for you."

Treya shows Leta that she was often depressed. Then she would become hyper to counterbalance. She knew she was supposed to be paying attention but she just could not really do it. This made her feel bad too.

"Do you feel different now?"

Treya conveys to Leta a sobering effect. Being away from everything and everyone she loved in a setting she did not understand had a big impact on her. Leta asks, "Do you feel like you know more now?"

Treya shows she has more skills but without context. She does not know how or when to use what she has been taught.

"Carol Ann wants you to know when you get home there will be a few places she will be able to take you but you will have to learn to wait in the car and sometimes to stay home. When you are out seeing people who know you there may be some feedback indicating that in some way you did not live up to expectations. People can be insensitive and not understand how it was for you. But you must remember how successful you are and disregard this kind of energy. You are fulfilling your destiny in being with Carol Ann and the pack."

Treya becomes wiggley happy upon hearing of the destiny vision. "Do you understand what I am saying about all of this?"

"Yes, I think so. I can just ignore any remarks if they do not feel right for me."

"Yes, that is very wise and perfect. Do you remember the day she took you to school?"

"How could I ever forget that?"

"In the moments that she was hugging you bye there was a man waiting to walk you to the kennel. Carol Ann was totally amazed how you were able to go with him so calmly and without fear. Part of this feeling was because during the ceremony you had ants in your pants and could not sit still. Can you tell her about this?"

"Yes, it was because I knew it was the moment of our truth. Her demeanour was what created mine. We both knew I had to do this and she was ready and so I had to be. I was very nervous in the ceremony as the moment was building up but then it came and I understood. What else could I do? I could not disappoint Carol Ann."

"Thank you Treasure. That is very moving. You are amazing."

Leta can hear my crying over the phone and shares this. "Carol Ann has tears in her eyes and could not be more grateful for you sharing all this with her. Do you have anything else to say?"

"Hurry, hurry, hurry come get me." She puts her paw up.

"Thank you sweetest puppy. Patience, your reunion is coming soon."

Next Leta wants to tune into Saber. He shows up before he is even asked. He is all smiles sharing, "I am so proud of you both, Carol Ann and Treya Treasure."

"Carol Ann is wondering if you had anything to do with Treya's coming back?"

Saber has a glint in his eye twinkling at Leta answering, "I did visit her. I talked to her during times she was resting."

"What did you tell her?"

"I told her to do her best but not to let her spirit die."

"Thank you, so you agree she is supposed to be back?"

"How else could it be for her joy puppy? She and Carol Ann have work to do together."

"Yes, Carol Ann has sensed the same thing. How are you doing? Do you come around the house anymore?"

He shows Leta a vision of him running free in the sky. "Yes, I check in everyday with all of them but I usually do not stay long now."

"Carol Ann wants to know any insights about Mystic puppy."

"He needs to be protected a lot. He has a broken spirit and heart that will take a long time to heal. He came into this life with it. He is a very special soul but it is hidden behind his wounds. He is very tender. I am so glad Carol Ann understands him."

"Thank you. She really misses you. Christmas was tough."

"I was there. I shall be watching the joyous reunion and do not forget to get balloons for Treya."

"Thanks wise boy."

Next we communicate with Mystic. Leta shares he is a magnificent spirit with a huge heart. "Carol Ann wants to tell you that Treya will be home soon. She has been very homesick and will require a lot of extra attentions. You will now have to share the affections of Carol Ann."

He just listens without any response. "You and Treya will make a great team and become best friends. How do you feel about everything?"

He shares his anxiety and the feeling of heartbreak Saber shared. "That is why you are with Carol Ann. Do not worry; she will take care of you. There are a lot of people with the same feelings. It can be very difficult but you will all help each other. Your life is going to be very good."

Leta recommends some flower essences for Mystic.

"Spirit can we check in with you?"

"Yes, I am here. It is great she is coming home. She can help with some of the chores."

"You are right yes. Carol Ann will start work with Treya so you can retire as a therapy dog now." She thumps her tail in happy agreement.

"Yeah, I know I am going to California to bust her out of school. That will be a big surprise, I can't wait to go in there and kind of shock Treya."

"Well, she knows you are coming."

She expresses disappointment that Carol Ann has told Treya already since she wanted to surprise her. "I am sorry, but she probably would have seen this anyway."

"Yes, you are right."

"Is there anything else you want to tell us?"

Spirit shows Leta she is being very solicitous with Mystic. He needs careful taking care of. She shows the day when Carol Ann was visiting a friend with an elderly Mom. She planned to take Mystic with her but the friend suggested leaving him in her backyard. She was not sure about this but left him. They were gone about an hour and when she came back to her friend's home he came charging up when she got out of the car. He had wiggled his way out through a grated gate with a screen over it and was running from house to house. He was a mess, whimpering and crying looking for her.

Leta checks back in with Mystic. "Do you understand that Carol Ann would never leave you for good?"

He understands but cannot be away from her at all at this point. "Thank you Mystic for staying close to the house. You were very strong and good to stay close and find her. She will be most careful with you from now on. You will always be her dog and she will not leave you."

Spookie comes in next and Leta asks if she misses Saber. "I cannot really miss him. I am aware of when he comes. I was worried about his condition and am glad he has left his ailing body."

"That is very good, Spooks."

"Yes, I can be a wise old gal."

"Do you have anything else to tell us?"

"I will be glad when Treya comes home. Those two puppies can keep each other busy and leave me alone."

Amber just wants to sleep. She understands about Treya coming home and is glad the two puppies will be able to play together and not interact with her. She wants to be left alone.

Leta checks in momentarily with Maggie at her home in Colorado. "Carol Ann wants you to know how proud she is of you. She understands what a difficult job you have. She knows that your girl Joy and her Mom love you very much."

"Yes, that is true. It is a different environment than what I grew up with but I am adjusting to it."

"Carol Ann says that she wants to be able to see you again sometime in the next few months."

"Oh yes, I hope that can be so. Thank you."

On December 30 all of us drive over to Linda and Cliff's. Spookie, Amber and Mystic are left at their home while Spirit and I head for the freeway and California. "Alright Lollipop, let's go bust that perfect puppy out of boot camp." Spirit lays her broad head contentedly in my lap with a big sigh. Both of us are breathing in the vision of our reunion a few hours away, all is in divine perfection. My first guide dog puppy career changed is to be by my side to adopt my CCI career change puppy who is my fifth and last dog to train. How magically perfect!

Upon arriving to the school Spirit jumps out of the car enthusiastically. With a prance in her step we enter the front door and introduce ourselves. "We are here to pick up our puppy Treya, who has been released."

The CCI lady admires my beautiful yellow lab. "This is my first pup that I raised for Guide Dogs for the Blind, her name is Spirit. She has helped to raise four more working puppies including Treya."

Spirit sits proudly by my side as I sign the paperwork for the adoption. "Ok, let me go get that girl of yours."

"Oh my, we like the sound of those words, don't we Spirit."

Both myself and Spirit pace back and forth panting with excitement. I hear the thud of a door at the end of the hallway. It is the entrance from the kennels. And there she is. A calm Treya on a loose leash enters. I cannot control myself and say her name. The moment she hears my voice she pulls on the leash. "Please let her come to me."

The woman drops her leash. Treya flies down the hallway crashing into the open arms of myself and Spirit. The three of us are enveloped in a big furry wiggley embrace. In the excitement their leashes get dropped. Both dogs take advantage and prance together running down the hallway entering the open door to a training room. The CCI woman charges after them. "Oh no!"

There must be someone in the room working dogs. I cannot help but laugh to think that both of my career change puppies in their last encounter with a school are both being naughty. She gathers both dogs and hands their leashes to me. "Thank you so much, it must be time for us to make our exit. Happy New Year's Eve."

The three of us head outside and into the car. I take them over to the building where the CCI ceremonies are performed. Both the girls charge around chasing each other. If I had four legs myself perhaps I could keep up. After a good run they jump joyfully into the car and we head to our motel room. We eat our supper and they enjoy peanut butter marrow bone treats and Treya falls into an exhausted sleep on the floor.

I lift her onto the bed without her even waking up and lay cuddled next to her. Spirit snuggles in close to both of us. In the middle of the night something wakes all of us up. I turn on the bedside light. Treya has a look of disbelief on her face when she sees me. "Yes, it is me for real sweet puppy. You are not dreaming." Then she sees Spirit, displaying another look of disbelief. In the next moment the two dogs burst into raucous play wrestling with each other. All three of us are laughing and rolling around on the bed together.

We all settle back into sleep and I awaken exhausted but blissful. It is time to head home. They have a good morning run and both fall back into deep sleep as we head to the freeway.

After lunch I find another place to run both of them. Treya settles back asleep with her head resting on my lap while Spirit snoozes on the back seat. I am in need of another coffee. It is not my routine to drink a lot of caffeine but my head to becoming too heavy and droopy. It is time to look for a stop.

After entering a freeway exit I notice a disheveled man with a dog at the side of the road. They are an odd looking pair. Something about him catches my attention. I drive on and get my caffeine fix. I sip it gratefully and head up the exit ramp for the freeway where to my surprise the same man with his dog on a long rope is now hitchhiking.

I study him as we pass. I park the car. I walk toward him, "If your dog is well behaved you could come with us. I have two labs in the car."

"He will be fine."

"Ok, good. I am Carol Ann."

He shakes my outstretched hand, "Thank you. I am Irish and my dog is Jack."

The three dogs make their own acquaintances with lots of sniffing. Irish climbs into the back seat with his arm around Jack. Treya resumes her navigator position. My own nose is getting a workout. After a few minutes all the dogs fall into sleep. I share the tale of my girls. Irish shares, "This Spirit of yours certainly is a groovy dog."

"Yes, for sure you are right about that. She is extra special indeed."

We chat with each other as I continue to sip my coffee. What a blessing this has turned out to be. I had become dangerously unfit to drive. I silently thank my angels and my husband in spirit who no doubt has played a hand in this event. Irish lives in Phoenix and is in no hurry to return home. After a couple hours of travelling together he says, "You can let us out anywhere there is services."

We pull into the parking lot of a McDonalds. I take a photo of the two of them as Irish proudly displays the dancing ability of Jack. As we shake hands I pass him a bill. "Safe travels to both of you."

I am rejuvenated as we head back on to the freeway this time without any more coffee. "Thanks girls, for both being so good with Jack. Tonight is New Year's Eve and we shall all start the new year in grand style." I lay my arm over my blissed out pup as she dreams of home.

All of the pack transitions comfortably with our perfect girl being home again. Treya becomes a certified therapy dog and Spirit settles into her retirement enjoying staying home more. I have had a custom made blue working vest made for Treasure which she wears on our outings to drive cancer patients. It has therapy dog embroidered on it along with her name and a butterfly. Every time she sees me picking it up along with my big bag she comes running. She is ready to work. Therapy work suits her perfectly and she wiggles her way into many hearts putting smiles where there previously were none.

Treasure Doghouse Day

Toward the end of May I throw a big dog party with all of our usual guests both two legged and four. I have been recently enjoying some new musical delights with the sounds of a didgeridoo. I put it on loud and jump in the pool thrashing around happily to the music. People look startled to the strange sounds. Linda goes inside and changes the cd to some jazz music. I say nothing but instantly feel my inner knowing talking to me. Thanks to her switching the music, I can literally feel a response within my whole being telling me, Carol Ann it is time for you to leave Arizona. I feel a palpable shift happening in the very moment the didgeridoo music is turned off. I am shocked yet pleased at the same time. Wow, could this really be true I ask myself. Again I feel a positive response overcoming me.

This sensation continues to grow and I know I have reached a turning point which cannot be ignored. It is a big decision to know where we shall go and I instantly think of Nova Scotia, yet the harsh winters would be too tough on us. I want to live near the ocean so next I think of Vancouver Island. Yes, that must be where we are meant to go.

I telephone my parents and family to share my plan about moving. It is now time to share it with Linda and Cliff. I invite them for supper. My news is greeted with stunned silence and then tears from Linda. "I cannot believe you are leaving. I have learned so much through our friendship. I understand why you feel the need to leave but I am not ready for this."

"I understand your shock but I truly cannot continue to stay here.

This will be very difficult for me to leave here. I value our friendship greatly and it shall not end because of this. Perhaps it shall grow in a whole new way because I believe this will be to the highest good for all of us."

I awaken in the morning numb and immobilized as I recall the evening with dearest Linda and Cliff. I need to clear my head and decide a leisurely desert drive is in order. The dogs eagerly jump into the Labaru and I head for Starbucks for a treat. As I wait in line to place my order the music plays a Linda song. She is always finding new favorite songs. This one speaks to lightening up. I am all smiles inside and out as I exit into the Arizona sunshine thinking of my friend. I know in my heart that we are both going to be alright. I take the dogs to the schoolyard for a good long run and then we enjoy a drive before heading back home.

It is now a week since making the decision to move. On May 1, I had been guided to pay off the small debt remaining on our mortgage. Thoughts of selling had never entered my mind and yet now I realize why I had done this. I remember that Linda had telephoned me on that very day. "Carol Ann, I am flying out of the Ontario airport and am standing looking at the large poster of your lovely guide dog Laverne Spirit." Roberto had been putting his stamp of approval on my plan in that very moment. Plus my Lollipop was guiding me also.

I leave a long message on the telephone of Aly about our future move to Vancouver Island. It is time to put the plan in action. I know a woman named Gail who is one of the top selling realty agents of the area. On June 3 she arrives to discuss my plan. I ponder our visit some more and telephone her the next day asking her to bring the listing paperwork.

As we sit at our lovely Mexican dining table I share, "Today, June 4 is Treasure's birthday and I believe it will manifest a prompt sale." I am all soul smiles as I gaze at my Bobby Perfect Angel asleep nearby. All is in divine perfection.

Within two days a woman views our home and presents an offer. She has the house inspected and then the roller coaster ride comes to a screeching halt. She cancels her offer. Obviously, she was not the right person.

On June 20 a realtor arrives to show our home to two men. It is the birthday of my youngest sister Gail. I am still home as one of them enters introducing themselves. "I am David and this is Michael. We like dogs, it is not necessary for you to all leave."

I am grateful and take the five dogs on to the kitchen patio to stay out of sight. After a few minutes the man waves me goodbye thanking me through the patio door.

I take the dogs into the backyard for playtime. I do my best to keep my thoughts focused in the present. I realize they have not left yet. They must be studying the inspection report because they are still out by the car. This seems a good sign that they did not just drive away. About twenty minutes later I hear the sound of the cars pulling away.

Later in the day Gail telephones to share that they are interested. Another day passes and I busy myself with finding things to give to the Salvation Army.

The next day I phone Gail. "Bring Rex with you for supper tonight."

I chat with my island realtor Wendy to see what she has come up with. She is still looking for a suitable property.

Gail and Rex arrive. We happily chat away as we watch Rex sniffing every inch of our floor. He is a little overwhelmed by all the dogs but soon relaxes and enjoys himself. I tell Gail that perhaps my asking price is too high considering the need to paint inside and out along with other work. She replies, "Perhaps so, but let's just wait to see if an offer comes in."

An hour later her phone rings. They have made an offer of $280,000.

"I am most insulted, that is ridiculously too low."

"Yes I agree, but I think you ought to counter back with a higher offer and perhaps you will settle in the middle."

I know I must keep my emotions out of this and think in terms of business. "I would like to suggest the number of $345." She leaves with the paper telling me she shall return soon.

I sit quietly thanking my inner guidance for inviting her to supper. This had been a good choice wise Possum, I tell myself. Prior to her arrival back my phone rings and it is Aly. She is now a nurse in Seattle. She is ecstatic with my plan. "If you only knew how often I think of you. I wish you could be beamed whenever you are in my thoughts."

We both laugh. Aly is the one person who knows firsthand of my life since that day of Sept. 1 when Roberto flew into the light. I share with her that I am a mix of sorrow and joy about leaving our desert home.

"Carol Ann, just as you have done before you will shine in this new venture. The energy of your home will carry with you and never leave you."

Her beautiful wise words soothe my heart. It is as if Robert has prompted her to call me today of all days. The day is truly complete with an offer on our home and hearing from our Aly.

Gail returns and we continue with our wine over desserts. Her phone rings again and I hear her say, "Good, that sounds good." I am in a state of numb disbelief trying to remain calm.

"We have a counter back at $325. I think you ought to reply with $330."

I pause and reply confidently, "Tell them my new number is $335. I believe that will work." It is now later in the evening.

"I will return in the morning with the new paper for you to sign."

In the morning I busy myself with chores doing my best to trust the highest good will come from this venture. All is well in my world I chant aloud to myself and the dogs.

A few hours later our phone rings and Gail shares, "You need to celebrate. They took your offer. You will close on July 30 and you can stay in the house rent free till the end of August if you need to."

Wowsers, that is a good deal. The day is June 23 and I realize it is my older sister Valerie's birthday. A most auspicious blessing.

I call the mortgage company to see when the recorded release of lien will be forwarded to the Maricopa County Recorder. I am told to call them. It was recorded on June 3 which was the day that Gail arrived to discuss listing the house. They say it will be eight weeks to be mailed so I ought to get it in August.

When I check the mail the next day to my surprise I see an envelope from the recorder office. It is my recorded release of lien with a mail date of June 23 and the recording date of June 3. Wowsers!

Some folk may not notice such little details, yet I take great delight in such discovery. It speaks to the universe supporting my dreams. I had envisioned a man would be making the offer on our home and indeed that was correct. As he had entered I sensed he must be the one and indeed my intuition proved correct. Thank you David and Michael.

My island realtor has found some properties and I decide a plane trip is now necessary. July 1 is the day I fly into Victoria. It is Canada Day and the air is filled with celebratory energy which in my mind speaks well to my trip. I meet a jolly faced Wendy and soon we are driving down the road with her Canadian flag on her hood waving merrily at me. Welcome home Carol Ann.

We pull into the Travellers Motel in Cowichan Bay so I can check in. This name is the same as the motel in Peace River, Alberta which was frequented by Robert. I smile silently telling him, "Ok my love, help me find our new home in some trees for the puppies."

Next we are off to look at the properties she has lined up. One of them strikes my fancy and we return to her home office to find comparables for an asking price. I am standing by her side watching the photos of listings scroll before her. Something catches my eye. "Stop, go back to that last listing."

She pulls it up and snorts disapprovingly. "That is not suitable for you."

"I want you to make an appointment. I need to see for myself."

About an hour later I am looking through the trees at my future home. I gasp in awe as we drive slowly up to the house which is situated on a treed two acre lot with a small pond. It is very large but I do not care. The moment I step inside I feel at home. The house is talking to me and I am in love. I wander down the hallway to peer into the bedrooms. Wendy is not enthused with the place. "This is far too large a home for you Carol Ann."

I ignore her negativity replying, "I have five dogs, each of them can have their own bedroom." This is not the truth of course but I am quite beside myself with this magical discovery. It was certainly no accident that I had just happened to see it on her computer screen.

We wander outdoors where the owner of the house is working. I introduce myself to her and say, "I am going to buy your home."

Wendy pulls me away hurriedly saying, "You cannot say that."

"Well, I just did. Do not worry so. This will all work out."

To her chagrin I continue to chat with the woman. "Why are you leaving here?"

She replies, "My husband is American and wants to return home."

I smile in reply, "That is just the reverse of my situation although my hubby is in spirit now."

I have had all the confirmation I need to know this venture will succeed. I fly home to Arizona on July 3. The phone rings on July 4, American Independence Day. It is Wendy. "Carol Ann, you have your home in the trees. Your offer was accepted."

On the day of signing the official paperwork for the closing of our dog house sale I take all five dogs with me. I have asked ahead if they could be allowed into the office and it is agreed to be alright. The meeting takes place with all five dogs underfoot. I execute the documents as a twenty-two legged dog thus including all of us with everyone's names. We all leave with the happiest of tail wags.

Victoria Here We Come

I want to make a last visit to see Elisabeth Kubler-Ross. She is now in a private care home which we have already seen her in. With my therapy girl by my side wearing her lovely blue vest we go see our friend and share the news about our move. "Have you ever been to Victoria?"

"Yes, I have been everywhere. You will love it there."

"Yes, I have been to Victoria in the past. We will be living about an hour north of the city in the country."

She wishes us well and we leave her company after the customary ET farewell. She has her life sized ET sitting at her doorway.

A few days prior to our departure I throw us a going away party and invite all our important two leggers and four leggers. I am not up to preparing the food so hire a caterer to deliver us a feast. I line up all the plants in the front hallway telling everyone to choose one prior to their departure. Linda and Cliff are the happy recipients of many a clay pot which are too heavy to pack without damage.

The next day I am working in the guest bedroom and catch sight of the bathroom mirror. Dearest Mary Kay who loves all of my Robert tales has left a message written in soap. "We love you Bobby." How special is that!

I am looking for the two wheelies which can be used on the drive to Canada. That was Robert's term for our compact suitcases on wheels. They were always stored in the guest room closet. Yet the second one is nowhere to be found. I realize that my ever silly love has taken his.

"Funny love, are you telling me that you are coming with us." His sense of humor still amuses me.

Mark has arrived and joins me in packing up. What an endless chore it seems to be. It has taken me two whole days just to pack all of my photo enlargements along with all the tabletop ones.

August 8 arrives and the United truck pulls up to the road. The Arizona heat is not making it any easier since it is an unbearable 116 degrees. Cliff and Linda have arrived with their dogs. The moving truck heads down the road. All of us wander from room to room our voices echoing our joint disbelief. My home really does look like a woodpecker lives there due to the innumerable nail holes in the walls from all my photographs. Tears are shed as big hugs are held with Linda and Cliff. It is time to depart.

The car is fully loaded with all five dogs in their places and a grinning Mark eager to depart. We head for Flagstaff to stay the night at the Arizona Mountain Inn which Robert and I had frequented with the dogs.

Our first day driving is very hot. I have not had enough sleep and need a pickup. "Mark could you pour some water over me to perk me up. We still have some driving to do and my head is beginning to nod."

This task gives him smiles as he happily pours away. "Ok, let me know when you want your next indoor showers."

Next stop is California where we make a phone call to Serna. Tamara and Ariana arrive with my Bobby lab to our motel room. It is a wild reunion with all the dogs and always such a thrill for me to see my working dog in action. She certainly is well loved.

Somewhere in the state of Oregon I find us a sandy park area and run the dogs. As we head back down the highway I am studying my map. I happen to glance in the rear view mirror. "Oh my God!" The map flies out the window as I pull the car to the side of the road slowly and jump out of the car running to the back. I forgot to close the hatch.

Poor Amber who is all alone gives me a perplexed look. "Good girl you sweetest puppy, I am so sorry for scaring you. What a great job you did not moving around. Your goofy companion forgot to make you safe and secure." I give her an extra-long hug and securely close the hatch.

I thank all of our angels for our safety and continue our journey.

Next we encounter a long delay due to road work. "Why don't you blow up some balloons for entertainment Mark. They are in the glove box. He happily agrees. Within moments he is releasing blown up balloons into the dogs faces. We are all laughing. The noise they make cannot keep us with a straight face. As he blows up the next one I take my pen and pop it. This does not go well with my brother. He is not amused. We wait a long time and are finally given the go ahead. We pass miles of cars. His mood is now returned to his usual jolly self and we continue on our way. He hollers out the window, "You better turn around, there is road work ahead, you will be sitting here a long time waiting."

I love to tease my brother who is such a good sport. "Hey Dude, which direction are we going now Mark?"

His navigation skills are not one a person ought to rely on. He smiles in reply, "I do not know Dudette, I guess it is the same direction as yesterday." He grins and we enjoy a good laugh.

The night prior to our approach to Seattle I telephone Aly to advise her of our location. She suggests that we meet in Tacoma and for me to phone her when we get checked in to our dog motel. As we are driving in the city for some reason I annoy a woman driver who zips past us honking. Mark yells out at her, "Lady, take a PMS pill. You better take two."

Our reunion is a wild time with all the dogs bouncing around welcoming our friend. Mark adds to the mayhem with his own labby happiness to meet Aly. We enjoy a very festive time sharing our tales and supper with the four-footed gang. The room is filled with many a boisterous hoot and some good barks as well.

Mark and I follow her out to the car when it is time for her to depart. She has pulled in next to the passenger side of my Labaru. "So Carol Ann, what is this orange mess on the side of your car?"

Mark and I both look bursting into hysterics. He replies with his big grin, "I found a bag of carrots on the floor that had gone slimey and emptied the bag out the front window while we were driving."

I respond, "Hey, it is a good thing that the back window was up otherwise Spookie would have had a splat in her face."

"Oh my God! You guys crack me up. Happy travels to you."

After a leisurely start to the next day we are ready to depart. "This will be our shortest day, Mark."

"I hope so."

My words are soon becoming unrealized as we inch our way through Seattle's bumper to bumper traffic. Upon reaching the border crossing a long wait is ahead of us. There are miles of traffic on both sides of the U.S. and Canada.

Finally our turn arrives to pull up to the Canadian border agent. He tells me that I can clear customs when I meet up with the United moving truck. He peers his head into the car catching sight of all my dogs. "Are all these dogs yours?"

His face is complete shock as I reply, "Yes, all five of them want to learn to bark in Canadian. I have their paperwork if you want to check it."

"No, never mind that. Welcome home."

I hastily pull the car forward whooping, "Welcome to Canada, puppies. You are now officially Canadians. Let's get ourselves to that ferry."

Due to the long delays in our border and traffic we have missed our reserved sailing and join the line of cars waiting for a ferry. It is a long two hours before we are waved on to an available ferry. I telephone our realtor Wendy just prior to getting on to advise her of our arrival and get directions.

Finally the ferry begins to move and I breathe a sigh of relief. Mark and I are too tired to do anything but stay in the company of the dogs. My small Canadian flag is happily waving. As we had approached the border of Washington I had been waving the flag at all the passing cars and making loud whoops of joy. I had put on my enormous pink plastic sunglasses also. It had been a very merry day as we got closer to our Canadian destination. Our excitement offsets our fatigue when we finally touch the soil of our new home, Vancouver Island.

It is now just prior to 8:00 pm. We do not have far to go so I wait to let the dogs out of the car again. They stretched their legs prior to getting on the ferry and I am now anxious to get to the house. We are to meet Wendy in Mill Bay. Yet my excitement has impaired my sense of directions and my two legged navigator is no additional help in pointing the correct way.

It is beginning to get dark. I realize we have missed a turn somewhere. "Mark, I do not know where we are going but this road is taking us into Victoria." I know we are going the wrong way yet I am compelled to stay in this same wrong direction.

We make a stop at a red light and someone hollers to me, "You are driving without any lights."

A moment later a police car makes a turn onto the street passing right beside us. "Oh boy, I trust he won't stop me about the car lights."

And miracle of miracles, indeed he keeps driving. "Look at that Mark. Man, that cop would have got an earful listening to me babble about our day and adventures."

"Crap yes, that is for sure."

"Mark, I have to find us a phone and telephone Wendy. Look where we are now. I do not know how we got here; but look, that is the parliament buildings. They are beautiful all lit up with white lights."

I am now laughing without any sense of worry but know we are in a bit of a pickle for sure.

We are now in the harbor area. I see a little shop with someone inside. I scramble into a parking space. "Ok Mark I will go find us help, keep the pups company."

There is no one else around as I watch a couple working together in their ice cream shop. I bounce into their presence announcing, "I am in dire need of your help. My brother and my five dogs are waiting in my car. We have no lights. I am late to meet my realtor in Mill Bay to get to our new home in Cobble Hill tonight. Can I please use your phone?"

I catch my breath as both of them look in disbelief responding, "Who travels with five dogs?"

"I do. They are my constant companions."

"It is impossible for you to drive anywhere tonight. You make your phone call and we shall help you."

The phone is answered by Wendy's husband Pierre. He is aghast with my story. "She has been waiting for hours. You need to call her in the morning from wherever you are."

The gentleman then begins to make phone calls on my behalf. I listen to him asking various establishments about availability for two people travelling with five dogs. A few minutes later he greets me with a big smile, "You are all set up. The Ramada right next door to us will gladly take you."

"You mean all the dogs are allowed?"

"Yes."

"Wowsers, thank you so much."

I am beside myself with grateful shock and start towards the door. I turn and ask him, "What is your name?"

"Bob."

I laugh and whoop my arms with joy as I charge out their door to the car. Mark cannot believe his ears when I tell him the news. "Yup, it is true. I shall return in a few minutes after I get us checked in."

The man at the check in counter greets me with a welcome smile when I tell him I am the woman with the dogs. "We certainly have never had five big dogs stay with us before."

"I am most grateful. We shall behave ourselves."

"I have one room left with a king size bed."

"That is perfect. Thank you."

I make the payment for the night and am delighted that no extra charge is made for the dogs. Plus he has given us a discount rate.

Mark and I take turns walking the dogs on the nearby grass and then head to the underground parking garage. "Ok, dear brother load up. We have to do this all in one trip." Needless to say, we both have our hands full with the requirements for us and the dogs. We slowly make our way to the elevator.

As the elevator door from the garage opens to the lobby a woman watching exclaims, "Oh my, look at the beautiful dogs. My goodness, there is more coming. Wow, five of them; aren't they all beautiful." Mark has charge of the older girls, Spookie and Amber. I have the three rowdies.

Suddenly Treya bursts loose from her leash which has not been adequately attached to her collar. She charges into the lounge. I move as quickly as I can with Mystic and Spirit in tow calling her back to me. Thankfully, she responds to my call and her leash is affixed securely.

We now head to the elevator for our room on the third floor. We successfully make our exit and start down the long hallway. A door opens at the end but slams shut instantly as the person sees what is fast approaching. I drop the leashes and the dogs are now running happily with their bells clanging loudly.

The door is opened and we all tumble inside. After a few minutes all the dogs are fed and watered. Mark and I collapse on to the king size dog bed and are joined by our four footers.

"You said this was to be our shortest day. Boy, were you ever wrong about that."

"Yeah, for sure but look where we are. Isn't this something!"

"I cannot believe that police car just driving past us without any lights. That Robert of yours must have made the cop momentarily blind because he should have stopped us."

"For sure. But you know if we had met with Wendy we would be sleeping in an empty house on the floor. The moving truck arrives tomorrow at the house. I reckon for my first night back in Canada after twenty-six years of living in the USA that Robert wanted us to be in comfort."

"Must be true. I still cannot believe about that police man. Holy smokes." We turn out the light and continue our giddiness in the dark.

I treat us to breakfast in the room and talk to Wendy. The ice cream shop has opened and I go inside to thank the couple.

The man asks, "So why did you react that way to my name last night?"

"My husband is named Robert and he died a few years ago."

He looks to his wife with a smile responding, "So you believe he helped you find us."

"Yes most definitely, he guided me and kept us safe."

"That is very beautiful. Please come see us when you are in Victoria again."

Wendy successfully leads us to our tree home and Mark is awed by the beauty. Awhile later the big truck arrives. We are now finally unpacking. Mark is having a great time opening boxes in search of a telephone.

A couple days later he is cleaning out the car. The pups are nearby and get surprise treats as he discovers old French fries. He is all laughter exclaiming, "Man, some of these are about to grow legs." As we drove down the road we ate many a French fry and I got chuckles throwing them in the car for the dogs.

In the evening all of us are exhausted lounging on the king size bed. It has become dark but I sense something flying around in the bedroom. "Mark what the heck is flying around in here. Can you see anything?"

He does not even move or open his eyes as he replies in a muffled voice with his head snuggled into a pillow, "It is probably just a bat."

"Just a bat! Are you kidding me? Did you leave that bathroom window open when you were showering?"

"Must have, yup guess so."

I jump off the bed and slam the door. "Well, Mr. Bat you better find your way out the way you came in."

"Don't worry, he is harmless."

"Maybe so brother mine but I am not too enthused to share my home with any bat. I must get someone to get a screen into that window."

I eventually calm down and join all the dogs and my brother in sleep.

October 10 Anniversary

It is our wedding anniversary. As I lay awake I cannot believe the task waiting my attentions. We had recently met a neighbour of our new tree house named George. A couple days ago George had telephoned me, "Carol Ann, would you like me to deliver you some beef lung for your dogs?"

I had replied, "Yes, anything fresh you want to bring them would be appreciated by all of us, thank you."

First I do our chicken chores with an egg for each dog. There are still several eggs so I shall be making myself some yummy egg salad.

After taking the remaining eggs into the house I walk down the long driveway to the garage. I envision an island cow and silently thank him for providing food for my dogs. George called last evening to tell me he had left a bucket by my gate. I went down and pulled it into the garage for the night. Now I stand gazing inside with the full light of day. "Holy cow, look at that dogs. Ok, let me get this up to the house."

I pull the pail slowly since it is too heavy for me to lift. All five dogs are sniffing eagerly at the aromatic morsels inside.

I phone George to inquire how to do this task. He makes it sound so easy. I leave the dogs inside the house and move my outdoor plastic table. I stretch out a couple big plastic trash bags and peer inside the bucket. Goodness gracious, this is humungous. He had put in more than just a lung. As I pull it out there is also the windpipe. It just keeps coming. There is a lot of weight to it. Plus he put in two lungs. Truly

I had no idea what I had got myself in for when I agreed to this man's offer.

Well, I cannot stop now. I say aloud, "Bless you cow and thank you. I release any fearful energy within you. May only energies of love fill you and in turn fill my dogs." I begin to cut and envision the island cows feeding on the lush greenery. Only a few hours ago this was a living cow.

The memory of Robert's death comes to mind. I marvel at the gift of two lungs and not just one. George could have brought different organ meat but this is two lungs. Robert had succumbed to lung cancer.

It may take George only a few minutes for this task but certainly it is taking me longer. I do not have any good sharp knives and am cutting this all up with a pair of scissors. Unbelievable! I need to take a break and get a glass of water. The vibration of my rubber boots hitting the pine floor is music to my soul. Boy oh boy, Carol Ann. You really are a country girl now. The dogs are licking my bloody fingers. "Be gentle, puppies. Those fingers are attached to the rest of me." I am sniffed all over as I stand at the kitchen sink for a few minutes.

I head back to the front door and have to push them all back inside as I close the door behind me.

The first lung is done and I begin on the second. The dogs are scratching at the door. "Patience, puppies. You will be getting some tonight." There are a lot of meals here. It is all bagged up and some of it is taken to the freezer in the crawl space under the house.

During the evening I am enjoying wine with my pack as I reflect on our new lives. This has been quite a transition living here compared to our life in a gated community where it is common for people to have multiple homes.

My old sense of Carol Ann would not have been ready for this. I am now feeling like a rebirthed being within the body of Carol Ann Joy. I help Spook up beside me on the couch and she enjoys a sip of wine. "Thank you beloved Von Spook, you truly are a testament to my transformation. I am so glad you have come into your joy. We have both shifted so much."

The extreme change in climate from the desert heat to dampness takes a toll on Spook's arthritic joints. One day she is not able to get up on her own speed. I take a trip in to Duncan for a remedy. At a health store I am guided to buy Silica gel which I treat her with. Miraculously, within about four days she is back to herself and motoring around tail wagging. I am pleased to have avoided a trip to a vet.

Sister Freida Raab

Even prior to leaving Arizona I sensed and told everyone that the tree house will be a stepping stone home with a short stay. I do not know why, yet it is a very strong intuitive knowing. As I am enjoying the breathtaking view from our massive windows overlooking our paradise yard I put my feet up and pick up a local newspaper.

My eyes catch sight of an article with a photo about a place nearby called Providence Farm. "Holy smokes!" I gasp in disbelief as I read the name of Sister Freida Raab who is to be in attendance at an event at this farm. Freida is the kind Catholic sister who helped me years ago when I was alone and frightened seeking an answer to my pregnancy situation while I was here on the island. When I was choosing an area of Vancouver Island to find our new home, my subconscious had coached me to the Duncan area yet my conscious mind was not aware why.

"Puppies we need to go for an explore drive. Put on your shoes and follow me." They need no encouragement and within a few minutes all five dogs are happily in the Labaru wondering where their Carol Ann is taking them now. We head northward out of Duncan and down a lovely country road and soon see the sign for Providence Farm.

Somehow I am able to track down a phone number for Sister Freida and the next day make the phone call. The timing is quite bizarre since it is the same day of the birth of Jade's daughter Erica on Sept. 28. Jade called earlier telling me of the birth of my granddaughter.

Freida had told me many years ago I could drop the sister from her name and thus I did. She answers the phone, "Hello Freida, it is Carol

Ann Arnim calling. I have recently moved up to the island and need to come see you."

"How lovely to hear from you Carol Ann. Is that Robert love with you?"

"Unfortunately no, Freida. He developed lung cancer and died in 1996. I have moved forward as best I can and got to a point that I decided it was to my highest good to leave Arizona. So here I am."

"Where are you living?"

"I live in a lovely treed lot near Cobble Hill with my five dogs. Where are you?"

"Your home sounds perfect for all your gang, my goodness five dogs. I live in Victoria, could you drive in?"

"Of course, I would love to." We set up a time in the next couple days.

"I look forward to our visit. We can have lunch together here and I want to hear all about your life."

"Thank you so much."

It is a lovely breezy island day when we head toward the city. The Sister of Saint Ann home is in a beautiful, quiet residential area and I tell the pups to have a snooze. With a grateful heart I make my way up the stairs and tell a sister who I have come to see. A few moments later I am greeted with Freida walking towards me with outstretched arms. We share a lovely hug.

"Come now, let's sit here where we won't be disturbed and you update me. We last saw each other when Robert and you came to the island."

"Yes, that must have been about 1994." I take a breath. Tears surface as I share my trauma about the death of the man who impregnated me leading me to Freida so long ago.

"You have been so brave, Carol Ann. I am so glad to have met your Robert. I was so touched that you took the extra time to track me down."

My story leads into the miracle of Bobby Magic Angel pup and the parade of puppies.

"I remember your two labs which were with you when we met. Do you still have them?"

"Saber died at the grand age of fifteen but Spookie is with us. She

242

was not enthused initially to share my affections with a rowdy puppy. The first puppy Laverne was released from training and became a Mom figure to the following four working girls."

"So what are your plans now?"

"I do not have a specific agenda. It has been such an adjustment for all of us coming to live here after my life of twenty-six years in the states. It is a whole new environment for the dogs since they grew up in the Arizona desert with a pool in their backyard. I spent those six years training dogs and helping cancer and hospice patients. It just seemed time to start focusing on Carol Ann for a change."

"That sounds very wise. Let's go have some lunch and you can continue to share."

She is still the attentive, patient listener asking questions. The conversation revolves around my life. We turn to the long ago past. "Freida, can you tell me where in Duncan we met? Where is the building?"

She describes it to me as I make notes. "I would like to find it and go back inside. That part of my life was so very difficult and serendipity has led me to you to help me retrace this painful past. This must be why I was led to live here. You have been most helpful in putting the puzzle pieces together; some of which were lost from my memory. I have learned a lot through my journey of healing and have started to write stories of my life for a future book."

"I hope I get to read it. It shall be a real page turner. Certainly God has very much blessed your life, Carol Ann. Let's go out to your car and you can introduce me to your four-footed angels as you call them."

"Yes, I would love to."

A few minutes later each dog is happily enjoying a pet from Freida. Warm hugs are shared and the woman who shall forever have my fullest gratitude walks back inside. I drive home with a heart lightened and ready to go further into my past. How uttterly remarkable to have been led to her.

The next day I find the government services building in downtown Duncan and make my way up the elevator to the floor she was on years ago. I can feel the fears surface as I push the elevator button. Yet when I go back outside I feel a sense of release. I walk along the shops nearby and go inside a lovely little store selling crystals and other treasures. It has the name of Wishes. I purchase my first piece of citrine.

When I step outside from the shop and look up the street my gaze rests upon the building I just came from where I met Freida. How perfect is that just coming out of the Wishes store. Many years ago my wishes were seen to and are again in this moment being taken care of.

I continue the tour of the Duncan shops and take delight in one with funky old things. The moment I catch sight of a small baby chair painted green with butterflies on it I squeal with amusement. I grab it up and purchase it without a second thought. At the farmers market store I find another tiny wicker rocking chair. It is too small for a baby and yet obviously my mind is very much in baby land. I find an appropriate place for my two items upon getting back to our tree house. The dogs charge around happily and go splash around the side of the pond.

I have been spending a lot of time exploring our green paradise since arriving to our tree house. One day I am led to the outskirts of town and find myself on Bell McKinnon Road. I recall now that my Uncle Russ and Aunt Ivah had a small home outside Duncan yet I cannot remember the name of their street. Magically I am on the right road although I do not know it. As I drive humming away, I see a sign for hair salon. I stop the car in disbelief. I am looking at the home of my Uncle Russ.

I cannot contain my excitement. There is a phone number yet surely she must get people who just drive in without an appointment. I slowly make our way up the laneway and park. I have been well guided for a moment later the woman exits the house and comes over to the car. "Can I help you? Oh my goodness, look at all your dogs!"

We both chuckle as she takes turns petting them all. "I have been in your home several times. A brother of my Dad used to live here."

"Wow, that is amazing and you just found us."

"Yes, I did not know the address of his former home but guess part of me remembered Bell McKinnon and that is how I found you. It would be fun for me to have my hair cut if you are interested."

"Of course, you must come in."

I bound out of the car lickedty split and follow her inside. After a little tour I find myself getting my locks trimmed as we chatter away.

In my mind I am back years ago sitting alone in this same house staring out the window looking for answers. Wowsers, I cannot believe where I am, I keep saying silently to myself. This is truly incredible.

In the space of just a few days I have been led to the exact places and the person responsible for helping me. As Freida said, God has blessed me well and continues to do so.

You Really Are a Screwball

There is a small village named Mill Bay within a few minutes driving distance from our tree house. We make our way there one day and I make an interesting discovery. Robert's youngest son John, went to a private school name Brentwood College in Mill Bay. During our time on the island we had driven in to the school. As I drive the residential area I see its sign. Remarkable. This time I am retracing happy memories with my Magoo, Saber and Spook.

Next I find a road which follows the shore and park the car for a stroll alone. It is not an appropriate place to let my hooligans run free so they must sniff the sea air from the car. There is a trail leading into some large cedar trees which I follow. I feel the need to go hug a tree and in doing so catch sight of my very first bald eagle. I am mesmerized and walk further out towards the sea catching sight of him over the water. It is a most lovely location. I am drawn back to this very same place with the majestic cedar tree over the next few days.

In doing so the eagle always makes an appearance and I feel a connection between us. I begin to hear a message, "You will leave here."

Every time I come back to this spot I get the same message telling me of leaving. I do ponder the fact that whenever I think of perhaps painting the bedroom at the end of the hallway I hear, "Just wait, just wait." I sense I am not to do any further improvements to the house. I did speak of it being a stepping stone home and staying a short time.

I find a safe beach to run the dogs. They all bound around enjoying the shore finding morsels to eat. I trust that their tummies will handle these gourmet delights since it is all new to them. Again I hear the message, "You need to live by the water. You need to be by the sea for your healing." Wow. Holy smokes, perhaps my time here is coming to an end. Yet it makes my head spin since it is so soon.

Our front yard has a nice sized pond and Treasure's favorite thing is swimming. One day we wake up to the pond with a formation of ice. Without any thought I allow the dogs to run down the hill with me to the chicken coop and wait for an egg treat.

This morning Treya has other ideas. I watch as she slides her way onto the ice and then a moment later falls through. Oh my God! I am at a loss to know what to do. She is thrashing about fearfully. She is the only dog who has gone out thankfully. I holler at her, "Come on sweet girl, keep going. Just keep pounding away." In my mind I am envisioning driving the car into the pond to rescue her which is ludicrous of course, yet I am terrified.

Thankfully, she makes her way out and comes charging up to me. She shakes all over as I grab her close to my heart. "Thank Godness you are alright. That was a terrible scare puppy."

"Ok guys, that is it. There will be no more coming in the front yard when the weather is cool."

We return to the house. I sit staring out the window at the pond which created this awful scare. Do I need to put fencing around the pond? I sense not because I know this is a message we are to leave. "Ok, puppy I guess you are trying to tell me something. It must be time for us to depart this paradise; but where the heck are we going to go?" I get out the map of Vancouver Island to study.

In the morning I awaken hearing the message, "Go north."

"Come on my happy dogs, we are all going for an explore drive."

We head up island. Nanaimo is not a place I want to live so we continue further onward. I am driving enjoying the lovely new scenery and after a while turn the car around and head home.

The next day I wake up and again hear, "Go north."

So we repeat the same as the day before yet we go further north towards Courtney Comox. As I drive the shore highway coming into

Union Bay I catch sight of a For Sale sign. I turn up the road. A minute later my eyes are gazing at the reason I have been told go north.

There it is, situated on a short no thru road with a nice sized yard. It is in a quiet neighborhood with a couple houses beside it. I like the look of it. It sits above the water so would have a sea view which I have been told I need. Perhaps this is to be our healing home on the water.

I write down the information. I had heard that somewhere in Courtney there is a small shop operated by a former Tibetan Buddhist Lama. I do not know the name or its location so ask my angelic guidance to help me out. I am driving happily along liking the look of this seaside town when I spot a window with familiar looking items from my favorite part of the world. Colorful prayer flags beckon me inside the shop.

I am greeted with a smiling faced young woman. I ask her if the shop is owned by a Tibetan. "Yes, it is indeed. He is my husband."

I seem to recall reading about monks coming to the west and marrying. What a monumental change of lifestyle this would be for them. I tell her about my plans of moving up island from down near Duncan. She replies, "The energy here is much better. You will love it here."

After a lovely chat I head homeward with a sense of mission accomplished. I telephone realtor Wendy and she is absolutely stupefied. "What the heck are you talking about, you only just moved into that place. You cannot move yet."

"Yes I can and must. I want to list the home on November 9 which is Saber's birthday. I have found the place I want to buy already and want you to make an appointment for us to see it." I can tell she is hanging up the phone shaking her head at this whacko woman who now claims to be moving within less than six months.

In the morning I awake with a sleeping dog nestled into my shoulder. I assume it is Treasure but to my delight it is Spookie. I wrap my arm around her snuggling her closer as she drifts back to sleep. It is now six years plus since my attentions to her became disrupted with the parade of raising five working girls.

Through my grief she truly had become a best friend. She had taught me about being a mirror. Since I had not wanted to live neither did she.

My joy this morning to have her so close speaks to her mirroring my healing since being in our paradise tree house. What a blessing, thank you Spookie.

Time to get up and feed the chickens. Today is Sunday and if there are sufficient eggs we shall put our cooler out at the side of the road with our eggs for sale sign. It is a fun venture and pleases me to see the honesty in people. As I head to the chicken coop I warn the mice. "Ok Mr. Mouse, stay out of my way." Last night I had been startled by one when I opened the door. Now the door is warped so I get my trusty little saw and cut off the side. Finally it scrapes shut. We have enough eggs in the house and now with the ones from this morning shall be able to put the cooler out.

I stand in amazement silently admiring our magnificent trees pondering the fact that we may be leaving here soon. Hard to believe since we have not been here that long. I thank my trees for their role in our journey. Since our arrival I feel more empowered and deep pains are releasing. My soul guided us here knowing I was on track with each step.

It is seven years plus since my torturous journey through the maze of grief and my Bobby still guides and supports me. Last night in the living room I could feel a palpable presence of his energy around us. I always keep my slippers by the front door but cannot find them anywhere. I think of my love wondering if he has been up to mischief. I then find them by the back door. The dogs are asleep as I sit in the big wicker chair in silence.

Spook is now awake watching me. I begin to feel very peaceful as I feel the tingling warmth of his presence. I know he is here. I hear him message me. "Yes, I did move the slippers. It delights me to see your smiles when you realize it is me. You have turned another corner. You do need the daily visual contact and healing power of the sea and so it shall be. When you see your path, you are unstoppable, forging ahead despite any outside obstacles. You are still a brick and more unbreakable now than ever before. Your progress astounds me but you never cease to amaze me. I know this is all making your head spin but it is all to your higher good as it is for all others in your close circle."

During these moments Spookie is pesting me. I realize she is participating in the Robert visit. She barks acknowledging his presence.

We make a trip to see the place in Union Bay. I walk through its front door to be greeted with a million dollar view of the coast mountains and Denman Island. I am sure this is the right place in the right time. When we head down the coast highway I realize that my Robert and I have travelled this very road. We had driven up to Courtney Comox to catch the ferry over to Powell River and drive down the sunshine coast back to our rental home in Anacortes, Washington.

With the help of realtor Wendy I make an offer. It becomes our second heavenly blessed real estate transaction. My offer on the sea home is accepted on November 24. My tree home has an offer within ten days of listing by a man named Travis. He has a similar type cedar home nearby but wants a bigger place. Our home is a dream come true for his family.

We will be able to be in our new home by Xmas. I share the news with everyone and call my favorite moving buddy, Mark. "Hey Dude, how would you like to help us move again to our new home for the holidays."

He is always ready for another adventure with the dogs and says he will get himself packed and ready to go. It is a shock to everyone's ears to be sure but I remind everyone that this had been in the works all along.

Sid and Betty are on my mind a lot. About a week ago I had phoned the house and she said Sid was being evaluated for hospice. This is a couple in Arizona whom Treya and I drove to medical appointments. Sid has lung cancer. I sense that he may have taken flight. On American Thanksgiving I phone their home.

My mind replays movies from our time together. They both had become very fond of my perfect working girl. We were always invited inside their home when we returned from our outings. On our first time inside with them, Betty asks, "Can I get the pup something?"

"An apple would be good if you have any."

She returns a moment later holding a knife with the apple. "Shall I cut it up for her?"

"Not necessary." She hands Treya the apple. Initially she plays with it rolling it around on their carpet.

"Look at her playing with it. Will she really eat it?"

"Yes, she is just being silly entertaining you. Just wait, it will be all gone."

Treya loved to perform the lap command for Sid. He enjoyed every second of her thorough face washings and kisses. I presented him a photo on our next visit. He had told Treya, "Go in the kitchen for your apple and see your happy face on our fridge, Treya."

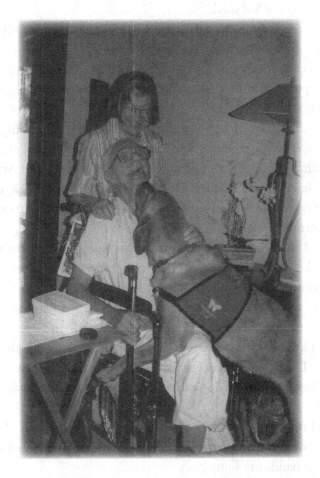

It had been a difficult last visit prior to leaving Arizona. Betty stood in the heat on her front lawn waving tearfully and I drove away in tears also.

After several rings she answers the phone. We chat a moment about my dogs and she says, "Sid died three days ago on November 24."

"I sensed this was so. Tell me more."

"He died peacefully with his eyes open. We had moved into a private care home. I had stayed on. You would not have reached me. I only just walked in the door an hour ago. You have called at the perfect time."

"Betty, I have to share a story about our moving to another home by the sea. Actually the day my offer on the new home was accepted was the same day Sid died."

"You are kidding, the same day! Thank you for sharing that. What has made you want to move so soon?"

"It was our funny girl Treya who put on her skates going on to the ice of the pond. A couple moments later she fell through."

"Oh no. Is she alright?"

"Yes, she thrashed her way out. I cannot continue living here so we have a new place. Betty you know how Sid had no belief in life after death. We talked openly about it and he always said, when you are dead that is it, end of story. He saw no possibility of messaging from the other side. I think Betty that now he must be smiling in on us. My home venture happened on the very day of his death."

"Yes, I must say that is a great thing. Guess that means we both have a stake in that new place. Give me a call when you get settled in the sea home."

While at the mall in Duncan a couple days later I see the van belonging to our friend Douglas. His dog Miss Ruff is sitting alertly on the lookout for him. I sense that he shall be returning any minute so I wait. The dog welcomes my strokes to her thick fur. Sure enough within a few minutes his dog catches sight of him. He is slowly walking up to me.

"Well now my young friend, it is good to see you here. I was just going to come out to your place to give you this." He reaches in his pocket and hands me some cash.

"What is this for Douglas?"

"I sold that old refrigerator for you."

"Well now you are a wonder indeed. Thank you so much. I am glad to see you because I have big news to share with you my friend. You better hang onto your barstool because you might topple over in shock from what I am going to tell you."

He pretends to be falling over as he replies, "Tell all. What are you up to now?"

I share my plan to move and what motivated me to do so. He looks at me puzzled replying, "You really are a screwball aren't you!"

"Maybe so Douglas, but I am a happy screwball."

Travis comes by with all of his family. He visits us a few times making his own preparations for his move. I had envisioned a special needs person living in one of the bedrooms and to my surprise this manifests. He works with special needs people and during one of his visits to our place I am introduced to the young man. He will be living in one of the bedrooms.

I telephone Sister Freida to update her. "I have been busy since our chat and done great walking through my painful past. The uncle's home I stayed in while I met you I discovered is now a hair salon. I actually had my hair cut in my Uncle Russ's home. I did spend a short time in the building where we met also. Thanks to my perfect Bobby angel pup Treya falling through the ice of our pond I have decided we must move. We have found a place outside of Union Bay which has a magnificent view of the water. It overlooks Denman Island and the coast mountains in the distance."

"My goodness; what a journey you are on with that blessed life of yours. I would love to come see all of you prior to the move. I plan to go up island the first Saturday of December so could pop in."

"That would be splendid. Yes please do."

Mark flies in on December 15 and assists in our packing adventure. Treya Treasure was released from CCI advanced training on December 20. Magically, the day of our move is the very same day. "Mark, I certainly named Treya right with her Bobby Perfect Angel nickname. Thanks to her pond misadventure we are now leaving here on the one year anniversary of the day her school advised me of her release."

"Wow, that is smashing. Good work angel girl. The sea shore awaits you. No more ponds for you."

Something Big Is Coming

Travis wishes us well as the five dogs along with Mark head out the driveway for the last time. The car is really packed to the max. Jade has just sent a Xmas floral bouquet which is resting by Mark's knees. Thankfully it is not a long drive. We pull up to our sea home and open the front door. My brother's jaw drops to the floor. "Wow, this is beautiful Carol Ann, you hit the jackpot again with this place. The view is spectacular, yes indeed."

I install a woodstove in the corner of the living room. Mark loves to take charge of building our fires. The large deck with glass railing is very private and we spend a lot of time out there.

We soon discover the closest beach is up the road a few minutes. It is a bit rocky to get out to the sandy area but all five dogs make their way. Amber is not really a water dog but dips her paws in. Her old dog buddy Spookie is by her side. There is another lovely beach with a long stretch of sand near the airport which becomes our favorite.

It is a very merry Xmas with a big mess of papers to clean up after the dogs open their presents and find the edible treats inside. For supper one evening I make a large pot of spaghetti. Mark gives both of us chuckles when he steps up for his serving with one of the dog bowls in hand. "Ok, my laughing labby Mark, enjoy." Naturally he is surrounded with all the dogs when they see him eating out of one of their bowls. It is a large serving and of course they all get some spoon fed treats for their patience.

Our month with Mark has flown by and we all drive him out to the Comox airport. It is always hard for us to say farewell with each other. We share such great camaraderie. He is so in sync with all the dogs.

Linda arrives from Arizona and we spend a lovely few days sharing the island with her. We take a trip down to the tree home to share where we just moved from. It is great to see the place again and see how Travis and his family are so much in love with their new home. It definitely was destined for them. The Tibetan Buddhist Lama is having a public function at his home which Linda and I attend. It is a small gathering in their backyard.

Next we receive a short visit from Maggie and family. Our large deck is full of dogs and much celebration. Maggie loves her play runs at the sandy beach.

Our next visitor is Aly who pulls into our driveway with the biggest smiles in her top down convertible. We have lots of exploring with her as well. One day I get a bundle of colorful bright mylar balloons and we go to the nearby beach with the dogs. I have written out a note which I affix to the balloons speaking to the old parts of Carol Ann which I desire to release. I am stepping more into my power and to celebrate this with dearest Aly is very memorable for all of us.

"I cannot believe you sleep with all five big dogs on this small bed."

The old four poster bed of Robert's is in the upstairs bedroom and the king size bed is on the lower level. All five dogs are still able to jump on the bed at night. If I don't get in first I have some manoeuvering to find my spot.

Spookie loves to swim. Sometimes we walk to the end of our short road and cross the highway and walk the few feet to the sea. She joins me in a swim in the swallow waters by the shore. We both shake off and make our way home with salty sea smiles. The rocky beach across from Union Bay which we frequent the most due to closeness has become too rocky for her. At the feed store I discover a huge Rubbermaid tub which is delivered to our backyard. I place a couple bricks at the side for a step which she climbs on. I need to help her out. Her legs are short so when it is full to the brim she can actually make a few turns around in it. She loves it.

One day our dear Amber loses her appetite. She is now about fourteen although I cannot say for sure since Vivian did not know her age when she rescued her from the Phoenix pound. Her life since our move to Canada has been such fun. Our sea home backyard proves to be a great race track for all the dogs. If one dog catches sight of something on one side of the house within a minute all of them are charging to the other side to find out what is passing the house. Amber joins the pack running as fast as she can barking the whole way. What a happy girl.

Her condition is not diagnosed but the vet agrees that she is approaching her end of life. After a few days of her appetite decreasing down to nothing it is time to let her go. With all of her family by her side I lift her onto our double bed and the vet releases her. Spookie is lying by her side and stays with her after death. It is September 27, 2004. Vivian will be welcoming her across the rainbow bridge.

The doctor refers me to a cremation man outside of Duncan. The next day I carry her body out to the car and we all take a trip down island. I am most touched by the kind man who greets us. He has turned an old grain silo into a cremation furnace. I lift her out of the car and place her on his table on wheels which he rolls inside. A few days later he delivers her remains in a lovely wooden box.

We all adjust to our life without our fluffy girl. She had formed a close bond with Spookie. I am so very glad that Amber got to live long enough to enjoy some of our Canadian lifestyle which was so very different from her former home in the desert.

Living by the sea has truly been a healing for me. The waters never seem to look the same. Spookie still loves to bark at boats. When Robert and I rented our seaside home in Chester, Nova Scotia, Spookie barked every time the ferry pulled out of the bay. Any boat on the water created loud barks.

She has not lost her love of this. This property keeps her busy. The moment she catches sight of anything on the water she runs toward the fence barking. It is very entertaining. There is a lot to watch on the water. The nearby coast guard station is often out practicing. Sometimes even at night I can watch a hovering helicopter as the swimmers jump into the sea to practice. Herring season arrives and there are many boats to keep Spookie busy. During the summer months in the evening I can see the lights of the cruise ships heading north and south.

In my mailbox one day I receive a letter from my friend Liz in Arizona. She has kindly sent me a newspaper article on the death of Elisabeth Kubler-Ross. I do not watch the news so am very glad of Liz's kindness in this gesture. I am relieved her years of suffering are over.

It has been a long time since my thoughts have been on the potential Robert walk-in. Somehow I come across a book about this unusual topic. Once again I am enthralled reading about this possibility. What a fantastic whopping tail of a tale that would be to happen. I am mesmerized all over again at the prospect.

I begin to write again enjoying the setup of my desk on the lower level looking at the happy dogs in the backyard. The door is ajar. They come and go as they please while I write about my dog blessed journey. We do seem to have a lot of planes over our home. One day I begin to receive a strange message, "Something big is coming." I am at a loss for whatever this could mean. What am I going to be doing next? These words become a constant refrain. Often they are in conjunction with a plane over the house.

We all very much love our new home yet the neighbour next door is not in love with us. Whenever Harold walks along the fence line Mystic charges and barks. My dog is not enthralled with this man. One day he has a friend with him and as they are passing into the backyard Mystic does his usual barking and running up to the fence growling.

The man calls out, "I could break that dog's neck."

I am at a loss for words and keep my eyes attentive for Mystic in the yard whenever we are outside. I do my best to keep Mystic away from the fence line and call him back to me whenever I see any sight of Harold. The man is obsessed with his yard work and mowing the lawn. The neighbours on the other side are very friendly although they are not home much. Yet anytime they are by the fence they wander over to pet the dogs and talk to them. Sometimes treats are thrown over for them.

On a weekend Harold and his friend are going into their backyard, Mystic catches sight of them before I do. He runs over growling at them. The unkind man is with him and again yells out, "I could break that dog's neck." I tell them I am calling the police. I do so but they advise me there is nothing they can do.

I do my best to keep out of his sight and keep track of where my dogs are, especially Mystic. This becomes very wearisome and soon I realize that I cannot continue to live like this. The life of dogs is shorter than humans and I do not want their lives to continue to be subjected to such stress. And of course it is not the best for me either.

Linda cannot believe we are still living under such conditions and is very happy when I share the news with her one day that we plan to move. I know that moving further north the real estate prices will be lower and I set my sights on the Port McNeill area. A friend who visits us with her golden retriever agrees with my decision. "Carol Ann I know a realtor named Robert."

I know with this as his name I am receiving confirmation that Mystic has guided us to leave here. The timing is very amazing because the birthday of my Robert love is February 22 just a week away. I list our sea home on that same day.

Within a few weeks realtor Robert shows our home and I receive an acceptable offer. As he sits with me at our dining table the tugboat dog toy on the top of the fridge makes a toot. "What is that noise?" asks Robert.

"It is a dog toy on top of the fridge which sometimes goes off." I am smiles inside and out as I know that my Bobby love has announced his approval.

I have found a realtor from Port Hardy who checks out a home I have found on the internet. She takes a look at it for me and we set up an appointment.

I have become friends with a woman named Margarite who I picked up hitchhiking one day. She loves the dogs and agrees to come stay with them while I go view our potential home. I take Mystic with me and leave the three girls in the capable hands of Margarite.

Mystic is thrilled to be my navigator and assumes his position in the front seat. His black nose eagerly sniffs the treed air as we head north. After leaving Campbell River there are no more stop lights. It is only trees and more tress. It feels like we are driving into the bush as I reflect on the days of meeting Robert.

The home is down a short winding hill at the end of the road. It is surrounded with trees and a very large open yard on three acres. There is a trail down to the Nimpkish River which we explore. The river trees are magnificent and seem to be welcoming us.

It is an interesting property and very unique so much to my liking. I talk to both of the neighbours to assure myself they will not mind living next to four dogs. Everything is perfect in their eye in this regard. It has a large wraparound deck and two small upper bedrooms. There is a tiny balcony overlooking the river and the yard below. It is charming. The owner is named Robert and lives in the north somewhere. The property has been rented for a while.

The realtor and I head back to her office to discuss my offer. That evening in our motel room the television set turns on without my effort. I turn it off. A few minutes later it turns on again. I know that my Robert love is talking to me through his turning the TV on; how amusing. I am comforted, thank you.

Once again with my real estate efforts I am well blessed. This is at the right time and meant to be. Thanks to Mystic we have found a new home on the river. People are surprised with my news but when they hear why we are leaving they agree it is appropriate.

During my trips to Courtney there is a store with sunrooms. My busy mind begins to dream of the possibility of adding a glass sunroom to the side of the home facing the river. I could put a futon inside and lay sleeping under the stars.

Mark welcomes our news with joy. This means another visit from him. This will be his third time to help us move in less than two years. A rainbow over the water blesses our good news. A couple days later another rainbow greets us along with a strange surprise on the fence line adjoining Harold's yard. It is a dead fish. Where the blazes did this come from I wonder. Then a double rainbow blesses us.

Over the space of about ten days prior to the arrival of Mark we have been blessed with four rainbows. Then I find dead snakes on the fence line on a day of another rainbow. There is no way a bird would drop more than one. There are four dead garter snakes lined in a row. This must be the work of Harold.

This is very sick minded person indeed. Mark arrives. We pick up our happiest two legged laughing labby at the airport. While playing in the yard later Mark is by the fence and calls me over. "What the heck is this? Come see this. Where did these dead snakes come from?"

"Mark this happened about three days ago. I disposed of the snakes but here are more. It is the work of the neighbor. Mystic has guided this transaction to leave here. Treya helped guide us to leave the tree house and now thanks to Mystic we are leaving this sea side home."

"Boy, sis. I am sure glad you are leaving here. That guy sure has a sick mind. He is one sick puppy."

"Yes, he won't be missed by any of us. Thanks to Mystic we are heading north into the trees away from any close neighbours."

"I can't wait to see this place you have found, it sounds neato."

"I think you will be pleased Mark. It is very private and quiet. Just what we all need. It definitely will be a place of deeper healing. On move day I will surprise Harold with a balloon. I have that neat big red balloon in the shape of a dog head which I got when we sold."

After the moving truck pulls away I take the red dog balloon and climb over the fence into Harold's yard. I affix the balloon to the door of his yard shed. Next I take several large marrow bones and with a black magic marker write the word thank you. I throw them into his backyard.

He will have his own shock when he returns home to see dog bones in his backyard. Perhaps it is spiteful of me but I am human. It has lightened my heart and is causing him no distress unlike his dead snakes and dead fish presents.

Time for us to depart our sea home. It is May 31 which is the birthday of brother Roger. The car is again loaded to the max. With each move the remains of Saber and young Mystic puppy were at Mark's feet. Now Amber's ashes join the other dogs. Goodness knows what else I have crammed on the floor but Mark is a little cramped. It is a three hour drive and we make a couple stops prior to arrival so he can stretch his legs. Even with the seat back as far as it goes he does not have much room.

Finally I introduce the Nicholson Road sign to him and we slowly make our way down the hill. "This is it, puppies your new home in the trees. Quiet and safe for all of us."

After the moving truck leaves the next day we need groceries and we head into Port McNeill which is a short drive. As I unpack our goodies and open the freezer door I am greeted with a surprise. For years I have stored my film in the fridge on the door. I am now looking at my film inside the freezer. I call out to Mark, "Hey, did you put my film in the freezer?"

He joins me in disbelief. "Heck no, I did not do that."

He has heard about my mischievous husband's antics but never been a firsthand witness to such. We look at each other forming a big smile. Mark responds, "Sis, I guess your Robert wanted you to know how pleased he is with this move. You must be in the right place."

The men from down island arrive to construct our sunroom addition. It is not a long undertaking. I purchase us a queen sized futon dog bed. Soon the puppies and I are sleeping under a starry blanket.

261

One night I awaken to look out at the night sky. I do not know what I am looking at. I cannot even describe it. At first glance one may think it is UFOs beaming around. I get up and go out on the deck with my head skyward. There is no sound. I am watching six or seven large, round, white circles which dance around above me. They are swirling to and fro very fast. I am mesmerized. I am unable to comprehend the significance of what this is. For several minutes I am entertained by this otherworldly phenomenon. I go back inside and lie down on the bed. Awhile later I wake up looking out but the mysterious flying swirls are gone. I whisper in the dark, "Thank you, whomever you are for allowing me to witness you."

"Puppy Communications"

Awhile after settling into the river home I contact the animal communicator Georgina whom I met in Courtney. When Amber stopped eating I had pushed food on her. I feel the need to connect with her. Georgina shares the voice of Amber.

"Carol Ann need not feel sorry for force feeding me since it was her way of making sure I was ready to depart this life. I was refusing to eat in order to let her know it was my time. She listened to her heart and the vet confirmed it. All was perfect and happened exactly as it should. She needs to remember that any choice made with love is never wrong."

"I felt very honored to be a part of her pack and was very respectful of them all. They all loved me and I loved them. The move to Canada was stressful for everyone. I found the air was crisper. I was able to release a lot of what I gathered in Arizona. I liked my Canadian life but missed Arizona and its energy because my heart is there with Vivian. I will reincarnate back into a dog life in that area."

I had given Amber a balloon ceremony after her death and Georgina shares her thoughts of this. Amber replied, "I was so honored she did all of that just for me. I felt humbled because I was just doing my job. It was an honor to the angels who not only guided me but to all of those others who just do their jobs. It made a huge impact on raising the energy of honoring those who serve as lightworkers. This type of thing should be done more often because it adds to the vibration as well as honoring what lightworker means. All beings who serve in the light need to honor what they do themselves and also to make an offer symbolizing what others are doing."

Robert comes in with a brief message to share. "My love, you need to move into another stage of your purpose. I am with you always. You need to open your awareness more and develop your senses. Saber and I will help you. Pay attention, sense us. Allow yourself to feel us and to feel into us......to be us......feel into everything. It is the secret, the key."

"You have done well my love. You conquered your doubts and erased your fears. You moved through the veil of grief and have accepted who you are. Now you are ready to be who you are meant to be and do what you are meant to do."

Saber comes in next. Georgina shares her impressions of him. "He is a wise benevolent being with such a grounding presence. He loved being a leader and teacher. He helped the other dogs to learn and everyone around him; humans also. He was very supportive and encouraging, always trying to change the energy into positive no matter what was going on. Everyone respected his presence."

He tells Carol Ann. "It is time and you know this. You have been waiting and preparing. There is nothing to fear. You need to connect and feel the energies allowing your spirit to do what it needs to do. Do not get caught up in trying to be anything or anyone. Just allow your spirit to do what it needs. Your job is to allow your spirit to hold the space for the vibrations to connect. The information will come through you and you will be simply allowing the energy to come through to start healing the planet. You have gathered this energy all of your life. Robert left this plane to work with this energy and assist from the other side. Trust you are safe and protected. There is nothing to fear, there is only love."

"In regard to your lightworker role, it has to do with writing. You need to write everything you receive from spirit or Robert. Everything is significant and you need to write it all down. Do not worry what to do with it. The time will come and it will fall into place, just trust. Your beloved guide dog Spirit girl also encourages you to keep listening and to keep writing. Stay tuned into the spirits and they will guide you. Just listen."

Georgina connects next with Mystic and senses he has a lot of fearful energy. He is not sure about his role with you. He feels he needs to be a protector but does not have the confidence to do so. He feels like he is trying to fill someone else shoes and does not feel he can do that.

"Whose shoes?"

"I feel I am supposed to do justice to Saber's spirit and presence but am unqualified to do so."

"Carol Ann does not expect this or want this of you, puppy boy. You need to be yourself." He relaxed and opened up a bit more. "I feel I am doing a poor job."

"You are an incredible being and a great dog. You need to let go of the past. Allow yourself to be a new dog every day. You can feel into each new day and feel yourself evolving into who you are meant to be now. It would be very exciting for you to feel your real self and to relax. Try to be nothing but yourself."

"I am very grateful to Carol Ann. I want to do the very best I can but I feel I can never do enough or be good enough. I am grateful for the closeness and love we share. I do not want her to give me away because I am not doing my job."

"We assure you this would never happen."

"How do you feel with Amber gone?"

"I miss her presence because I loved her so. She held such a strong leadership role."

"How do you like your Canadian life?"

"The energy is different here and is more relaxed. I do not know how to respond to it."

Georgina connects lastly with Treasure and is awed by her grace. "She carries such a huge presence of love and joy for all she meets. She loves to play and chase fairies and plant devas. She feels all of the frequencies around her and tunes into them. She absorbs and transmutes energies. She is a doer and not much of a talker. She is an angel dog. She works to clear energies. She is here to help you open your awareness."

She asks Treasure, "At what point did you know you were to be with Carol Ann instead of a service dog?"

"I always knew but wanted to encourage her with the training. Carol Ann finally realized that I was not supposed to leave her. Part of the lesson was about being able to listen to the voice in her heart instead of her head and also learning to listen to my voice also."

"Can you share with us about falling through the ice of the pond?"

"Yes, it was because we needed to move. Also, the energy there was stagnant. She needed to be where there was more flow. She was isolated from the energy she needed to connect with. She had to be near the ocean to clear herself and open more. She listened well. She was really amazing and intuitive. It is wonderful to see her trusting this more and learning how to listen and understand. I am proud of her for allowing herself to work in those energies more."

"I like to challenge her inner abilities and to work with her learning. I find it fun. I love her very much and just want to be with her. I am proud she has seen the fairies. They hang around the outside of the doors and she can feel them greeting her. They are happy giggly fairies."

Saber Rainbow Balloons

I am standing at the edge of the stormy sea with my beloved Spookie wandering nearby. It is three years today that her Dad Saber died. We are enjoying a stroll on our favorite sandy beach. The storm is reminiscent of the night that Robert died. The Arizona desert skies had rumbled loudly that night welcoming my love home into the light.

Spookers and I are joined with our new friend, Kelly. At the grocery store recently I had pulled in next to a car with a young couple. Both of them stood admiring the dogs for a long time and we chatted. They were living in a beach cabin near our favorite beach. We shared phone numbers and I called Kelly to see if she would like to join my Saber celebration. She agrees. The rest of the pack are left at home. I want special alone time with my first puppy girl. I have purchased fifteen pink balloons.

Kelly gazes on as I affix the bouquet of balloons to the collar of Spookie. I wrap the strings around extra tight since I do not want the island winds carrying them aloft until I am ready. She is quite pleased with herself as she prances before me with our bundle of pink love for her Dad. We are all smiles. She looks like she could take flight as the balloons tumble around her. I find a stick and draw a heart message in the sand. "We love you Saber."

After walking along for a few minutes I decide to let them fly. The rains are pouring now all around us and the sky is brooding. "Ok, angel puppy, let's release these for your buddy. Go find Saber." I loosen the strings and off they go. At first it looks like they are heading out to sea but the wind shifts and blows them back toward land. They become stuck in a tall tree. Guess my Saber balloons have another plan. We walk over to the tree.

Kelly and I watch mesmerized. "Look, they are forming a heart shape now." Then the wind blows them another direction and Kelly laughs saying, "They look like a chicken to me now."

The rain is pouring now as a man is walking toward us. It is the same man we passed earlier with his wife. He now stops to pet Spook. The woman asks if they can take a photo of Spook. I share our story. "Her Dad named Saber died three years ago today and the balloons stuck above in that tree were being released for him."

They continue on their way while Kelly and I make our way back towards the picnic area. Both of us have brought fixings for a picnic. As we approach the area there is a woman with a chocolate lab entering the beach. "Look Kelly, there is a chocolate lab coming. I have to say hello to that dog."

The dog comes over for a pet. The woman says she lives in the neighbourhood and brings her twice a day. "She is blind and her name is Muffin."

I am all smiles inside and out as I recall that one of my nicknames Robert used had been Muffin. I am amazed and ask Kelly to take a photo. Miraculously, while we have been visiting with the chocolate lab a magnificent rainbow has appeared over the sea sky. Kelly captures a lovely shot of me with my arms wrapped around a chocolate lab with the rainbow in background.

A moment later as I release the dog, Muffin happily trots down the beach with her partner. She is totally aware of her surroundings and walks without any hesitation.

Kelly and I find our table and set up our food. I continue to share aloud my grateful delight in our little miracle of the Saber rainbow. Spookie eagerly awaits a treat and is soon rewarded as Kelly puts a generous helping of potato salad onto a small plastic spoon. A second later she squeals, "My God, where did the spoon go?"

I am all laughter as I retrieve it from the ground. "You must watch out for our Spookie girl. She is a real snapping turtle when it comes to food. Anything you give her must be with a flat hand or you might be missing a finger."

Both of us are enjoying another good laugh. Kelly was a bartender and is now happily shaking a martini shaker to make us cosmopolitans. Spookie's eyes are growing larger when she sniffs the salmon only a foot away from her busy nose. She is well rewarded. We clink our toasts to Saber and enjoy our crackers and salmon. "You know this is a great memory for me. On the day of his death our dearest friend Linda joined Saber and I for a special last meal with him. I carried him onto a grassy knoll and we spread out a feast for all of us. It was a very special time. He died just before his fifteenth birthday."

"How old is Spookie now?"

"She is fourteen and a half."

"I cannot believe that. Plus she is still standing after that long walk we just had."

"Food is a great motivator for labs; but you are right she has done really well today with all the walking."

"I noticed she seems to be very bow legged."

"Yes she certainly is in her hind legs. Our Robert used to love being in the pool with both the dogs. He would sing to Spook. I love to swim with bow legged women and swim between their legs."

"How funny; that husband of yours sounds like quite the fellow."

"That is for sure."

After a leisurely time and a full tummy by all three of us we head to the car. I drive Kelly back to the beach cabin where her Dean is waiting. He asks, "So how was your time? Was it a sad day for you Carol Ann remembering the death of your dog?"

"Not at all. We had a great balloon release although they got stuck in a tree. Awhile later we met a woman about to walk her dog who is blind. It was a chocolate lab and a rainbow came in the sky so we have a great shot of me with a chocolate lab and a rainbow."

"You are kidding me! Wow, how cool is that. So what do you do with your time Carol Ann?"

"I like to spread my light and joy with whomever crosses my path. I have been writing stories for a while now so spend some of my time writing."

That evening I crawl into bed with a peaceful vision of my bundle of pink love flapping in the breeze in the tree. A couple days later I decide to take all the dogs for a walk on the beach to see what has happened with our balloons.

This beach is situated near a road with homes so it does get a lot of walkers. I park the car by the tree when I see that the balloons are still stuck. The dogs get out and run around. There is a man admiring them. I share my intent of the balloons to which he responds, "That is how they should be. They look great there. This way more people can see them and wonder what they represent. My dog died recently and I am at a loss."

"I understand. I do hope you can find another dog someday. Your dog in spirit wants you to be happy."

After he departs we all head down to the beach for a long walk. There is no one else about at the moment. We head back up to the road by the balloon tree. There is now a couple standing with their heads turned upward. The man is throwing rocks at the balloons. I stop to chat. "Those are balloons which I released a couple days ago for my dead dog Saber. The winds carried them back to land and they got stuck."

The woman shares, "We were on the beach having a fire smoking hot dogs when my husband asks, what is all that pink stuff in that tree. So we got up to investigate."

After a brief visit I walk away chuckling. This grown man has found his playfulness thanks to my balloons. Guess they are serving a higher purpose after all. Nature will free them in time if they are meant to go. Perhaps someone will see them float away some day and contemplate their purpose.

I realize many folks walking this beach road will have seen them by now. Pink is the color of love so we are sending love to everyone who sees them. They were meant to be shared with more than just Kelly and myself. As we head into Port Hardy to shop I see a rainbow. With each place I exit a rainbow is blessing my vision. Incredible.

As I drive home there magically is another rainbow at the entrance of our Nicholson Road. This has all happened over about a three hour period and I have been blessed with the sightings of more than three rainbows.

Spookie Reunites with
Saber and Robert

Spookie's breathing has become labored and her mobility is back in decline. A few weeks ago I took her to a vet in Courtney who had given her a chiropractic adjustment and some Chinese herbs. My beloved lab who could not get up on her own had been revived within a day. Miraculously, she was mobile on her own steam again.

Yet now this is different. With heavy sorrow in my heart I leave her on her bed and walk outside to contemplate what to do next. Our home on the Nimpkish River is well blessed with an abundance of bald eagles which sometimes swoop low over the backyard. The young dogs love to bark as they chase them with their heads turned skyward.

As I consider my situation with my first puppy Spook I look to the trees and am rewarded with the company of bald eagle. I stop in awe as I feel a message come through to me, "Yes it is time, you know this. You need to let her fly free."

I recall the wonderful book, "I Heard The Owl Call My Name," by Margaret Craven. Here now I am hearing the bald eagle calling Spookie back to her home in the light. "Ok, I shall go call the vet, thank you my wise sky friend."

The vet needs to check her so I help her into the back of the car. I ask the vet to come outside to examine her. After a brief consultation the eagle's message is confirmed. "Can someone come to our home to assist her?"

"Yes, we shall do this for you Carol Ann." If possible I time dog

271

deaths on auspicious days and magically the day of March 31 is Mystic's birthday, two days from now.

This is to be the death of my puppy from chocolate lab Saber whom my love, Robert had brought into our lives. She is indeed a most important dog. All my dogs are for they all have special roles and times they appear in my life. This beautiful black labrador had manifested in the lives of my husband and I at a most crucial time after the suicide of his son, Mark.

Over the years I have always thanked Mark Stephen Arnim for his death, in that it opened the door to my life with puppies and magically the heavenly line began to form of all those spirits awaiting their lives in dog form that would bless my life over the coming years. Out of any darkness there is always a blessing in disguise waiting if one can open your eyes to its message.

So it is now time to prepare myself to say earthly farewells to my first puppy that shared and took on all the pains of my grief in the death of my husband. March 31 arrives. I spend my time nestled next to her watching her enjoy apple treats. She gets a bowl of ice cream next.

I take photos of her lip smacking enjoyment as we wait for the arrival of the vet. Despite her challenge in breathing she is very vocal. She is not about to leave this life without voicing her feelings. She barks and barks looking at me with her sparkly brown eyes. My Arizona friend Margaret, who later lost her sight completely, thankfully was able to see her eyes. "Wow, that dog Spookie has the loveliest eyes I have ever seen, they just have little sparkles in them don't they."

Indeed Margaret was right; Spookie's eyes are very unique and exceptional. They speak to the voice of magic. I think her fairy angels during her birth must have spilled a bottle of their fairy dust over her because they truly do glisten and sparkle.

The vet arrives and Spookie is surrounded with her pack. All of us are very sombre as she leaves this earth plane. The three dogs stay by her side as I walk the vet to the door. "Do you have anyone to come be with you, Carol Ann?"

"No, I need to be alone with my four footers; I do not desire human comfort or companionship. Thank you for your sentiments."

Since the most painful death of my beloved Saber I have grown a lot and have the strength to do this without anyone by my side. I know I have Robert and Saber with all of us and this is enough.

My heart is heavy as I return into the house. I telephone Linda in Arizona, yet she does not answer. Spookie has a lovely brass bell on her collar with a very distinctive ring. While Robert and I lived in Chester, Nova Scotia, we found hand-made brass bells which he lovingly affixed to both collars of Saber and Spookie. When they ran loose we could then keep better track of them.

I leave a message on Linda's phone using the bell. "Linda, Spookie has flown away, this is now the only sound left of her." I shake her collar vigorously allowing the bell to sing into the phone and without saying another word, I hang up. Spookie was often a very vocal dog. I recall the death of Robert during his burial. As she stood beside me next to Saber she barked and barked.

Our river home has a wraparound deck with the main door being on the upper level. After purchasing our home I had a long ramp installed instead of the stairs so old dog Spook could easily come and go. I am very grateful for this. I go out to the yard and bring my little red wagon into the house. This will be Spookie's transport out of the house tomorrow.

Prior to our bedtime I move her lifeless form onto our bed and place her where she has always slept. The north island does not have a dog crematorium. The closest one is in Duncan which is the man I used to have Amber cremated while at the sea home. Yet my state of grief over her death is too deep to make the long drive to deliver her body.

The vet said that I could have her body frozen and put on a greyhound bus to be delivered to the cremation man. That seems to be a good plan.

The next morning I place her body into the red wagon and pull her down the ramp. The first daffodils have magically come into bloom. Her fairies had seen to this miracle. I cut some of the island's wild greenery and make a wreath putting a daffodil on it and write a love note which I attach to the wreath.

I call the cremation man to advise him of Spookie's arrival by bus and instruct him to cremate her with the wreath and note in place.

I take a last photo of her pack next to her in the red wagon. All three dogs look on in solemn quiet as they witness her being put into the back of the car onto the dog bed. "Ok, puppies jump in, we all need to go take our Von Spook to the vet in Port Hardy."

I find out the time of the bus she would be going south on. It stops in Port McNeill. A few minutes prior to its arrival to Port McNeill the three dogs and I pull into the bus station. Tearfully, I envision her frozen body in the cargo hold of the bus. "We shall see you again my dearest angel puppy, thank you for blessing our lives."

The bus slowly pulls out and I follow it up to the highway where it heads south. With my pack of three we head home.

My pack of five which I had arrived home to Canada with is now only three. This is another big change for all of us. I ask Spook to somehow give me any message she could from the other side. My wish is indeed granted. I have a red valentine heart shaped bowl which I had placed next to her dog bed for her water. Inside it recently I had placed a very large quartz crystal. A couple days after her spirit flight I notice that the crystal has been moved. It is now outside of the bowl on the floor.

"Oh my goodness Spookie is here. Thank you my angel dog for your message." I am very much immobilized in my grief and knowing her presence is with all of us is very comforting.

Her totem animal is a deer and although there are a lot of deer around our property I have never seen one. Our neighbour complains a lot about the deer getting into her garden. To my surprise I just happen to glance out our kitchen window one morning and see a deer in our back trees. Holy smokes, puppies. I open the door to go outside and of course my always on high alert boy Mystic charges out the door. The deer bounds away out of sight. All three dogs fly down the ramp barking as they run the fence line sniffing. "Wow, now that is a most lovely message of your presence, Spookie, thank you again."

Another way she talked to me from the other side was by the telephone. After Robert died I would hear the phone ring and go to answer it. There would be no one on the other end. I instantly had known that it was him sending me comfort as he witnessed my grief. Over the next week every night about seven p.m. the phone rang and no human was on the other end. My Robert and Spook were talking to us.

My grieving for her is comforted with these heavenly confirmations and always with my highest gratitude. When I get her cremation box I place her on the kitchen counter with daffodils. She was always underfoot in the kitchen.

Anytime I see a greyhound bus or any kind of a passenger bus I always get a vision of Spookie and I send her my loving gratitude.

Awhile after her death I have animal communicator, Georgina connect with her from the other side. She conveys that Spookie is a very powerful presence with a strong spiritual strength and a knowing of all. This is her message. "Spook helps you to find the answers you seek and encourages you to move into the intuition of the being that you truly are. She says that you hesitate to go there and it has been calling you for a long time."

"She says that as a child you always had abilities that were very special but that you were afraid to use them. Even as an adult you have had things happen to you that were unexplainable but you did not want to acknowledge them. She says you have very special gifts and that it has made it harder for you since your husband's passing, but she wants you to know to trust in your feelings around that. She says there is absolutely nothing you should feel guilty about and that Robert knows how much you love him. You need to know that he is still there to support you in your times of need. She says that you know when he is around. He is still there with you to help you to become who you are meant to be. He also says that you have huge gifts within you. Spookie says that she works with him a lot and helps you to connect with him and that you know that. Yet you do not want to feel vulnerable and that you have a lot of fears of going there, but there is nothing to fear, only love."

"She says you need to embrace the love with love and that it will take you to the peace that you are searching for. She says she is very much here for you, but you need to find the real you, it is your reason for being. She says you are a lightworker and you need to embrace why you are here. Wow, I have never had a reading come out quite like this, I hope it all makes sense to you, Carol Ann."

"She says she loves you dearly and thanks you for all of your care. She got quiet when I mentioned about her messages to you after her death. This must be something special between you. Her constant barking on her last day was her vocalizing her immense love for you. She thanks you for her ability to live such a valuable life."

Her death is just prior to the grand old age of fifteen. Her buddy and father, Saber, also died at fifteen. Definitely, my first two labradors have fulfilled their roles of companion, healer and teacher, to the fullest.

I grieve deeply for my beloved lab. Mark feels my pains and asks my family to call in on me. This is such a sweet gesture and much appreciated. He asks if he can do anything for me. "I will find you a small black lab to cuddle and mail it to you."

My parents telephone and share something very heartwarming. They had been with me at the burial of Robert when I had everyone in attendance release a yellow balloon. Upon hearing of the death of Spookie they purchased a balloon which they had released in the park across from their home. Thank you Mom and Dad. Spookie is well pleased.

A short time later Mark has mailed me my Spookie cuddle pup. "She is lovely Mark. I am cuddling here now as we speak. Thank you."

My brother Mark is a rare jewel who needs to share his love with another. He has a very big heart and I send my intents out into the universe for him to manifest a match. I foresee him with the perfect woman and I also sense he shall manifest his love before I find my new old love.

Paul to the Rescue

The beautiful sunroom proves to be faulty. To my dismay one day I hear a drip, drip. The contractor who built it was to come install a vinyl decking for me. Phone calls to him turn into endless frustrations. I do not know what to do. I discover a neighbor up the hill who is a contractor and make a call to him. I do not want to deal with the folks from Courtney for any further work.

My angels are watching over me when Paul comes through our gate. He is very thorough and professional. We make a deal for him to install the vinyl deck with a glass railing. I happily begin to pull off the countless wooden spindles of the deck throwing them to the ground below. Next I get my crowbar and begin to pull up the planks of the deck over the carport. There is plywood beneath.

Paul proves to be worth the money and soon we are enjoying our vinyl deck with an uninterrupted view of the trees thanks to the glass railing. What a magnificent improvement. Next we discover that the cedar planks of the house are splitting. He suggests vinyl siding which he can install over the cedar. Big spender awesome Possum decides this would be a marvelous addition and add good resale value. I know at some point we shall leave this paradise. It is a very big job with a big price. However, the end result is worth every penny. Our home now looks loved. It had indeed been neglected by its absentee owner and realtor Mary had cautioned me but I charged ahead believing in my vision of living there.

A few weeks later we are blessed with a visit from Linda and Cliff.

My brother Mark also arrives and we enjoy a wild reunion and grand time sitting on our back deck overlooking our bubble of trees. My Arizona friends love to sail and treat the three of us to a day on the water sailing northward. Unfortunately the island winds are not cooperative yet it is a lovely treat to enjoy their company with the sea and sky. We share a lovely beach picnic before sailing homeward. Mark has enjoyed his solo day with the three rowdies.

The river trail is well worth exploring. After our arrival I found a neighbour who was willing to climb the tall trees to trim the boughs. After lots of ruckus with his chainsaw I am now able to have a much better view of the river below. My visitors take delight in my throne. I had Mike carve me a throne from a large stump and he even carved a heart in the back.

The sunroom continues to leak. Paul offers a solution which seems quite drastic. "Your best option Carol Ann is to remove it."

"Good God. What the heck would I do with it after that?"

"I know someone who could purchase it from you to reassemble it for his own home."

"That sounds good. I cannot believe it has come to this but I trust in your judgement so get the ball rolling."

"We can install a window the same size as the front one and put some French doors in for you."

"That was its original look." He has a couple other jobs to finish first.

My parents bless us with a stay to our river home. The large Mexican dining table has found a new home at a resort by the sea. It was ridiculously too large for this place and certainly I cannot move it again whenever we leave here. I have found a comfortable smaller dining table which my Dad helps put together. They enjoy the peacefulness of our quiet place. One evening I entertain them with playing my various crystal singing bowls by candlelight. It is very soothing and peaceful.

A few days after they depart Paul gets to the task of removing the sunroom. The job proceeds smoothly and soon our home is downsized. I breathe a sigh of relief and write my last cheque to Paul. His wife comes over to admire our home presenting me with a very large red bow. I have a heart shaped wreath on the front of the house which I attach the bow to. It adds a very happy note to catch sight of this when you drive through our gate.

My ill feelings to the Courtenay contractor are assuaged with an idea. I take a photo of our new look without the sunroom and put it on the front of a card. I tell him I forgive him for his inadequate and unprofessional manner. I thank him for his role in our magical home. I have no idea what his response shall be but I am doing this for the highest good and seal it with this intent.

A Spiritland Namaste

As I come inside our front door one day I see that my lovely Namaste plaque is not in it usual position by the telephone. I check around but cannot find it anywhere. It is not something that is moved around since it is kept at my entry table.

My mischievous lovie boy must be up to tricks. I call aloud to him, "You know how fond I am of that plaque. It would be nice to have you return it silly love of mine."

The new year is coming. I receive a phone call from Paul, the man responsible for improving the look of our river home. "Carol Ann, we would like to invite you for New Year's Eve supper. You can join our family get together."

Just as I am about to decline I surprise myself responding happily, "Yes, that would be lovely. Thank you for thinking of me."

I am pleased with my decision upon hanging up the telephone. The New Year's Eve always marks my own celebrations due to it being the anniversary of the beginning of my love with Robert. Spending it with two leggers would be good for me.

It is a month or so later I am looking through the drawers of the telephone table. There is some piece of important paper I am attempting to find. To my delight I discover the Namaste plaque. "Oh thank you Magoo, you finally put it back. You know my ways all too well. There always comes a time when I am rooting around looking for something."

Namaste is a Sanskrit word which I have carried with me since my study abroad program in Nepal during college. Its translation means,

"I honor the place in you in which the entire universe dwells. I honor the place in you which is of love, of truth, of light and peace. When you are in that place in you, and I am in that place in me, we are one."

My love and I certainly are still embracing the Namaste spirit as he continues to bring me smiles from the other side.

Brother Rog is keeping up with our activities at the river home. While I visit with him for some mysterious reason I notice the name Robert slips out instead of Roger. How very odd. Wendy and he have been thinking of leaving Vancouver Island. They have closed their little gift shop in Sydney named Treasures. They have made the decision to go live on Prince Edward Island. He plants a seed within me. I smile as I hang up the phone.

Already I have begun to feel the stirrings within me to leave our bubble in the trees. Robert and I very much enjoyed our time in the maritimes and spent three days exploring PEI. The winters of the north island here are very gentle in comparison but we will adjust. Roger led me well before as I followed him out west. Now perhaps I am meant to follow him back east.

I love our river home yet I am now in need of seeing the horizon. I desire to be back more in civilization. There are so many trees here which impair my view of the sky.

My ponderings take hold and I find myself a friendly realtor named Debbie. In June, 2007 on the day of a new moon a For Sale sign is attached to our gate. About this time I begin to hear a repeated message, "Fasten your seat belt." Thank you for whatever that may mean.

I do not have internet and brother Mark offers to find me a realtor on Prince Edward Island. Soon I am conversing with a man with Royal LePage in Summerside. I fill him in with my desires for our new home.

Orca Guide to Native Guide Dog

While at the grocery one day I notice a bulletin for a book signing. The authors of a book I purchased about orcas are doing a presentation at Telegraph Cove. I decide to go. While living at the sea home during our explore drives heading north out of town I was always mesmerized by the signs for whale watching at Telegraph Cove. Every time I saw the sign I felt drawn to go there. My guides of the deep blue sea, the orcas were calling to me. Our river home is situated a short drive from Telegraph Cove. It is my favorite place to go on the north island. The dogs love to wander through the trees of a campground which leads out to a secluded bay and lovely beach.

The two authors are seated at a table. As I hand them my book for their autographs I say, "Thanks for the important work you are doing to assist the whales and educate the public. It is a necessary worthy endeavor and most appreciated by myself."

I wander close by their table as two women sit nearby. One of them gets up and helps her husband with a drink. She catches my eye responding, "My husband is blind."

I lean over him whispering, "Have you considered getting a guide dog?"

He replies with a smile, "I have one."

"What school is he from?"

"My boy is named Native and he is from Guide Dogs for the Blind of San Rafael, California."

"Holy smokes. I raised two puppies for that school."

The wife excitedly tells the other woman, "Arlene, this woman raised dogs for the same school Native is from, isn't that amazing."

It has been years since I worked with guide dogs yet still it impacts my life profoundly. My passion continues to draw working dogs across my path. Puppy excitement fills the air and I ask the author. "Where is your guide dog now?"

"He is on vacation staying at a friend's who lives in the country. He shall be having a great time. Yet anytime I leave him after getting home he has his nose out of joint."

"That is because he knows his place is with you. His dedication and commitment is to be by your side all the time. What type of dog is he?"

"Native is a yellow labrador and is my second guide. I worked at the Vancouver Aquarium. I began my search for a guide dog when it became difficult for me to walk through the trees of Stanley Park."

"My first two pups were yellow lab females. My first came back to me as a career change puppy and the second graduated as a breeder. Next I raised three girls for CCI that trains dogs for wheelchair and the deaf."

"Are you still raising puppies?"

"No, I stopped prior to moving home to Canada. It was my driving force and passion which guided me through the worst of my grief after my husband's death. It was very difficult turning in the dogs. My turn in of Laverne, my first puppy was excruciating. But the miraculous ending was I got to adopt her and rename her Spirit. I had been blinded in my grief and from the moment she was placed in my arms she became my guide dog." Tears have formed but they are tears of joyful gratitude instead of the pain of grief.

The woman is shocked by my unabashed public display of emotion. "My God, you are really crying. Will you be coming to the talk and slide show tonight? It will be worth your while."

"I had not planned to which is why I am here now. Yet perhaps I shall. Could I bring my guide dog Spirit?"

"Yes, you should bring her."

Later that day Spirit happily follows me to the car as the young hooligans are left home together. She prances by my side glad to be included in this outing. At the entrance to the whale museum where the talk is to be I am told the dog cannot come in. I explain that the blind author told me I could do so. Thankfully the right person overhears me. "Yes, you can bring your dog with you. Go inside."

We find a seat and the folks nearby greet Spirit with smiles and pets. She settles by my feet as the speakers begin. Above us hangs the skeleton of a whale. Last year in honor of celebrating the day she had come into my life as guide dog puppy Laverne I took her out to Telegraph Cove for a run on the beach. Then we walked the boardwalk and spent time in the whale museum in which we now sit. At that time the skeleton was on the floor being assembled. I was allowed to have Spirit with me and I got a great photo of her standing next to the whale remains.

Every one of the crowd is enthralled with the slide show and the tales of the deep. I sense the spirits of those great creatures of the sea are well pleased. A question period begins. Spirit begins to scratch and in doing so her paw keeps thumping the floor. The speaker chuckles saying, "The dog must have a question." The formerly serious energy pervading the room is now taken over with infectious laughter as everyone becomes lighter in heart and body as her tail thumps continue. Good work girl. I lean over to give her a hug. It gives me great satisfaction and pleasure to know that all the audience is now aware of her canine presence.

My mind shifts back to the raising of CCI girl Maggie, when she had made her presence known at a public gathering. We were at a function presented by the British author and medium, Rosemary Altea. One could have heard a pin drop in the room as everyone was rapt in her words. As she spoke of receiving insight or messages through nature and spirits, Maggie let out a woof. Rosemary responded, "I see that someone's dog is having a connection with a spirit right now."

At the end of the presentation I waited in line for her book signing. The moment she saw adorable angel Maggie, her face lit up with a huge smile. "Oh my, what a light you are. I can see why you received something through her. She is radiance personified. Such a lovely adorable angel." My whole body had responded in truth bumps as I call them for when we speak or hear our truth the body knows.

Spirit nudges me as I return fully to the present. I am so grateful for those days of raising my five service dog puppies.

The presentation ends and Spirit receives welcome attention as we make our way outside. "Great job, Lollipop. I am so glad we both got to come to this event. That was so special for you as well I know. It is always great for me to be able to share your background and have you appreciated as you so well deserve."

I drive home with a sense of gratitude and expectation for the day that my own book shall be out in the public eye. A guide dog named Native confirms this shall be so, I know it is meant to be. This is a powerful synchronistic confirmation I myself have a book to share about my passionate dog blessed driven life.

In a few weeks the Christmas holiday will be upon us and I call Mark to see if he would like to come visit. Another grand idea comes to mind as we chat. "Would you like to meet our son Jade?"

"That would be smashing Carol Ann, yes. Thank you."

Mark arrives first and Jade comes after the new year. The dogs welcome another visitor and within minutes utter mayhem ensues. Mark and Jade have an instant rapport which is no surprise to me. I am most pleased. When Mark walks into our home he greets me with an enthusiastic, "Wow, look what you have done to the place. Holy smokes."

"Yes, it needed some cheering up."

He loves the bright golden yellow of the kitchen and living room. The bedroom is lavender and bathroom a lime green. "Hey, look at the paw prints on the stair."

"I had to replace the steep stairway. I did not want carpet so painted it green. Spirit is very cooperative with anything I ask of her. I took her to the top of the stairs and dipped her front paws in yellow paint. The paw prints are from her. I placed all my colorful clogs on the step for added color and fun."

"It sure looks neat, good job."

We share a huge turkey and a great feast. I am thrilled to enjoy the boisterous entertainment of the two of them. The living room is gifted with the sounds of farting and roof raising laughter. It becomes a competition. Boys will be boys as the saying goes. We take the dogs to a nearby lake and enjoy tossing sticks and getting wet along with the dogs. All our tails are wagging happily.

Jade heads back north. The pups and I continue a great time with Mark.

During any time I share with Mark when I call Mystic the name comes out as "Marr" as I am about to call him Mark. "Hey, I have discovered why the dog is sometimes called your name. It may sound far-out."

"I am listening."

"Since the name confusion happens so often it got my curiosity aroused. I know there must be meaning to this. An animal communicator asked him if someone had guided him into my life. Is it someone I know? Mystic responded, Yes, it is your brother Mark. It would also explain the instant rapport the two of you shared when you met."

"Hey cool. That is really neat. Sometimes you even call me Mystic."

"Well brother you do call yourself laughing labby."

"I want to go share that with Isabel. She would enjoy such a story." Mark has been with his true love Isabel for a short time now. It is a woman who crossed his path years earlier yet they both wisely agree that the timing was not yet right for their union. Divine timing is ever wise and always magical. I prepare us supper as I listen to my brother's whoops of delight and laughter while chatting with his love.

Margaret Hugs

During the winter months I take our home off the market and relist on the first day of spring 2008. I receive a spring card from my Mom with a note, thinking of you. Just as I am about to turn off the highway onto Nimpkish Road I stop to admire the realtor sale sign pointing up the road to our place. I happen to notice a big truck approaching. It is a United moving truck. They are my moving company. When I get home I receive a call from the realtor telling me she has another realtor named Joy who has a couple to view our home.

The showing is for April 6 which is my Mom's birthday. I telephone Stratford to share about seeing the moving truck with a showing by a Joy on her birthday. "Did you go out on the highway and wave down the United truck?"

"No Mom, but it certainly gave me a good feeling."

"All these signs certainly are a good omen for you."

On the day of the showing two cars pull up to the gate. They have arrived early. I talk to the couple who tell me they have two dogs. One of them is a black lab. It would be perfect for our buyers to have dogs. I receive a good report from Debbie about the showing and a couple days later the couple come through and stay for another long hour plus. This is a very good sign. An acceptable offer is made and we have a deal. They have a home in Nanaimo. The offer is contingent on that sale.

In early May my maritime realtor advises me he has found a suitable place. He emails many photos which I study over and over. I gasp in disbelief at one of them as I see an apparition in the doorway of a room.

It is Treasure. I think it is likely table legs which are her same coloring and yet my eyes definitely see it as my dog in our future home. My neighbour who can see into the unusual has the same response when she first sees the photo. "You mean you see the dog too?"

"Yes, for sure. It is Treasure."

"You and I are the only ones who see it. Thank you for sharing what you saw."

It is confirmation for me we are destined to live there. I do not have a suitable person to stay with my three labs so I decide I will buy this place sight unseen. It is in the country outside of Summerside on six acres of land. This is the challenge to property there because many of the places in the country are in farmland so have acreage. It is a small one storey property with lots of trees and very private. Every room looks different so it is a very unique place. I share the photos with my realtor and she says, "It looks like it suits you. I think it has your name written all over it. Very unique, just like you."

The place has just been listed in April. My realtor places my offer and agreement is reached. On the signature line I sign my name along with beloved labs, Spirit, Treasure and Mystic. The deal is made on May 11 which is Mother's Day. Six years ago on this day was the graduation of my Serna trust puppy. The incredible synchronistic tapestry of divine timing astounds me. Bow wow wowsers! In the evening I check the TV schedule for movies. Anne of Green Gables is playing. My new home is located in the area of the island called Anne's Land. Magic.

People are amazed with my interest in dates and how I connect events. For me it speaks to the support of the universe. We thank those we love who gift us. Synchronicity is a gift of love from the universe and the universe is really made up of all of us. Proper acknowledgement is vital. Plus it is a fun tool. When one pays attention with an attitude of awed gratitude it opens the door for more blessings. All of us want to keep life's blessings coming our way.

My parents have now been married for sixty-five years. In honor of this milestone they have travelled across the Canadian rainbow by rail. I arrange to meet them in Vancouver when their train pulls into the station. I enjoy my short flight from Port Hardy to the mainland.

There are several people on the train who have heard about me coming to meet them from the island. After our happy reunion I am greeted warmly by folk my parents befriended. My parents have certainly enjoyed a festive time sharing their anniversary with strangers on a train. We go for a tour by trolley car. My Dad snaps photos as he is hanging on to the bar.

We share a lunch and spend some quiet time in a lovely old church across from the restaurant. Our time together is brief and yet is worth every moment to share a memorable time with my parents. I fly back to my north island home.

I want to make a trip to Arizona prior to our move to Prince Edward Island. I want to spend some quality time with dearest Margaret. Her son Don died a year ago, which has been extremely tough on her. The two of them had wanted to come visit our river home although in reality it would not be suitable for a wheelchair visitor.

I have seen a lot of the couple, Fraser and Coraley who made the offer on our 910 puppy home. They love our dogs and agree to stay with them when I travel to Arizona. I am most grateful. I have to leave in the dark of the morning so they have come to stay the night. I lay awake my mind abuzz with anticipation about my trip.

There is another loud buzz coming from upstairs. My Roberto was known to be a good snorer on occasion and now I am being serenaded by Fraser. He could definitely win the prize for the loudest snores. Occasionally they subside and I know that Coraley has given him a big nudge, something I used to do myself. I am unable to stop myself from rolling in laughter. What a most timely gift to hear this sound after my twelve long years without my companion, on the eve of the day I am flying back to our former home. It seems like a propitious sign of a blessed trip. The snores subside and I am lulled into slumber.

I fly out of Port Hardy into Vancouver on Sept. 12. I have a couple hours wait to catch my plane into Phoenix. I have chosen to wait at a small coffee bar sitting on a tall seat overlooking the countless people parading left and right. A few minutes later the seat next to me is taken by a young woman who immediately becomes engrossed in a book making notes. How so like me I muse. I am curious what could create such serious undivided attention and discreetly catch a glance at the book. It is about the law of attraction. I am witnessing firsthand evidence how like energy draws like energy. I am about to converse with her when I catch sight of an airport vehicle moving through the crowd. Instantly I see why I am gifted to look that way because there is a black lab in it. I sense it is a working dog. My little girl self gets up right away to get a closer look.

I am rewarded with seeing a lovely soft black lab in a guide dog harness and on it reads Guide Dogs for the Blind. I walk up to the team once they are off the vehicle. She senses my presence. I greet her happily commenting on her beautiful dog. "What school is your dog from?"

I know what her reply will be but want to hear the words. "She is from Guide Dogs for the Blind in San Rafael, California."

I cannot contain my excitement. "Wow, I knew it. My name is Carol Ann and I raised two pups for them years ago."

"You are kidding. It is really something to meet you," she replies with the same enthusiasm. Whenever a service dog person and puppy raiser mix the air becomes electric with an unspoken bond of gratitude. I walk along side with her and the airline employee who is escorting them. I have plenty of time so follow them into an elevator.

My big red shoulder bag has a black lab on it with the phrase, "Well Bred." The airline lady notices and shares this with the blind woman. I laugh in reply, "Yes I am a well bred lab puppy myself. I have three labs currently so I am really a fourteen legged dog. I raised two pups for guide dogs and then three for CCI. My second guide dog pup became a breeder."

"What is her name?"

"Terrace. Her last litter of puppies were birthed on the 9/11 tragedy day. Today is Sept. 12 so her pups will have had a birthday as of now. It is most propitious to meet you on this day."

"This is Trixie and she is my second guide. I am small myself so wanted a petite dog and I got my wish with her. She is three years now. Where are you from?"

"Stratford, Ontario."

"Wow, I live in Guelph, Ontario. Trixie and I are flying to Portland for a guide dog reunion."

"My goodness, I went to that campus with my first puppy, Laverne." The airline lady speaks of helping a couple other guide dog teams yesterday. It seems there will be several Canadian teams reuniting in Portland.

She is about to head into the customs area so we say our farewells. I walk back towards the coffee bar with a marvelous sense of peace as I pass lines of people waiting to check in with faces set in exhaustion and grim determination.

The woman who was reading is still immersed in her book. I do not feel the desire to chit chat with her yet am compelled to wish her well. I approach her chair and put my hand on her shoulder saying, "I trust you will achieve what you desire."

She is startled with my voice and words yet responds with a smile, "How did you know?"

"I was sitting next to you earlier and happened to see your reading material. You were not aware of my presence."

"No, I had not seen you. I was oblivious."

"Yes, I know. But it is a lot of fun when one pays attention. It does help get your needs met. I wish you success."

"Yes and I wish the same for you."

I walk away to spend a few minutes outdoors. I had followed my heart and in doing so I know imparted a little joy into hers as well. It is time to head to my gate. On the plane I listen to my cd of the pacific coast whales that lullaby me into deeper serenity as I contemplate landing in Phoenix. As we make our approach into the valley of the sun tears begin to roll as I the feel the sorrows of years ago surface. I have been well guided to do this trip at this time. Roberto was buried in Montana on Sept. 6. It is now Sept 12 and I return on Sept. 21. I intentionally did the trip during this time span to assist me in healing that chapter of my life. I know this trip will be a catalyst for further transformation. This year is my first time I am not with my Laverne Spirit on the anniversary of our reunion at guide dogs. That day was Sept. 18. I saw on my calendar when I planned this trip that was also the day I had returned into Phoenix after Robert's burial.

The essence of my beloved potential Laverne Spirit was guiding me even from the other side so many years previous. Far fetched? Perhaps not. It was a synchronistic blessing of my future although consciously unknown to me at the time.

Linda and I share a happy reunion and head for the home of Margaret to pick her up for supper. The three of us are joined by my good old friend, Liz. What a happy time. It has been a long time since seeing Margaret. She is now totally blind yet her zest is intact. A friend of Linda's who is out of town allows us to stay at her home out in the Carefree desert. I awaken to gaze upon the majestic saguaros which had been part of my daily life for sixteen years while living in the desert.

The next day we drive to the private care home where Margaret resides and head out of town. The three of us chatter away as Linda drives us to their home outside of Patagonia in southern Arizona. Cliff and she have been living in a charming home in the hills of Patagonia near the Mexican border. There is no room to accommodate Margaret and I so we have made reservations at a lovely B&B close by. It is named the Spirit B&B.

We check in to it and then make the drive up to the hilltop home of Linda's. Cliff greets us and lifts Margaret out of their truck. She is thrilled with the canine greeting. I sit on the floor next to her as the dogs make their acquaintance. Linda treats all of us to a lovely supper and drives us back down the hill to our lodging.

Our room has two twin beds. Margaret and I can reach across and touch hands. We share many a giggle about this and that as we both fall into contented slumber. In the morning I share with Margaret some of her chatterings from in the night.

"You mean I talk in my sleep?"

"Yes, you do. Plus you talk quietly to yourself while still awake. I also have picked up that habit. You were dreaming which was fun for me to overhear since it involved a puppy. You were with Don, telling him, ok puppy go find Don, go find him."

"Really! I am so indebted to you for helping me through my Don grief. He suffered so much in his life and his cancer only added to that."

"Yes, I understand Margaret but he was very brave."

"Why did he have to suffer so much? I cannot bear to think of him in any pain."

"Remember our past conversations when I told you that in death you leave behind your diseased body?"

"Yes, you said I will be able to walk again and no longer be blind.

You also told me he can hear me talk to him even though he is dead. I used to think he could not hear me. Yet thanks to your stories about Robert I do believe now. I often talk to him and sing like I do for your Spirit."

"Spirits on the other side do not want to see us in such pain and grieving so deeply. I walked the deepest depths of that myself and if there is any way I can alleviate it for you or anyone that is my task. I know that Don is around you a lot helping you."

"Oh, I sure hope so. I think maybe he is. A few days ago I was sitting in my chair talking aloud to him when I felt a hand on my shoulder. There was no one else in the room but me. Do you really think it was him?"

"You thought so initially so yes I am sure. You can believe in these things now Margaret."

"You are my angel Carol Ann for helping me."

"I think we all carry angel energy. We are all angels in training."

She giggles at this prospect. "Oh I like that idea."

"It is an uplifting mindset so why not. Shall we go get some breakfast now my dear friend?"

"Yes, that sounds good. Linda will be here soon too."

Breakfast is delicious. While we wait for the arrival of Linda, I walk Margaret slowly around the place. I give her a tour with my eyes and she uses her hands to admire all the beautiful old antiques and various treasures.

We spend another fun day with Linda and the dogs. Our last evening is supper at a Mexican restaurant. The conversation turns to talk of her son Don. As we chat during our meal I sense Don is with her listening to his Mom talk about him. "Margaret, I do believe he is with you right now."

"Oh Carol Ann I hope so. Do you really think he can hear me? I want to believe so much, I miss him more than I can say."

Linda shares a story. "Margaret you know how rainbows are an important messaging sign for Carol Ann. I have wondered whether we would see one while Carol Ann is here and while I was driving last night after taking you to the B&B I saw one. I knew it was a Robert message for all of us."

"Really, how marvelous," Margaret's sorrow turns to smiles.

"Hey Linda, thanks for sharing that. I am so glad it was you to see the Bobby rainbow."

In the morning we take several photos and Linda drives us to the car rental. I rent a car to drive her back to her home in Phoenix. Margaret and I visit happily as we enjoy the three hour drive back into the city. She is very excited about our potential move to PEI. Every time I spot a United moving truck I announce its sighting. "Boy, how many have you seen now Carol Ann? You definitely must be moving soon to keep seeing so many of those big trucks carrying people's belongings to new homes. Oh how I wish I could visit you there."

I help her get settled back into her room and give her the biggest hugs. She is teary eyed at my departure. "I will see you in a couple days friend. Linda is driving us back into the city so I shall see you again prior to flying home." I make the drive back to the home of Linda.

We spend the next afternoon exploring Tubac. In a shop I find a snuggle pup with a pocket and a pink heart which fits inside the pocket. "I am going to present this to Margaret when we see her. She can cuddle this."

I am treated to a trip down memory lane when Linda and Cliff take us into the Tubac Resort which was frequented by Robert and I along with Saber and Spook. It has grown since then but we sit outside sipping yummy margaritas overlooking the golf course.

I have contacted the present owners of our former Carefree home and the next day Linda drives us back into the city. Being back inside the home of where my Roberto died will be a healing for me. We drive slowly around the neighborhood and pull into the driveway. The house looks very different. The two men Michael and David who had purchased it did a complete renovation of it for resale.

Thankfully, the saltillo tile walkway is still in place and I am greeted by the paw prints of Saber and Spook as I approach the front door. The former heavy wooden carved doors have been replaced with glass and we can see a full view into the backyard area. The former plants in the patio have been removed and a fountain babbles away. It is very beautiful. I am very much in shock.

The couple greet us warmly allowing us to wander on our own

from room to room. I sit for a few minutes alone in our former bedroom envisioning that life changing day in 1996. I breathe myself back into the present and go into the backyard to gaze over the pool. Everything looks and feels so different yet my mind is busy playing various movies. There are lots of dogs and splashing in the pool. After a few minutes I return inside to join Linda and the couple. I explain about my life with Robert and the dogs and his death in our bedroom. They are very empathetic.

The former laundry room wall has been knocked down and now the dining room and kitchen are all part of the large living room area. I cannot get over the changes to our beloved Toad Hall. Thankfully, the saltillo tile flooring is in place. I share with them the significance of the various custom tiles.

I capture several photos inside and out. I am so grateful to have been able to come inside our beautiful home. I loved it as it was but its purpose had completed with me and thus it had to be transformed itself, to accommodate new owners. As we drive away I call out, "Farewell Toad Hall, thank you."

Linda next takes us on a tour up into the Carefree highlands past Robert's first home. We drive past Vivian's and Margaret's as well and around the town of Carefree and through Cave Creek. It has been a wonderful worthwhile time to do all of this reminiscing and retracing of my desert life as best I can.

We stop in for a brief visit with Margaret's long-time friend Mac. He and I became acquainted when I was helping Vivian. It is great to reconnect with him and takes me down memory lane again to when I first moved to Carefree. Mac lives in the very same complex of my first studio apartment of 1987. I ponder whether we may have seen each other back then and said hello. How amazing that years later Margaret entered my life thanks to a dog. Our paths were not intended to cross at that time. My divinely timed meeting of Margaret, Vivian, Amber and Mac was meant to be when it was to the highest good for all of us. I am again awed with the conductor of my life's symphony. It is a celestial orchestration of our joint souls and our mischievous heavenly flyboys.

My last visit with Margaret is a tough farewell but she puts on her bravest face. "What are you wearing today Carol Ann?" She always loved to hear about my colorful attire.

"I have a pink linen top with cotton capri pants which have butterflys all over them."

As I present her with the snuggle pup and enjoy our farewell hugs she says, "Take those butterfly pants home. Happy landings Carol Ann."

Next farewell is with dearest Linda. My plane lifts off and I gaze out the window as I fondly say farewell to the Arizona desert.

I have a long wait in Vancouver before I can catch my flight up island to my river home. I go to the ground level to spend some time outdoors. The international arrivals and customs is nearby. I sit and watch a tall young man exit with a luggage carrier with a big, long box labeled bike. He removes the bike box and I go get the luggage carrier to put my own heavy suitcase on it. There is a piece of paper laying on it which I pick up to read. It is a receipt for foreign currency exchange. I am instantly fascinated and walk over to the man asking, "Hi, where are you from?"

"I just flew in from Auckland, New Zealand."

"Wowsers, welcome to Canada. I presume you plan to tour and camp with your bicycle."

"Yes after a couple days in Vancouver, I plan to ride around Vancouver Island."

"Good show, there are lots of cyclists over there. I live on the north end of the island. I have a long wait for my flight up island and would love to watch you assemble your bike if you do not mind."

"Not at all, we can be a good distraction for each other."

"I have to share why this is so special for me. Several years ago I flew my bike from Edmonton, Alberta to London, England. After the wedding of my sister in Scotland I rode all around Scotland, Ireland and Wales for a month. I slept in a pup tent and knocked on people's doors for permission to camp in their fields. I do not remember who helped to put my bike together but it certainly was not me."

This process of assembling takes quite a long time and I am glad to have a good way to pass the time. He is finally done and asks, "Do you mind watching this while I go inside?"

"Absolutely not, feel free to take your time. I still have some time to wait for my shuttle to the other terminal."

While he is gone I notice a bag with a label with Kathmandu in the name. When he returns I say, "It looks like you have been trekking in the Himalayas."

"Yes, I was there in the nineties for a trek. How did you know?"

"I saw your bag referring to Kathmandu. I lived there for a semester while in college in 1979. I had a period of trekking in the mountains and ten days at a Buddhist monastery. It was a life changing experience and I loved every minute."

His eyes get very big and he stops what he is doing. "Wow, it must have been something to be there back then. Now it is so westernized. The mountain villages have signs, apple pie served here."

"Yes, I know that would be true. The nonstop constant march of trekkers, mountain climbers and curious travellers have forever changed the face of Kathmandu and Nepal."

We seem to be a pair of kindred spirits who are drawn together by a bicycle box. How amusing indeed. "Time for me to go for a test drive."

With a boyish grin he wheels away and returns a few minutes later. "Can you watch over this while I go inside again?"

"Yes, feel free."

I am pleased to be of assistance for him. I notice a spot on one of his packs where the zipper is not fully closed. I am guided to send him off with a little note. I take one of my colorful pages from my notepad and write, "Happy magical cycling to you Jeff. Thank you for our time. Keep smiling. Blessings to you, Carol Ann Joy. Namaste." I tuck it into the pack and securely close the zipper. He returns a moment later attired in his biking outfit along with a glorious smile.

I shake his hand and he is off. "Safe travels to you."

A few moments after boarding my south terminal shuttle bus I catch sight of a man exiting the airport to sit on an outdoor bench. I look again when I notice he is a blind man walking alone with the aid of a white cane. I recall my visit with the Canadian woman and her beautiful guide dog Trixie. I chuckle as I wonder what the conversation would have been if this man had crossed my path. The details of his story are unknown to me but I silently send him an intent to find a guide dog if this is his choice. May you be drawn to finding your four-footed angel so your life can be blessed beyond your imaginations of this moment in time.

My own beloved guide dog and the two hooligans are overjoyed to welcome me back home. I have checked in with them by phone a few times and Coraley always had good reports.

The next day as I am lounging with my labrador rainbow I catch sight of a message from my love.

I have many butterflies around our home and I had one placed over a photo of Jade and I with Spirit. Now it is perched atop my half-moon Mexican piñata. Robert has made his pleasure known. In my mind I hear, "You are my butterfly girl. Keep going. You have your butterfly wings and the world awaits transformed Carol Ann Joy."

Star Lady and Medium Rosemary

It has been months since listing our river home. We do have the offer from the Nanaimo couple yet it is contingent on them selling their home. This real estate transaction is not evolving in the same manner as my previous three. I do know we are meant to leave here but the wait is becoming frustrating. I want some answers. The astrologer I worked with previously is on holiday. Somehow I am guided to another woman from Victoria named Samantha Kane-Kennedy.

I set up an appointment with her which falls on the six year anniversary of Saber dog's death. I seek answers from my stars as to why I am still stuck in our river home. I have an instant rapport with her and very much like her style of communicating the clues she unearths from my chart.

The answers I receive leave my head spinning.

I share with her about my life with dogs and their meaningful purposes on my journey through grief and healing. Samantha shares, "You have definitely been guided to your current home for healing. Your dog Spirit's soul devotion to you shows me that she will not want to depart this earth. She will hold on for as long as possible."

"You have put yourself into a place of sanctuary in this home. Your grief has been monumental and it still shows in your chart at this time. Carol Ann you have had so much happen to you, I do not know where to start with this chart of yours."

"For years you have not wanted to be here and your body has started to shut down. You need to tell your body that you are here to stay. Your kidneys, lung and blood are still poorly. You need to make your food fun and liven it up with beets and greens. Your breath has been too shallow far too long. Cinnamon is a blood cleanser, so cinnamon toast would be a helpful tasty treat for you. Red and white ginseng would be very beneficial for you and help build you back into your body."

"You can visualize connecting with mother earth bringing her energy up through your feet to help ground you. Breathe down through your crown. The breath can help connect you to be more consciously here in your body. You are on a precipice at this point in time and need to make the move fully into embracing life. Your Robert needs to go on."

"I have told him he can go on."

"Maybe so, but he still hovers very close to you and is with you. He does not want to let you go, he has been waiting for this point for you to make the disconnection from him. He is still concerned for you. He has been carrying you. Carol Ann, it is now time for you to be fully on your own two feet. He is doing great work on his own but needs to fly free. You must find your path on your own unguided by him. He needs to go. You are holding back your own growth due to this dependence on him. It is holding him back."

I am gasping in disbelief and do not know how I can possibly do what she is suggesting. I have embraced life more fully and here this woman is telling me I am still holding on to my lovie too tightly. What am I to do? I continue to listen.

She goes on. "This is the hardest thing you will do in this lifetime. Robert has witnessed you doing other tough things and he knows you can do this too. I know there is nothing deeper than this, it is core deep. This is a huge transition period for you at this time. Robert made your life more bearable but releasing him will be a culmination of your whole life's purpose."

"Your purpose is to find your ownness, to truly become authentic Carol Ann. This is a monumental shift for you in this lifetime. The depth of your grief for Robert will not be repeated. You will not grieve this way again. This is a major turning point in your path. Until you work through this it would only duplicate itself again so this is a must that you release him. Do you understand what I am saying?"

"Yes, I do but it still seems like a very difficult thing to accomplish at this time."

"Your home will sell and a new journey will begin for you in 2009."

"Thank you for this bright news."

"Your life on PEI shows time spent writing. There will be a lot of self-realization work unfold. Your writing is your career and will lead to publication. You will be of great positive influence. Your intuition continues to grow steadily. There are spirits waiting to connect with you, this is a part of your work."

"You do have enough in the way of money although you are too impulsive and sometimes careless with your monies. This will improve however and you will become more discerning. You will develop prosperity consciousness and know you can live in abundance. It is about embracing prosperity within and not about prosperity in the bank."

"You can transfer all that love for Robert into yourself and build your own self love. You must shed the layers of disconnection and become your true self."

Our session ends. I am very grateful yet now sit perplexed as to what next. With a couple phone calls I am able to track down the ginseng she recommends. I sit looking at my beloved guide dog and ponder my Robert love. Yes, I know this wise woman as spoken the truth yet I am feeling lost already at the thought of cutting the tie to him.

The next day I awaken exhausted and nauseous. I am in and out of tears. As I stand looking at my Robert photos I know they need to be put away. Without any hesitation I begin to pick them up. I have six alone in my bedroom. As I tally the total count of them everywhere I have thirty-three in various sizes. I feel almost embarrassed to admit this. This is the jolt of reality I need however. I had not been able to see this prior to now, I was not fully ready. It made me realize I must let him go. I cannot hold him back or myself.

I take all the Robert photos into the basement except two. I get a glimpse of feeling lighter but it remains buried in the grief. I have another night of restlessness. Again I awaken tired, numb and lost. I am in a void of blackness. I am sickened that I have held him back. I go to the grocery in a daze reminiscent of the intense grief after his death. In my despair miraculously I receive a peek into my future.

I catch a glimpse of my future self in our new home. I see a triumphant, jubilant healed Carol Ann full of light and joy and peace. The window fogs over and I am back in tears. The waves are knocking me over. We return home and I wander the backyard. My love whispers, "Look at the big picture. Remember why I fell in love with you. I saw your potential." His words repeat in my mind bringing me out of the nausea and pain. It is short lived as another wave of sadness hits me. Yet I feel his coaching me as he shares, "Your most important contributions await you. The work of the past with the dogs and people was all highly valuable of course but you will exceed beyond all of that."

I do sleep. In the morning there is only the one Robert photo to greet me. The second one is in the upstairs bedroom. I ask myself how I feel about this and to my shock I hear my inner knowing say, I like this. Wow. Yes I think I like this. This new truth begins to emerge through my shock.

I then remember another pivotal moment from my days of Arizona. One day while lying in our bed, which is the bed in which he died I said aloud, "Thank you Robert for dying." The moment the words were spoken I felt a whoosh of release flow out of me and then utter shock. Now with the words to myself, I like the Robert photos gone from sight, I feel the same intensity. A surge of independence takes hold and I realize I can now fly solo. I want to gift him the same. I shall be unstoppable.

I know he is fully supportive to my efforts. I slowly begin to feel a huge weight lifting off me. I stand in front of my bathroom mirror saying aloud, "I, Carol Ann stand on my own. I relieve you Robert of your need to be concerned for me. I wish to set you free. May you follow your own path and I follow mine." My body responds with tears and trembles. This will take time I tell myself. This is a huge step so I am going in the right direction. In the days of my past intense grief I never would have imagined a day that I would sincerely thank my beloved for dying and being pleased most of his photos are gone from sight. Wowsers!

I recall that last new year I put some photos away but a day later they were right back where they were. I know that flower essences will assist and I place an order from a store down island. Walnut will help ease me through this and Impatiens. I am now conversing daily with my high self, my I Am presence. Through the Sedona magazine I am guided to purchase a book regarding the I Am presence. My order of ginseng has arrived in the mail. Thank you star lady. I know this will help me.

Every cell of my being needs to shift but the process has begun. It will take some time so I am doing my best to be kind to Carol Ann. I gaze out the window to see a rainbow over our river trees. What a gift. My mood still fluctuates from one hour to the next. As I lie on my couch I envision myself inside a large green pyramid. It is very comforting. My home actually resembles the shape of a pyramid with the huge deck forming a base.

Dear Arizona Linda surprises me with a phone call. I share about the astrologer Sam visit and the depth of my despair over my task of launching myself into solo flight. "It seems like I take steps forward and then I fall into my black pit and am going backwards again." She listens patiently and encourages me the best she knows how. I am so grateful for our friendship. "I do believe the how to my puzzle is being presented. Serendipity has paved the way. While in Port Hardy today I caught sight of a yellow flyer on a door. There is a medium coming to the north island around November 9 which is Saber's birthday."

"Good, have you made an appointment?"

"Yes, it is for the ninth and I shall have Spirit by my side."

"I look forward to hearing all about that. Good work CA."

"Thank you. Awesome Possum must find her way and thus I shall."

I look out the window. The sun is shining brightly and it is raining. I telephone my parents to share this unusual combo of sun and rain at the same time. Mom asks, "Have you seen a rainbow?"

She is familiar with my affection for rainbows or Bobby rainbows as I have called them for years. "No, there are no rainbows at the moment but I saw one a couple days ago."

Saber's birthday is here. Happy day to you dearest Saber dog. Today is a pivotal day in my life. We all drive to Port Hardy. I am full of anticipation and butterflies.

While Mystic and Treasure wait in the car I march inside with Spirit to meet a medium called Rosemary. I smile at the name remembering the talk I went to with Maggie by British medium Rosemary Altea. This must be good confirmation.

Rosemary welcomes both of us and asks that Spirit be placed by the door rather than between us so her energies do not interfere. She guides me through a relaxing colorful meditation leading me up through my chakras. My main goal is to let my lovie go and she leads me into visualizing a large pair of scissors which will cut the cord between the two of us. "Are you ready to do this now Carol Ann? There is a strong male presence beside you now which is your Robert."

I take a breath and make the cut. She responds, "Whoosh. There he goes."

It all sounds so simple. I am amazed. I have cut the cord but not the love. The dependence is gone. We are now both free.

"Now I want you to envision standing in front of an elevator. Step inside and push the button to the top floor and see yourself as the truest essence of Carol Ann." I am grateful for this fun vision as I sense myself zooming upward.

"I think you will benefit from watching a delightful movie entitled, "Over Her Dead Body," which will solidify for you what you have just gifted yourself and your husband."

She shares also that she sees us leaving the island within the next few months. "You need to look at your paper since I see something in it which will benefit you. Also I see that skipping would be very beneficial and of course fun as well."

Spirit receives a big hug and we make our way back to the car. I have a couple other stops to make but soon find myself very tired. Upon getting home I lie on the couch and feel a new appreciation for what I have just done. It is beginning to feel good. I know this has been very necessary and very right. I am so grateful to my wise star lady and my discovery of Rosemary.

The next day I feel quite spacey with a slight headache. I have found my skipping rope and jump in the kitchen. It makes me laugh. Later in the day as I go down the ramp into the yard I notice the deck gate is wide open. I always leave it closed, a habit developed living with old dog

Spookie who had to use the ramp. I ponder perhaps Robert is sending me a message of his departure.

Spirit is being treated with antibiotics for a small cyst which ruptured. She does not need any surgery to remove the growth since it has shrunk.

The local paper which Rosemary referred me to has an ad for volunteer help with a group for young girls. It is called girl power. I check it out and am accepted. I have opened a new door. On Tuesday evening I drive into Port Hardy to spend time with a small group of young teens who need some extra attentions.

I have left a long message on the phone of my star lady and she returns my call the next day. Sam expresses her joy and amazement over my huge progress since our initial talk. I tell her about the open deck gate. "Yes, I agree with you about a message from Robert. This is symbolic of his leaving. Also he is leaving it open for you to step fully into your future as authentic Carol Ann whom he fell in love with. That was the self he saw hidden beneath you."

At girl power the next week I offer to give them a talk about working dogs. My supervisor agrees to this suggestion. The next week Spirit demonstrates her ability to ignore food treats. Treasure also joins the talk and next I bring in Mystic. It has been a fun time for all of us. My three dogs and I leave with happy tail wags.

The government assistance office has a few women who use their services which require day care for their young toddlers. My supervisor asks if I am interested in a few hours of work. This is something different for me so I agree. I spend a couple hours one afternoon a week babysitting about four or five toddlers.

For a special outing for the girl power I suggest that they could all come out to our river home. This is agreed upon and the three dogs take turns entertaining all of them. One of the native girls is rather frightened by the big dogs but a lot of giggles reassure her all is well.

Spirit has developed an unpleasant skin condition and I make a call to Samantha for suggestions. She seems to think perhaps she is allergic to the chicken the dogs have all been eating recently. She sends me a recipe for vegetarian dog food. "Sam, I must share about good news with my guide dog Spirit. She had a ruptured cyst which is now all healed over. It is magical in sync timing with my inner shifts."

"You are a locomotive moving so quickly with your acceptance and shifts. I am very happy for you."

"During our session you referenced a man on the distant horizon I believe."

"Yes, there is a man. I did not go into it because my intent was for you to release your Robert. You were not ready for the info just yet."

I thank her for another wondrous visit and trust in her wisdom.

I am off to the grocery for the new food items for Spirit's veggie diet and that evening ease her onto the new diet. It is easier to feed the other two the same way so they also begin the vegetarian regime. She responds positively to the food quickly. I then feel the need to go cold turkey myself. All of us become vegetarians. Amazingly, I have no challenge in this regard and it all flows without any effort. Once again my guide dog has led us to a new path which in the long run is healthier for us and the planet.

In the basement is a zipper jacket of Robert's. I have made use of it a few times living here however it is time to let it go. It is a calm day without any high wind so I start a burn pile in the yard. I toss his jacket into the fire.

In the night I have a dream about Robert. I am walking along a street and see him marching alone on the other side. He has not seen me yet. Just as I am about to run across to greet him I am startled awake. I realize I can rescript the dream and close my eyes to recapture it. Despite not falling back into sleep my intent speaks to my new Carol Ann self. This time in the dream instead of joining him I watch him go his way and I go my own alone. Hey good work. That did feel better. My shift has truly anchored in.

My Mom has been hospitalized due to heart challenges. When she returns home I make a trip to see Mom and Dad. It has been decided she will benefit from a pacemaker. One evening I ask her to braid my hair. She is surprised by my request but soon I am with braids. Dad happily captures a photograph. It is a special memory I take home when I head back to the north island to be greeted with a most exuberant puppy welcome.

Remember to Laugh

The dogs and I are home unpacking our goodies from a trip into Port McNeill. We are now all settled into our respective couch potato positions enjoying the view of the Nimpkish through the magnificent trees. The telephone rings.

"Carol Ann, it is Sue from Robin's Pet Shop. I have your Arctic Oil you purchased."

"What? Yes, I noticed that it was missing when I got home."

"I was driving home about to make the turn onto the highway when I saw a bag near the side of the road. So I stopped to check it out. It turned out to be your purchase. The Arctic Oil was in the bag but the six little dog treats were gone. I guess a squirrel must have found them."

"I do remember putting the bag on the top of the car when I left the store. I have done that trick before. One time I was driving to California for one of my working dog events. I was very distracted and left my down pillow on top of the car. I used to travel with my own pillow. I got out onto the freeway and happened to look in the mirror and saw it flying off the rooftop. It got hit and feathers were flying everywhere."

"What a funny sight that must have been."

"Yes and rather annoying that I had lost my favorite comfy pillow. I am glad to hear from you. I cannot believe that I got all the way up to the turn before it fell off the roof of the car. The RCMP would not be stopping me for speeding at any rate right!"

"I shall come see you tomorrow after the shop opens to pick it up.

Thanks so much for calling and for your attentiveness. Most folks would not notice or else just keep going."

I hang up the phone giving Spirit girl a big nuzzle as she lays cuddled next to me on the couch. "Thanks to you Lollipop we have another funny story. Awesome Possum left your oil on top of the car and it flew off the roof. Sue found it on the highway."

Sometimes events in life just happen to help us remember to laugh.

To You Mark Stephen Arnim

As I contemplate our future move to Prince Edward Island I remember the rifle hidden in our basement. It is a commerative rifle which belonged to Robert. I do not want to move this item a fourth time. It was disturbing enough to me when I lied to the Canadians customs upon entering Canada about not possessing any firearms.

I recall that Fraser, the man with the offer on our home, is a former RCMP and decide to telephone him for advice. We have become friends as we await the sale of their Nanaimo home.

He answers the phone when I ring. "Hi, it is Carol Ann. I need to pursue your input about a matter which has been challenging me. I have an old rifle which belonged to my husband and it is stashed in the basement. It is time to get rid of it. Since you are a former policeman I thought you would have the best answers for me."

"Sure thing, be glad to help. Coraley and I can come over tomorrow to take a peek."

I go to bed with a sigh of relief that perhaps soon that dreaded possession will be gone from sight. I ought to have let it go while still living in Arizona but it was too overwhelming to deal with on top of everything related to leaving our Boulders home. My brother Mark had bothered me to do something with it but alas I never heeded his promptings. When we moved from the tree house up island to our sea home I received a phone call from Travis telling me that he found the rifle. It was tucked to the back of a shelf in a closet. The dogs and I had to make a trip down island to pick it up.

In the morning our visitors arrive and we go into the basement. Fraser carries the rifle upstairs and examines it. He thinks it is quite a beauty which I suppose it is yet I hate any kind of firearm with a passion especially since Robert's son, Mark commited suicide with a shotgun.

"If you like I can google this on the internet and find out a possible value for you so you could perhaps sell it."

"Ok yes, that might be good."

The next day he phones. "Carol Ann I have your hat here. It had been on the table and somehow got stuck inside my jacket sleeve and I found it upon returning home. You could come pick it up if you like."

I am chuckling as I drive over to retrieve my hat. He tells me, "You know the RCMP office is a minute away. They will not give you any grief over this since they are glad to take in any firearms."

"The fact that I lied about it in my possession after entering Canada will not be an issue."

"No."

"Ok, then thanks for the tip. I shall go over there right now."

I have never been inside such a place and I walk slowly asking for assistance that this issue resolve itself quickly and easily. I take a deep breath and tell the person greeting me at the glass window, "Hi, I need to report having a firearm and would like you to come get it."

"Do you want it destroyed?"

"You mean you could do that?"

"Yes, there are a lot of firearms which are taken apart and destroyed."

A few moments later a young Mountie follows me out to the car standing admiring the dogs. "I have a yellow lab of my own at home."

This puts me at ease and even more so when he shares his name. His first name is Mark. I feel a goosey relief fill my being and I know that my Robert and Mark are assisting. When the other policeman arrives they get in their car and follow us home. I open the basement door with the three dogs following us. I point to where it is and Mark pulls it out of the cabinet unwrapping the tablecloth hiding it.

The other policeman shares, "Would you sell it? I have a collection at home and this is a beauty. Once it is cleaned up it would be lovely."

We all walk back outside to their car and Mark puts it into the trunk. They head slowly up the hill and I stand with arms outstretched to the sky. "Hey there you guys. Roberto and Mark I sense you are helping with this. Big thank yous."

I decide I do not want to sell it. I do not need or want to take money from such a source. There is a firing range across the river from our home. Sometimes you can hear the shots echoing through the trees. The prospect that this cop may be over there doing target shooting with this rifle gives me the creepies.

When I go into the police office next the officer who wants to buy it greets me. I share, "I have decided to have the rifle destroyed."

"Ok, let me go prepare that paperwork for you to sign."

A few moments later he returns and I put my signature to the document. "Thank you for allowing me to do this."

"Yes, you are right, there are enough guns in the world. I reckon I already have enough of them anyways."

I leave the building with a lightness to my step and stop prior to getting into the car. I sense a gratitude hug from Mark with his father Robert my husband at his side. Without any doubt this has been a divinely orchestrated blessed endeavor.

My 910 Puppy

In honor of my huge inner shifts I feel the need to do something really silly. This river home has truly been a work in transformation itself mirroring my own shifts. Our address is 910 Nicholson Road. I now call it my 910 puppy since it reminds me of my working dogs' transformations. Would it not be fun to put some dog leashes around my glass railing? I am laughing at the prospect of finding enough leashes to go around the large deck but sense the dollar store is a place to start.

My trip to town results in the purchase of several colorful leashes. It takes two to cover the length of each glass panel so this project will evolve with time and exploring to find sources for enough leashes. Someone viewing our home may ponder what the heck are these leashes doing here but then again likely they won't notice. The river trees and the home will be their attention. With the three dogs by my side I finally attach the last leash. Our glass railing now has the longest dog leash wrapped around it.

Spirit has been batting her paw on the back of my leg. It is time for some affection with my beloved guide dog. This is a new ritual between us. When I walk in the yard she often pesters me with a paw. She is demanding a hug. I do my best to never ignore the affections of any of my dogs. I happily comply with her wishes and enjoy a long soft cuddle embrace.

After coming home one day from town I cannot enter our front door. I pull and twist the door knob but it won't open. I walk around to the French doors off the river side and walk inside. I discover that the dead bolt has been placed in the lock position. I chuckle, thinking my pups are very talented yet they do not possess this ability in their bag of tricks. However my love in spirit certainly does. He has been allowed to fly free unhindered by the cord connecting us and yet he seems to have gifted me with a wonderful sign. A locked door means someone else is living here.

A week later I see that the brass bell is missing from Treya's collar. This is most disturbing because I am very fond of this bell. When Robert and I rented our Chester, Nova Scotia home he found two handmade brass bells which he affixed to the collars of Saber and Spook. In the morning when we let them out for their strolls we did not always know which direction they had gone but the bells helped us to track them. I look through the car but cannot find it anywhere.

On our next outing as I am closing the gate ready to drive away I happen to notice something gold colored on the ground. I gasp in disbelief and stoop to pick up the brass bell. "Thank you Robert, I know you did this." I never walk the dogs outside the gate since I prefer to run them lose at the lake or beach. "This must be another sign from you of our departure. The bell is from Nova Scotia so we must be heading east soon, thank you."

My bicycle which I acquired while living at the sea home and I have made many a happy pedal together. On my birthday I tie a birthday mylar balloon to my handlebars and ride to the sea shore. There are a lot of hills and my route takes me over an hour. My favorite part is always resting to enjoy the view over to Sointula Island and the distant mainland mountains.

At the end of February our 910 puppy home is shown to a young couple. I receive a good report on the viewing and wait to see what happens. I smell scent of cigar smoke while I am outside on the driveway. In the upstairs bedroom I notice that a card has been moved and placed next to a couple red hearts and a photo of Robert and me. The wording on the outside of the card reads, "As you journey trust your heart." Thanks for the support messaging lovie. Although I cut our cord his puppy like devotion continues to support me. I know he is comforting me, telling me patience. Hold on, the deal is coming. The next day my realtor phones to tell me an offer has come in. A settlement in price is reached. Today is spring equinox. It is a year since I re-listed our 910 puppy and the future owners have arranged for a water test.

It is purchased by a young couple. The man is with the RCMP and has been transferred to the north island. They have two dogs and are expecting a two legger soon. Yeah, my 910 puppy shall be turned in to its new owners with their own happy tail waggers.

I make the good news phone call to the maritimes and set up the last minute details of our arrival to Prince Edward Island. Roger welcomes our happy news and shares they are very happy in their new PEI home. Again I have a slip of the tongue calling him Robert. He never makes an issue of this. Mark offers to be our moving buddy again. However this time I want to do it solo. It will be a long journey across our Canadian rainbow with three labs yet I am now a more empowered Carol Ann. This trip must honor this.

At my last evening with girl power I am gifted with a handmade farewell card.

My 910 puppy has proved to be a very healing space. I recall my decision to finally put a headstone on Robert's grave happened in the first year of living here. Each year since the death of Robert a floral shop in Livingstone, Montana, delivers a plant or floral arrangement for his gravesite. I had called Livingstone to make arrangements for a headstone. I was in shock to realize it is ten years that it took me to do this difficult task. I wanted it to be something unique and very special.

It is one large headstone with his name and dates on one side and mine on the other. At his name they engrave the head of a mature labrador and on my side is a smaller lab. I have paw prints placed between the names joining each other. On the bottom is written in quotes, "One Spirit" with a paw print. I receive a photo and am most pleased.

Jade's adoptive Mom has lung cancer which is most disturbing news to me. It is quite bizarre that his birth Dad died of lung cancer and now his adoptive Mom is facing the same prospect. Unbelievable! I had a good phone visit with her recently and decide to share our home sale news with her. She is able to visit and our conversation turns to the past.

"I have often wondered if you had Phillip as your obstetrician. Was he your doctor as well?"

"Yes, he was. Did he give you my letter?"

"You mean you wrote to me?"

"Yes, within the first year of having Jade. I wrote a letter and gave it to him to forward on to you. So you never got it?"

"Sad to say, but no. Yet I can treasure your intent and the vision of you working on such a compassionate endeavor. That was very kind of you and thank you for sharing that. When we leave the island for our new home on the eastern end of the Canadian rainbow I plan to go see Jade, so trust we shall see each other."

"Yes, that would be lovely to see you again as well."

I am at a loss for words upon hanging up the phone. I do trust I shall get to see her again and ponder why Phillip would not have mailed her letter. How very unkind. Perhaps he thought it would be more hurtful. How could he know? It is over and past but I am very glad that Jade's puppy raiser and I had a heart to heart chat.

I take my lavender paint and place some hearts on the stair and under the deck. I paint a large message, we love you 910 and sign the names of the dogs.

The new owners come over the next day for a visit and spend more time in their potential home. "How do you guys feel about bats?"

"They are good since they eat the mosquitoes."

"So you are not freaked out by bats flying around."

"No, not really."

"That is good because you bought a big bat house. The cedar shingles are home to the bats."

All of us are chuckling with this as I share my first encounter with them. "I was not too enthused when I initially discovered they were around. I was out on my deck at dusk enjoying a glass of wine when they started swooping everywhere. They were emerging for their nightly adventures. I did get used to it with time but you best be careful keeping things closed up at that time of day. The first time I had one flying around in our bedroom was rather unpleasant."

"Thanks for the tip."

Mary Jo

On April 17 we drive up the hill of Nicholson Road for the last time. I gratefully thank all the countless trees of the north island as we make our way south. The dog motel in Courtney is our home for the night. We have been there a few times in the past. During one visit with Mark we had made a shopping trip down island and a couple other times it had been trips to take Spookie to the vet in Courtney.

The next day we board the big ferry heading to the mainland. We exit the ferry with a very exuberant hallelujah. "Ok pups, we are going north now. Our Bobby boy Jade is waiting for all of us." He lives in Chetwynd which is out of the way for us heading east but I cannot miss the chance to see him. Plus I want to see his Mary Mom who is now on hospice care.

After a few hours driving it is time to find a place for the night. The town we are in is not very dog friendly. It takes me three tries before I find one for tail waggers. By now I am very tired and collect all the things we need from the car. A few minutes later I am back out the door looking for something. But the car door does not open. I peer inside with frustration seeing the keys in the ignition. Holy smokes man! I go to the front desk and they suggest someone who can help with my predicament.

About an hour later with some cash to the palm I have retrieved the keys and the necessary item from the car. The dogs gather around me to mooch some of my supper. After a glass of wine I tumble into bed.

Treya and Mystic jump from bed to bed and finally settle into slumber. All of us need a good sleep.

We are being blessed with some beautiful driving for sure. Some of it is not to my liking and I hug the middle line down the road as best I can. I do not allow my eyes to gaze below as we climb higher in elevation. There is a sign advising to fill up on gas. This is the last station for the next sixty miles. I look to my gas tank thinking no problem, we can get that far without having to fill up our near empty tank. The years of Robert working in the bush he liked to make sure he had enough gas and I can recall one time he was driving my mustang while we were in Denver. He had not checked my gauge and to his dismay we ran out of gas. "Poss, Poss, when will you learn to drive on a full tank?"

"Well my love one does not stay on a full tank long." The two of us chortle.

The road we are now driving is very hilly requiring a lot of shifting of the gears which does require more gas going up and down and around all these mountainous twists and turns. I am happy as a clam and ask my angels to get us safely to a gas station. The gas empty light is flashing at me now.

I put the car into neutral allowing us to coast on the downward parts of the road. Maybe this is not really saving us gas after all. I do not know how much further we have to go until this gas station will be in sight. The gauge is now past empty. Another uphill climb presents itself and I moan in dismay. Please let us get safely to a station. The road has very few other travellers.

A few minutes later I breathe a long sigh of relief. At the bottom of the next hill I see a big sign. We roll in. I am all chuckles inside as I read the sign, "Lightfoot Gas." That is a great pun, thank you.

It is not far to meet up with Jade and I make a call to him. He advises me of a place we can meet. Big grins and hearty hellos are shared. "I need to go see Mom, can you follow me there?"

"Absolutely, yes I want to see her. Lead the way."

We head out and a few minutes later I am walking into the small hospital of Chetwynd where his Mom used to work as a nurse. I pause at the doorway letting my eyes register what is before me. A couple women are standing by the window and Mary Jo in her bed. She smiles in greeting. "Come in. This is Carol Ann, the Mom of our Jade. These are my sisters, Dawn and Lynn."

I allow Jade to make his hello first and follow him inside. "Come over here Carol Ann and sit next to me."

I lean over to hug her and prop myself on the edge of her bed. "Carol Ann used to raise service dogs. How are the dogs and tell me about your plans. You must be excited about this move. You have a long journey ahead of you."

That evening we have supper with Jade's adoptive Dad, Norm. The next day Jade and I spend some time together and go play with the dogs. We go visit the hospital again. His daughter Erica is with them along with the two sisters who have not left her side. Norm is there. He tells Erica, "This is your Gramma."

She looks at me puzzled. "No she isn't. I already have a Gramma."

Norm replies, "Yes, she is, you just don't know it yet." I am touched by his sentiments.

Jade and I plan to leave in the morning for our drive through Jasper to stay the night. It is time to say farewell. I hug Mary Jo whispering, "Thank you for taking care of my Bobby boy."

"My pleasure and thank you Carol Ann."

Jade makes his goodbyes and we slowly walk outside to the car. He asks, "Are you sure it is going to be alright that I take this trip with you? I do not want her to die while I am not here."

"I do not want that for you either Jade. Yet you must trust it will be alright otherwise I would not be taking you on this little road trip."

The next day we have an interesting landscape of ever changing weather to drive through the Rocky Mountains. One mile it is totally clear and then the next it is whiteout conditions. We are both a little disappointed in the visibility of the mountains being obscured. It is still overcast when we drive into Lake Louise. We get all three dogs and walk the trail into the lake. There is a busload of Japanese tourists who scurry out of the way when they see the big dogs.

When we arrive into Jasper I tell Jade,"I am not going to the extra hassle of finding us a dog motel. I am not mentioning them when we check in so you will have to help me. I will ask for a room at the end."

Our needs are met without any difficulty and we all tumble into our dog motel. I have purchased a big pizza which is well sniffed by the pups.

The next stop is Calgary. I have made him a ticket to fly back into Fort St. John. As I drive he studies the map. "So where are we now Jade?"

"I do not really know. I am not too good a navigator."

"Holy molly, really. Well that is a surprise." We both chuckle.

After a while of driving I find us a place to walk the dogs. It is very windy and we end up walking along a train track for a few minutes.

I have not made any reservations for the night and it is a struggle to find a dog friendly motel close to the Calgary airport. After a few tries we are finally guided to the right spot. It has a pool so Jade enjoys a swim before supper.

In the morning I drop him off at the departures. I watch my Bobby boy walk inside to catch his plane. We turn and now begin our trip to PEI.

Land Ho!

Our journey through Alberta and across the prairies is uneventful. I drive the whole time in silence. Ontario seems to take forever. I am enthralled with the countless inukshuks lining the highway. An inukshuk functions as a guidepost. They were created by the Inuit of the Canadian north to show travellers their way. They are composed of a variety of rocks placed on top of each other often in the shape of a human. They prove to be a great distraction for me and keep me focused. I stop to collect some neat rocks and place my own little inukshuk with a Tibetan prayer flag. I take a self-portrait.

The car is beginning to lose power on the long uphill climbs which there are many of through this country. One does not realize how big the province is until you pass through it. I am now looking at a warning light on my dashboard. I do not know what it means but the car is definitely not driving properly. I pass a man with a young woman sitting on top of a huge boulder. I pull to the side of the road and park. I holler out the window, "You guys win the prize for being for being the best looking inuksuk."

They both laugh and come down off their perch. It is a father and daughter. She is on her way to live on Vancouver Island. They are having car trouble and are waiting for help. He looks under my car hood and advises me I ought to make it into Wawa if I drive slow.

Indeed we do. I recognize the big goose welcoming us on the hilltop. I find our way into Canadian Tire. The dogs and I wait in the waiting room for a diagnosis. I am told, "Your oxygen sensor needs to be replaced. We have disconnected it so you can safely drive to Stratford but you need to replace it once there." When we are back on the road again I ponder about the oxygen sensor. Guess my beloved Labaru is talking to me. No doubt my breathing is too shallow. Whether we are in good shock or bad shock often we forget to breathe deeply. I am not allowing enough oxygen into my lovely lungs. I am quite excited about reaching our new home. I make a conscious effort to pay better attention to my breath.

We do arrive safely into Stratford. Our stay is at the Queens Hotel in downtown. I make a call to the Subaru dealer and the next day our part is installed.

After a couple nights with Mom and Dad we head to London to see Mark and Isabel. I stay at a dog motel because their seven cats and my three dogs would not be a compatible mix. I pick them up after checking in and get them a big bucket of Kentucky fried chicken. I enjoy lots of cole slaw with rolls and dessert.

The next day we take the dogs for a long walk on the outside of the city. We find a good spot with lots of grass. Spirit has taken a shine to Isabel. Instead of staying by my side she is with her. Mark shares, "Wow, look at big girl. Isabel, she is normally always with Carol Ann. This is not usual behavior for her."

On the same road there is a Buddhist temple which looks deserted. We drive in slowly. The place has had a fire. For some unknown reason there is a lot of stuff under a large canopy tent which has been abandoned. Why it has been left is a mystery. I feel very badly for the abandoned Buddha statues. "I am going to take a couple with me."

"Do you think we should?"

"Why not, they will have a better home than left here to the elements. At least they will be appreciated. Someone has left them here and is not coming back." There is a trailer with a door hanging off. The three of us collect some treasures and put them into the car.

The next day is time to depart. I surprise Mom and Dad pulling in just prior to them leaving for church. "I had to come and say a quick goodbye. Mystic would like to sing farewell to you." Both my parents cannot believe that my dog will sing on command yet howl he does.

And we are off. My parents stand waving as we turn the corner off of Water Street.

I do not want to drive the 401 freeway so we go the back route. This does take much longer. We arrive into Ottawa about five and my decision to stay downtown is changed. We make our way past the Parliament buildings. We pass the Chateau Laurier where Robert and I stayed with Saber and Spook. That is not in my budget at this time so we begin to look for a suitable dog motel.

We head out of town. I do not know where we are going and ask my angels to help us find a place. Next I find myself going across a bridge and before I know it we are in Quebec. Ontario is behind us and I do not want to turn back now.

I drive looking but without success. I stop in to what looks like a hotel but dogs are not allowed. I am given directions for a dog place nearby. Their directions are amiss or my hearing is. I am now not sure where I am going but am thoroughly exhausted. It has been a very long day for all of us. The pups have been out of the car only once.

Finally I see a Holiday Inn sign. I park and go inside. I rest my head and arms on the counter in front of a startled employee who greets me in French. "Can I please stay here with dogs? I am willing to pay extra." The woman disappears and another employee appears addressing me in English. "Yes, we can accommodate you with your dogs."

Wow, what a relief. This is a high rise which requires entry through the lobby. I could not have sneaked three big dogs in if I wanted to. I get out my map laying it on the counter. "Can you please show me where I am and how to get back to the highway heading east?"

"It is very easy. When you pull out of the garage turn right and at the second stop light you make a right which puts you onto the highway."

Hallelujah, this is the perfect location for us. I walk the dogs and take them inside across the beautiful lobby. We go up an elevator and down a long hallway. They eagerly charge into their home for the night. Next I head to the underground parking and carry in what we all need for the night and morning.

The room is a step above our normal lower priced dog motels yet we all need some extra comfort tonight. I order myself room service and relax. In the morning I am in no rush to leave so we get a later start to the day.

The next night we stay in Edmundston, New Brunswick. By mid-afternoon I need gas and ask how far it is to the confederation bridge. I am told it is about an hour away. The confederation bridge over to Prince Edward Island is a very long eight miles or thirteen kilometres. I have been very nervous about the prospect of driving this since I do not like heights over water.

Awhile before arriving to the bridge I run the dogs and tell them to settle down. It will take a few minutes to cross the bridge and I need my full attentions on my driving. I have my Bach flower essences rescue remedy at the ready. The bridge is approaching in the distance. I am terrified. Ok awesome Possum, you can do this.

I take a deep breath and start on to the bridge. Every couple minutes I dose myself with a squirt of rescue remedy which is for stress and trauma. To my horror I see there is a slight bend in the bridge and it goes up in elevation. Holy cow. Thankfully all the dogs are quiet. I keep my focus on the road hunched over the wheel hanging on for dear life.

When we hit the downward stretch I see land and begin to breathe normally. Ok pups there is our new home. Land ho, land ho. I pull to the side of the road and get out to kiss the ground. I cannot believe we are actually here and all of us are safe. I repeat my gratitude over and over thanking all of our angels. It is May 5, 2009.

I do not know where to go but head toward Summerside. At a stop light there is a sign for Water Street. I smile thinking this is a good sign since my Mom and Dad's home is on a street of same name. I must be guided this way for some right reason. A few minutes later I see the office of my realtor Royal LePage. It is closed. A moment later a man pulls up beside us on a motorcycle.

"You must be Carol Ann."

"Yes, how did you know?"

"I saw your British Columbia car plate with all the dogs hanging their heads out the window. I am a realtor. You are expected. Do you have a place for the night?"

"No, not yet."

"Come inside and we shall find one for you."

He makes a call to the Country Inn outside town. I had seen it driving in and it looked great.

"Can you tell me how to get to our home?"

"You want to see it now?" He is surprised. "You will not be able to find it."

"Of course I can. I just want a quick peek. I have just driven all the way from the north end of Vancouver Island without getting really lost, so I think I can manage this assignment."

He provides me with directions. After we check into the dog motel and take care of the dogs we head out. Grahams Road has a large white church on the corner. I smile.

I am mesmerized and thrilled with what I see as we pull into the driveway. Yes this is our new home. We do not take possession for a couple days which is a blessing. The dogs and I need to rest. We have been well blessed in a safe journey from the western to the eastern end of our beautiful Canadian rainbow.

Crossing My Rainbow Bridge

The moving truck has come and gone and all three dogs are busy sniffing their new digs. I make phone calls to family and friends. Jade has sad news. His Mary Mom has flown into the light. I am very grateful for the gift of meeting her and the timing of our last visit.

It is a big transition settling into our new life on PEI. Our four years on the north end of Vancouver Island was quite isolated. We had to drive two hours to see a stop light. Now here I am shopping in the humungous Superstore for groceries. My first time in Walmart is too much for me. I find my item and am out the door in five minutes. All the people and cars everywhere are too much.

Thankfully our home provides the solace of solitude we have become accustomed to at our river home. Unpacking occupies all my time. Soon I am sharing the painting job with a painter to do the outside of the house. It had been a very drab grey which depressed me any time I looked at. Soon it is a lovely happy light sunshine yellow with green trim.

The living space is much smaller than anticipated. I decide to sell the large Mexican furniture pieces. This was from my life with Robert and I know that my new love awaits. My nickname for our place is the heart home for this is where my new old love shall manifest.

I am stunned to be selling furniture after moving it four times yet it does not suit this maritime home. Yet I do not believe in mistakes so do not chastise myself. Now that we are here I feel a strong need to remove as much of the Robert possessions from my life as possible. That was my past and the future awaits. Our best is yet to be.

I find a place which will take the pieces on consignment. Spirit is having difficulties getting on to the high king size bed. It is time for it to depart. It takes up too much of the bedroom anyway. It is the bed Robert died in. The Salvation Army takes it away for us. We now sleep on a queen size futon very low to the floor. Spirit happily climbs up with smiles of approval.

Roger checks in with us to get updates on our new adventures. Again I call him Robert. After some time settling in with all the various projects to make the home the imprint of Carol Ann I decide to make an unplanned visit to Roger. He and Wendy are indeed surprised to see me but he happily gives me a tour. He shares all of his handiwork. It is very lovely indeed.

Books and I have been lifelong friends. One of my favorite pastimes is to wander in a bookstore scanning the shelves waiting for that special book to catch my eye. I am now in the possession of a book entitled, "Balance" by Susan M. McDonald.

Susan has bravely written of her journey to heal an advanced form of cancer through natural means. I have the greatest respect for such people due to my horrific journey through traditional medicine with my husband's death of lung cancer. Inside the pages of her book I discover a hidden jewel when she discusses a life altering program she participated in called the Way of the Heart. My focus in on healing and opening my heart so this sounds like a good match for me.

Roger has undergone testing to discover the cause of buildup of fluid in his lung so the timing of this book is interesting. Synchronicity is holding my hand once again. It is cancer. I have come to realize the significance of my slip of the tongue in calling him Robert, instead of Roger. This began over two years ago at the river home and still I do it. I have foreseen his future.

On the day of his fluid drain, I drive in to the hospital in Charlottetown and thankfully am able to track him down while he is still waiting. He does not know I am coming. As I open the door to the waiting room he catches my eye greeting me with his customary wink and a smile. "Hey CA, what a sight you are."

It is awesome to connect with him as we share a good heart to heart talk. I sense his fear. "You are something else, CA. How can you sit there with that big smile on your face ready to hold my hand after everything you have been through?"

"It is exactly because of what I have been through which allows me to be here. My journey with Robert was horrific and yet now thirteen years later it is me alone who is fated to be here with you. I had to come."

He smiles from his heart and then says something I shall never forget, "CA, I believe you have found your pot of gold at the end of the rainbow and it is you."

He sheds a tear as my arm rests over his shoulder and we continue to talk quietly. A few minutes later his doctor bounds up to us and Roger introduces me. "Can she come with me?"

After he changes into his hospital gown I am allowed to sit with him while he waits for the doctor. "So what were you talking about out there CA, about other options for me?"

"Well, Rog, traditional medicine does not hold the best answers in healing various illnesses such as cancer. One need examine all the diverse ways of healing; going within and examining the spiritual aspect of illness, nutrition and detoxifying the body. There are many forms of energy healing to remove blocks within the body without difficult side effects. It is a whole big world of choices if you open that door."

His doctor is running late yet eventually rushes in. He is a most friendly soul and I can feel the connection between the two of them. I know he is in good hands and I make my exit. I pause in the hallway looking back into the open room and draw a big heart in the air. I then point to my heart and to him. He smiles.

A couple days later I make a phone call to the maritime contact with the Way of the Heart referenced in Susan's book. I am enthused with what she shares and I tell my like-minded new island friends, Debbie and Valerie. "There is a Way of the Heart class offered in Amherst, Nova Scotia." We all agree to participate. In my excitement I take charge, "We can all meet at the bridge and go together." In that moment I realize this will mean that I would have to drive across that terrifying long bridge to get to the mainland. What the heck are you thinking Carol Ann? Already my tummy is in a knot with the thought alone.

Many of us have fears of some nature which have no logical explanation. I do not like heights, or long bridges. This bridge takes ten minutes to cross after all. Yet I know that my heart is guiding me to do so. This must be a catalyst to possibly open me more to embrace my divine self and path. I have no choice but to jump into this opportunity.

At some point after arriving to our maritime island home, there have been several times during a day that I happen to catch the clock time always being eleven minutes after the hour. I believe this is no mere coincidence. Perhaps there is meaning to this number eleven. Can numbers talk to us? I believe so.

Prior to actually driving the bridge on the day of our class I decide it would be in my best interest to go up close to the bridge to just look at it. I have seen it from land awhile after my arrival to the island and was very astonished and also horrified when I saw it for the first time. It truly did frighten me to think that I had actually driven across such a monstrous long creation. You can actually see the curve in the bridge.

The three dogs get a run on a beach nearby the bridge which allows me to get another good view of it from afar. Holy smokes, I am about to cross that long sucker again, can I do it? A few minutes later I am parked at the grassy area next to the bridge. I walk alone over the grass and take photos up close. It truly is a creation of engineering beauty. I find a new respect and awe for it. Back inside the car I sit in quiet meditation talking to the bridge. "Ok bridge, I want to become friends with you so I can be confident and stress free as you carry me across the flowing waters to Nova Scotia."

It is a simplistic yet empowering step for me to "be with the bridge" focusing on my intent of a strong brave heart at the end of its crossing. I am very pleased with myself that I had listened and followed my inner guidance to come sit with the bridge. As I head home I am rewarded with the tail end of a rainbow.

"Holy PEI cows, look puppies, there is our rainbow." My earth angel pups are silently watching my antics and questioning what this might mean for them. A couple minutes later the whole rainbow appears before us. I pull the car to the side of the road, ready to open the car door when Treya sits up interested in our whereabouts.

"No puppies, you must stay in the car, I am going to talk to the rainbow." I am filled with the highest sense of joyful gratitude and awe to the point of tears. The fierce winds of lovely Prince Edward Island are blowing the tears across my face as I get back into the car. "Wow, puppies that is indeed a magical treasure to behold. The timing of this is truly unbelievable is it not?"

In the past whenever I saw a rainbow, I always thought first of Robert and yet this time I am seeing empowered Carol Ann Joy. I ponder aloud to myself and my four leggers, "Hey puppies, I am having the most delightful musings in my mind. You know this can mean only one thing. I have made a wise decision. No matter what the outcome is from the class I am destined to cross the bridge without the terror."

I am rewarded with another rainbow and this time it is the full rainbow. I drive into town to shop a bit and then head for home. Just as I turn onto our country road I am again greeted by the tail end of a rainbow and then moments later the full rainbow appears. This rainbow would indeed be shining directly over our little home up the road. Within a period of a couple hours I have seen three full rainbows.

I am filled with awe and gratitude for this very special gift and later share it with Valerie. "That is indeed extraordinary Carol Ann, my friend." A few days later I want to go talk to the bridge again prior to the actual drive day and Valerie agrees to join me.

I park the car and get out to silently commune with my bridge friend as the island winds blow my skirt to and fro. A vision comes into my mind. To my amazement I am seeing a rainbow over the bridge and I am in the middle of it. "Wow, thank you, I know this will be a wondrous opening for me."

I get back into the car with the dogs and Valerie. "You are very nervous about this Carol Ann. This bridge crossing really frightens you."

"Yes, just sitting here looking at the bridge imagining our drive I have knots in my tummy." I drive slowly around feeling this deep fear within me. Tears come to the surface as my upper body heaves and sighs at the same time. I feel a small sense of relief and park the car on a corner to talk. As I glance at the car clock it miraculously reads 11:11 a.m.

"Holy jumping PEI cows, Valerie, look at the time. I want to share with you that for a long while now since coming to the island I have seen the eleven after the hour on the clock. Do you know what this could be telling me?"

"Yes," she shares. "I have read about this. I also have had my own experiences seeing the same time on the clock. Eleven is a portal, 11:11 represents a vortex of energy and a bridge is a crossing. Eleven is a portal between worlds."

"So perhaps I ought to be actually driving us across the bridge at this very time then?"

"Yes, that would be very powerful."

Valerie was at our home recently and spent a lot of time admiring my many photos. It is thirty years ago this very fall that I was living as a student in Kathmandu, Nepal. During my trekking period I crossed a rope swing bridge which was a very fearful endeavor. I have a photo which shows me at the start of the bridge holding a brave smile. It is indeed one of my favorite photos.

"You could have that photo of you about to cross your Nepalese rope bridge with you in the car when we cross the bridge. That was a different type of bridge but definitely not a simple hop, skip and a jump across for you I am sure, just as this PEI bridge is now for you."

"Hey, I like that idea, thanks. I shall do that."

The awaited day of our Way of the Heart class arrives. Valerie and I meet kindred soul friend Debbie at the bridge. Prior to the crossing, I take us to the same place I had gone a few days ago in preparation for this day. Again, it is a fiercely windy day as I get out of the car with my camera.

"First I need your help to put on these lovely butterfly wings so you can photograph me wearing them."

"Oh how pretty, you are going to wear these?"

"Yes, of course, for I call myself a butterfly girl you know. The west coast First Nations believe a butterfly represents transformation and I definitely am a study in transformation."

All three of us are sharing good chuckles in my photo session. We head to the bridge. "Ok confederation bridge, here comes brave

Carol Ann. I need to ask both of you ladies to maintain silence while I concentrate on this endeavor."

Both my friends respect my wishes of silence as I slowly head into my fear. My body starts to react to the bridge beneath us as I feel deep sobs shaking my chest and tears begin to roll. I have put a soothing musical tape into my player so I put my focus on its tones and my breathing. "Be still my heart, be still my soul," plays in my ears as I silently put my intent into making this a crossing to its highest good.

The car clock shows the time of 11:11 which I share with my silent passengers. "Ok ladies, we are now at our vortex of 11:11, this is very exciting and wonderful. I am very grateful to have you witness and share this. Thank you both for being here today. Oh boy, oh boy, this is going good." I feel myself forming a slow smile as the former frown and tensions begin to fade. I ask Valerie to take a couple photos of me as we continue to cross.

"Yes, this is going good you guys, this is much better than my initial time I drove this a few months ago." I am sensing an inner shift happening within me as I say aloud, "Good bye to you my old Carol Ann self. I am leaving you behind on this bridge and driving into my new Carol Ann and my new path." As I continue to drive I begin to enjoy the experience as I look out at the ocean waters surrounding us. The Light and Love music cd is now skipping and stalling.

"So why is it doing that skipping about, what do you think is the reason for that?" It is a specially chosen cd filled with light and love to assist in keeping me in calmness.

Reiki master Debbie in the back seat replies, "You do not need it now, so it is skipping."

Valerie, also a reiki master agrees to the meaning of this magical phenomenon; that my car's music is giving me a message. I am empowered enough now to cross my rainbow bridge without the initial necessary aid of soothing music. I remove the cd from the player. Wowsers, good job, Carol Ann.

Indeed by the time we reach the shores of the mainland I feel I have left behind me a load of fearfulness. I am now ready to embrace a more enlightened self. The three of us enjoy the Way of the Heart and leave with a sense of enthusiastic higher purpose and possibilities. This has indeed been a life altering day for me.

I must cross that glorious long bridge to get us all back to lovely PEI. This time is different and conversation is being enjoyed by all of us. I do feel some inner turmoil to some extent. "My palms are still sweaty so guess I still have work on this and will have to do it again soon." Yet I find myself actually enjoying it at the same time. The sun is about to go down and upon landing us back on the island I get out of the car with my camera. The fierce island winds are welcoming us home and I capture a sunset with the bridge. "Thank you my bridge friend you have been a good teacher."

Indeed this bridge crossing has turned out to be a most divinely guided experience. Thanks to this I plan to cross it solo very soon when I go to enjoy an evening with Deepak Chopra in Moncton, New Brunswick.

A few days later I am shopping and when I get back to the car I discover a business card on the windshield. I need to find us a dogsitter for my trip to the mainland to see Deepak because it will require an overnight stay. To my utter surprise I am now looking at a card from a dogsitter, named Cheryl. How perfect is this. I had not heard the dogs bark at all which is unusual. Mystic normally does not allow someone so close to the car without a big scary woof. This is a good sign she is the right person for my dogs.

We connect by phone and Cheryl is able to come stay with the dogs. I depart knowing they will be well taken care of and I head to the confederation bridge. I am determined to make this crossing both ways with a lighter sense of self. Thanks to my previous journey over it recently this time is much easier. I even look over the side of the bridge to the waters below. Good work Carol Ann.

The evening listening to Deepak Chopra is very memorable. The arena is packed. I chat briefly with the woman next to me who shares she is an aspiring writer. Deepak is the synchrodestiny man, so this speaks well to my own future. I smile with delight. At the end of the evening I stand to salute him with my own Namaste greeting.

My hotel room is very lovely and I treat myself to room service and enjoy my wine. After a leisurely morning I head back to the bridge.

As I approach it I am calm and filled with smiles. I drive across it with loud cheers to my bravery. I recall the elevator vision gifted to me by the medium Rosemary who had helped me to cut the cord with my Robert love.

That day had been one year ago yesterday on Saber's birthday. This is powerful synchronistic timing. My mind replays her vision of pushing the elevator button to the top floor to embrace the truest essence of me. I have now stepped more fully into the freedom of my authentic self. One year from the day of releasing my Robert love I am now embracing the authentic truth of Carol Ann.

I recall the messages of something big is coming and fasten your seat belt. I always reply, ok I am ready thanks. Whatever that means, I am ready. Leaving the sea home to live in remote north Vancouver island was something big I think. Thanks to Roger I am guided to the other end of the Canadian rainbow, driving solo with three labs to live in a home I purchased sight unseen. Now that is something big in my mind. Yet I know there is something else.

I do believe now that my inner message of something big is coming has yet to arrive. I crossed my Canadian rainbow shore to shore and now my rainbow bridge. I am consciously merged with my authentic self. I am connected and empowered, listening to my authentic truth so I reckon something big is in the island winds. Why PEI is called the gentle island is beyond me because the winds are not gentle. Yet perhaps this something big requires these ferocious winds to blow it my way.

So it sounds like that something big has yet to arrive. Whatever or whomever could it be? I am trusting in knowing my best is yet to be.

Excerpt from "On the Wings of Butterflies"

I am on the couch doing my daily quiet time and hear Archangel Michael whisper, "Close your eyes and be the blue sky." I am a great sky watcher so this is an easy vision for me to follow. I go into the vastness of the blue. I tell Michael, "I understand you can be everywhere. That is such an incredible idea to envision."

"Yes I can. Just like the blue sky I am everywhere and with everyone." I continue with my sky visualizations thinking of Spirit alone in the den.

My blue sky turns into her beautiful labrador head with her brown eyes intently examining me. Often in the morning she puts her nose to my face to sniff me and check me out. This is our normal ritual. In the vision she is now gifting me she is up close to me. Then she turns herself into a young puppy body. She runs playfully into the glorious sunlight teasing me with her tail whispering, "Follow me, follow me." We are in a huge limitless meadow with yellow flowers. As far as the eye can see it is an ocean of yellow and vast blue sky overhead.

It is a glorious vision. I question her, "This is lovely Spirit, do you have a specific reason you are showing me this?"

"I am sharing this with you Carol Ann because this represents the sunshine glow of your heart which you are sharing and will share with the world."

"It is incredible. It goes on forever, the field has no ending."

"That is right. The same as you and I have no ending. We all go on forever."

She then points with her lab tail, "See look."

There in the sky she has made the word eternity from yellow flowers. "You see your sorrows can be shed for here we are in eternity."

"Spirit, we are you now?"

She has disappeared and calls out to me, "Come here and put yourself in this flower."

I smell the scent of daffodils fill my living room. She now leads me to a daffodil and is going inside it with me. My ever wise lab and I are immersed inside a giant daffodil. I am surrounded with the glow of brilliant yellows and golds. "Oh my, you know this is my favorite spring flower. I feel like a little girl exploring in here; it is so magical. Thank you."

"Feel the joy of the daffodil, be this joy. Stay inside the flower and become this energy."

I am touched and overwhelmed by this image as tears slowly roll down my face. I continue to listen. "You now have another visionary tool to work with to enhance your radiant glow into a peaceful heart. Combine it with the blue sky image from Michael and this shall induce bliss in you."

The next day during our quiet messaging together while she is in the den and I lie in the living room she gifts me with a lovely image. She leads me through fields while she runs in her young puppy body making heart shaped crop circles. She takes me above the field to see the message she created, "Love to all angels."

"Wow, Spirit that is beautiful. Yes for sure all the angels appreciate such sentiments from us. Thank you."

Next I see a vision of "Love to Carol Ann" written all in the shape of hearts. I see Spirit's tail pull on the end of the letters and all the hearts fall on top of me. She then takes me through a field of clover where I run with a multitude of exuberant puppies. "Who are all these silly puppies?"

"They are all the dogs of your past, present and future."

We are now all running through the scented clover. I look above and magically the "Love to Carol Ann" sky message has reshaped itself against a blue sky. I am now rolling down a clovered hill with the pups tumbling over and around me as we all laugh in unison. I get up smelling of the scent of young puppies and puppy kisses. "Marvelous visions, Spirit. Thank you."

Later as we all get into bed she faces the end of the bed and a minute later she sits up. "What you are doing big girl?"

She turns herself around and plops her lovely head over me. I fall asleep with her nestled in my neck and a smile gracing my face.